VIOLATION OF HUMAN RIGHTS BY THE POLICE

September 2011

PREFACE

Human rights are significant for every Man ever since he came into existence in this world until he breaths last. It has emerged as solemn legal premise after the Second World War. Law has been framed to protect the human rights due to its significance both nationally and internationally. Police is entrusted with the duty of protecting the life, liberty and security of persons in a State. However the protectors, many a times, turn out to be violators. The Police in India are known for their violations of human rights. There is always hue and cry about violation of human rights by the police in India.

The research study attempts to unravel the extent of the human rights violation by the police in India generally, and in Kerala particularly. The study also focuses on the reasons for the violations, the adequacies of the existing law to prevent violations, the problems related with prevention of the violations by the law effectively.

The study reveals that there takes place a large number of human rights violations by the police. The existing law, to a certain extent, attempts to prevent the violations of human rights by the police. However, more additions to the existing laws are necessary. The lack of proper implementation of the existing law intensifies the problem. There should be clear mechanisms to properly monitoring and implementing the law.

With specials laws, both substantive and procedural, in dealing with violation of human rights by the police can reduce the extent of violation as is seen today. However, proper monitoring, speedy and effective redressal mechanism, training on human rights, training on new technique to investigations and interrogations can improve the system and reduce the human rights violations by the police.

Dr. A. Prasanna, the Principal of Government Law College, Kozhikode, On Deputation in Institute of Management in Government, Thiruvananthapuram was my supervisor. I am extremely thankful to her for the sincere guidance and constant supervision in completing the research study.

My thanks are also due to Jusitce R. Natarajan and Advocate K.E. Gangadhhran, Members of Kerala State Human Rights Commission; Justice Dinakaran and Justice V.P. Mohan Kumar, former Chairpersons of the Kerala State Human Rights Commission; Justice A. Leksmi Kutty, Prof S. Varghese and Dr. S. Balaraman, former Members of the Kerala State Human Rights Commission; Mr. S. Pulikesi, Additional Director General of Police (Training), Kerala; Dr. Alexander Jacob, Additional Director General of Police (Prisons), Kerala; Mr. Asokan, Assistant Inspector General of Police (Public Grievances Cell), Police Head Quarters, Thiruvananthapuram, Philip M. Prasad, Advocate, Thiruvananthapuram, K. Mohan Kumar, Advocate, Thiruvananthapuram and C.D. Anil, Retired Additional Chief Judicial Magistrate for their cooperation in collecting information and data on various aspects related with the subject.

I am also thankful to staff of the Libraries of Kerala University library, Thiruvananthapuram; Department of Law, Kariavattom Campus, Thiruvananthapuram; Government Law College, Thiruvananthapuram and the School of Legal Studies, Cochin University of Science and Technology. I am also indebted to the staff of the libraries of the High Court of Kerala.

Table of Contents

PROTECTION OF HUMAN RIGHTS FROM POLICE- POSITION IN REGIONAL SYSTEMS

TABLE OF CASES

I

Chapter 1

INTRODUCTION

The concept of human rights is as old as the coming into existence of human beings on earth. These rights are inherent in every person by virtue of his birth. However, these rights were referred to as natural rights until recently. In the eighteenth and nineteenth centuries in Europe, several philosophers such as Thomas Paine,[1] John Stuart Mill[2] and Henry David Thoreau[3] proposed the concept of "natural rights", the rights belonging to a person by nature by virtue of being born as a human being. The concept of human rights emerged as a solemn premise after the Second World War due to the barbarous atrocities and massacre committed by Nazi Germany prior to and during the War. Although the expression "human rights" came into general use after the Second World War, yet Henry David Thoreau is considered to first use the expression "human rights" in the previous century.[4] The concept of human rights can be traced from Western Philosophy to Stoic natural law doctrines.[5] The ideas that originated with Zeno of *Citium* and the Stoics teachings that there were pervasive laws of nature and hence, the Man's conduct should be measured in accordance with those laws, have roots in the development of the concept of human rights.[6]

Human rights can generally be defined as those fundamental and natural rights that are attached with human beings and are essential to consider a Man as a human being. They are not the creation of any State or law. They are inherent in every Man by virtue of being human and are ascribed naturally by virtue of being born as a Man.[7] It is equal in every human being. The Universal Declaration of Human Rights 1948 declares that "all human beings are born free and equal in dignity and rights."[8] They are endowed with reason and conscience, and should act

1

towards one another in a spirit of brotherhood. This profound proposition is central to the Charter of the United Nations which affirms its faith in fundamental human rights and in the dignity and worth of human person.[9]

Human rights are universal across all nations. They are based upon the belief that each individual should be treated with dignity and respect to which, as human being, they are entitled. Human rights are part of what each person needs to be human. Human rights, defined in Constitutions and legislations are the attempt to express how people's humanity should be respected by those with power over them, particularly the Governments and their law enforcement agencies like police.[10]

There is no exaggeration to submit that generally, the police in India do not hesitate to violate human rights to any extent. The behaviour of Indian police is colonial and dreadful towards common man. No doubt, the police as protectors of society play a vital role in the administration of criminal justice by preventing and detecting crimes. While ensuring safety and security of the people they must also ensure that no member of the society is put in peril and no person's human rights and dignity are curtailed. It has always been a difficult task for the police to find out the culprit and set justice in motion to punish the delinquent without tampering the interest and dignity of human beings and the rights appended therewith. Police investigation, interrogation, arrest and detention have always been controversial for the non-compliance of the procedural requirement which put the accused and other persons in difficulty, violating their human rights and dignity. Attempts have always been made to . make the investigations, interrogation, arrest and detentions fair and free from coercion and "third degree" influences so that the minimum protection could be guaranteed. Nonetheless, police commit large number of

2

human rights violations irrespective of all the measures taken to protect the human rights of the people. Here comes the relevance of the research study.

1.1. Problem identified

The researcher has conducted a pilot study in Thiruvananthapuram, Kerala to find out the instances of violation of human rights. It is found that instances of violations of human rights are more on the part of police officials. So the researcher selected the problem "Violations of Human Rights by the Police" for the research study. An attempt has been made to explore and analyze the extent of violation of human rights by the police in India. Since all the States in India have more or less the same problems regarding the violation of human rights by the police, an empirical study has been conducted in Kerala to gather first hand information on the topic.

1.2 Objectives of the study

The objective of this research is to make an in depth study on the extent of violation of human rights committed by the police in India and to assess the effectiveness of the control mechanisms in the light of national and international legal framework.

1.2.1. Specific objectives

The following are the specific objectives of the study:

- ◆ To assess the extent of human rights violation by the police;
- ◆ To analyze whether the human rights violation by the police takes place as a result of lack of awareness of rights of accused person or any other person coming under the realm of investigation, interrogation, arrest and detention;

3

- To study the attitude of the police towards the human rights of accused person or any other person coming under the realm of investigation, interrogation, arrest and detention;

- To examine whether the present legal frame work is sufficient to tackle and control the violation of human rights by the police;

- To evaluate the legislative, executive and judicial action for prevention of human rights violation by police and its reactions and/or impacts;

- To put forth the suggestions for proper checks and balances and efficacious steps to be taken to curtail the human rights violations by the police.

1.3. Hypotheses

The hypotheses of this research study are:

- Human rights are violated by the police while arresting and detaining persons.
- Laws on human rights protection need improvement.
- Existing laws for the protection of human rights is not properly implemented.

With the above hypotheses, the researcher has inquired into the following problems:

1. What is the extent of violation of human rights by the police in India?

2. Is it because of the lack of awareness of human rights of accused person that the police commit violations?

3. What is the attitude of the police towards human rights of accused, arrested persons, witnesses, or victims of crimes?

4. Is the present Constitutional and legal framework sufficient to tackle the problem effectively?

5. If yes, why there is growing human rights violation by police?

6. What factors influence the police to commit violations of human rights of accused/ arrested persons, witnesses, complainants or victims of crimes?

7. What is the extent of protection given by the Judiciary, National Human Rights Commission of India, and the Kerala State Human Rights Commission from the violations of human rights by the police?

8. What protections are provided in relation to violation of human rights in other Countries?

1.4. Sources of Data Collection

The primary and secondary sources of data have been extensively utilized for conducting the research study. Constitutional provisions, statutes, books and available literature on the topic have been surveyed to find out the extent of protection afforded against the violation of human rights by the police in India. International conventions and declarations on human rights have also been analyzed to assess the extent of protection available under the international legal framework against violation of human rights by the police. Reported cases of the Supreme Court of India and the High Court of Kerala have been extensively analysed to find out the role played by the judiciary to provide protection against violation of human rights by the police. Case Reports of other State High Courts that are relevant to the subject have also been used for the study. An empirical study has also been conducted in Kerala for collecting the data for the study.

1.5. Methodology Adopted

The research work is partially doctrinal and partially empirical. Constitutional provisions, statutes and international legal documents have been carefully examined and critically analysed to find out the protective safeguards against arbitrary arrest, illegal detention, torture and other police excesses. The extent of constitutional and legal protection of human rights against violation by the police is assessed by critically evaluating the decisions of Supreme Court of India and High Courts of different States. A comparative legal analysis has been made to assess the protection afforded to human rights in other regional systems such as Europe, America, Africa, Arab and Asia. Such an analysis is made with a view to evaluate the effectiveness of those systems for the protection of human rights of individuals from being violated by the police. Valuable data have also been collected through empirical study to support the hypothesis. The Empirical study has been conducted with the help of questionnaires. Victims of human rights violations, officials of the police department, Chairperson and Members of the Kerala State Human Rights Commission, professionals, human rights activists, and witnesses have been interviewed to collect the data for the study to find out the extent of human rights violations by the police and the legal measures needed to improve the system.

1.6. Analysis of data

International conventions, Indian Constitutional provisions, statutes and judicial decisions on the protection of human rights from the violation by the police are collected and critically analyzed. Data collected from the empirical study has also been analyzed to find out the extent of human rights violations by the police, the adequacies of the law to safeguard human rights from the police excesses and the problems involved in the implementation of the law to control the police atrocities. Suggestions given by the experts to improve the protection mechanism, the law and the system to prevent the violation of human rights by the police have been recorded and analyzed to find out solutions for the problem.

1.7. Scheme of Work

The entire research study is divided into thirteen chapters in six parts. Part I is 'introductory' consisting of two chapters. The first chapter provides an introduction about the research study. It outlines the thematic sketch of the study summarizing the major issues connected with the subject under the study, the hypotheses, the research questions and methodology adopted for systematically conducting the research. The second chapter deals with historical retrospect of the growth and evolution of the concept of human rights.

Part II deals with the "Legal Aspects" and it consists of four chapters-chapters three, four, five and six. The chapter three defines the different concepts discussed in the thesis. The chapter four provides an insight into the legal framework relating to the international human rights protection system related with freedom from torture, arbitrary arrest, illegal detention, unlawful searches and seizures. It critically analyses the Universal Declaration of Human Rights 1948, International Covenant on Civil and Political Rights 1976 with its Protocols, the UN Convention Against Torture or other Cruel, Inhuman and Degrading Treatment or Punishment 1987[11] with its protocols related with the protection afforded from the violation of human rights by the police and the extent of India's participation in such mechanisms. How effective is the protection mechanisms that are made available in these declarations and conventions are also analysed here.

The fifth chapter analyses the Indian Constitutional provisions that are set out for human rights protection during investigation, interrogation, arrest or detention. Dealing with

Constitutional provisions inevitably imports various decisions Supreme Court and High Court of Kerala on the subject. An analysis is made on such decisions in relation to the protection of human rights by the Courts and prevention of its violation by the police. Though the Indian judiciary on its part has been dealing effectively in preventing the violation of human rights by the police, the violations only seem to increase day by day. An attempt has been made to find out the reasons for the rise in such violations.

The sixth chapter deals with statutory protection in India from the violation of human rights by the police. Here, an analysis of both procedural and substantive law is made with a view to identify the problems in controlling violations of human rights by the police. The main focus of analysis is on provisions of the Criminal Procedure Code with its Amendments in 2005, 2008 and 2010, the Indian Penal Code1860, the Indian Evidence Act1872, the Indian Police Act1861, the Kerala Police Act 2010, the Protection of Human Rights Act 1993, *etc.*, in the protection of human rights violations by the police.

Part III deals with "the Institutional Protection" and it consists of two chapters-chapters seven and eight. Seventh and Eighth chapters account the agencies for the human rights protection in India such as National Human Rights Commission at the national level and State Human Rights Commissions at State level. Here, the functioning of the National Human Rights Commission, State National Human Rights Commissions and the working of the Kerala State Human Rights Commission are analyzed and studied with a view to understand how effective these institutions are in protecting human rights violations by the police. Though these institutions are active, they face many issues such as lack of authority to enforce its decision, jurisdictional conflicts between National Human Rights Commission and State National Human

8

Rights Commissions; budgetary control by government, *etc.* Possible solutions for solving such problems are discussed here.

Part IV deals with "Empirical Study in Kerala" and it consistsof two chapters- chapters nine and ten. Chapters nine and ten deal with incidents of human rights violations by the police in Kerala, on the basis of first hand information gathered through interview from police officials, victims of police excesses, Members of Kerala State National Human Rights Commission, Experts on the subject and Human Rights Activists. Data collected are carefully analysed in order to arrive at a viable conclusion in determining the extent and the causes of violation of human rights by the police, and possible solutions to reduce such violations.

Part V deals with "Comparative Study" and it consists of two chapters- chapters eleven and twelve. Chapter eleven deals with protection of human rights from being violated by the police in different Regional Systems in other Countries. This chapter analyzes the human rights protection afforded by regional Conventions and Charters such as European, Inter-American, African, MISNK Conventions and Arab Charter. These systems are analysed to find out the effectiveness of different systems in the world in protecting human rights violations by the police, and the perspectives of such systems for the protection of human rights from being violated by police in India. Chapter twelve analyses the United Nation's guidelines on the exercise of police powers. It is an assessment of the international standards of human rights and policing. It examines the UN Code of Conduct for Law Enforcement Officials, Basic Principles and Rules, UN Declarations and Conventions related with standards of police and their dealings with accused, arrested or detained persons. It also examines the victims of abuse of power and the treatment of women and children in the hands of the police.

Part VI consists only one chapter and it is the "Conclusion". Analysis of the foregoing chapters, summary of the discussions and deliberations on the subject, the conclusion of the findings with main recommendations for strengthening the system more effectively are presented in this chapter 13.

A fair investigation, interrogation, arrest and detention with the minimum procedural guarantee is an essential prerequisite to ensure that the people are safe in the hands of police and their human rights are not violated. Nevertheless, there are numerous complaints against police about atrocities which culminate in the gross violations of human rights. The literature on this subject is not scanty. However, before proceeding to the details of the literature, it would be cogent here to comprehend the historical review of the concept of human rights.

A fair investigation, interrogation, arrest and detention with the minimum procedural guarantee is an essential prerequisite to ensure that the people are safe in the hands of police and their human rights are not violated. Nevertheless, there are numerous complaints against police about atrocities which culminate in the gross violations of human rights. The literature on this subject is not scanty. However, before proceeding to the details of the literature, it would be cogent here to comprehend the historical review of the concept of human rights.

Endnotes

---

[1] Thomas Pine, *Rights of Man,* Reprint (1792), p.25; In part 4 of 16 entitled "Being an Answer to Mr. Burke's Attack on the French Revolution" Pine claims ". ....that all men are born equal, and with equal natural right, in the same manner as if posterity had been continued by creation instead of generation.... Natural rights are those which appertain to man in right of his existence".

[2] John Stuart Mill, *Essays on Liberty*,Reprint (1973), pp.15-17, John Stuart Mill though not directly using the term "natural rights", but he claims that a set of rights that must be protected by society as they are natural or god-given and also ultimate utility of individuals.

[3] Henry David Thoreau, *On the duty ofCivil Disobedience,* Reprint (1842), p.14.

[4] Peter Halstead, *The Comprehensive Guide to All Facts: Human Rights* (2010), p. 16.

[5] Stoics is a group of philosophers founded in Athens by Zeno of *Citium* in early 3rd century and existed until 529 AD when it was closed down by order of the Emperor Justinian I.

[6] See *supra* n. 4, at p.17.

[7] Brian Orend,*Human rights: concept and context (*2002), p.38.

[8] Universal Declaration of Human Rights, Art. 1.

[9] See Preamble of the United Nations Charter 1945.

[10] GopalBhargava, *Meaning and Source of Human Rights* (2003), p.15.

[11] Hereinafter referred as "the UN Convention Against Torture".

Chapter 2

PROTECTION OF HUMAN RIGHTS – HISTORICAL RETROSPECTIVE

In the classical world, there was no concept of theories of rights, dignity of persons or status of individuals. In ancient Greece and Rome the status of individual was determined by their relationship to the State. According to Ancient Greece writers, the god establish a law which stand above obligations and prohibitions imposed by the rulers of the community.[1] However, Susan Ford Wiltshire claims that a doctrine of human rights could never have evolved if the ancient Athenians had not invented the revolutionary idea that human beings are capable of governing themselves and if the ancient Romans had not created their elaborate system of law and the rights.[2]

In ancient India, there were two norms, *viz.*, *Dharma* (Justice) and *Danda* (Rod for beating) which were provided in the administration of criminal justice.[3] The King had the authority to administer justice in accordance with the law, but he was himself bound by the law.[4] Later, torture and inhuman treatment of prisoners were prohibited under Ashoka's administration.[5] Therefore, there were traces of protection of human rights in ancient India.

However, the concept underwent several transformations during the Middle Ages in the Continental Europe and in England before it came to justify a theory of natural rights.[6] Nonetheless, a real concept of protection of human rights started emerging from England after the signing of the Great Charter or the *Magna Carta* in 1215.

2.1. *Magna Carta*

Magna Carta, popularly known as the Great Charter of Freedoms,[7] was signed by King

John of England at Runnymede in 1215. The two most important legal clauses of *Magna Carta* that are relevant for the protection of human rights of man from the arbitrariness of State are:

(i)　　Clause 40 which affirms that *"to no one will we sell, to no one will we deny or delay, right of justice"*, and

(ii)　　Clause 39 which promises that *"no freeman shall be taken or imprisoned or dismissed except by lawful judgment of his peers or by the law of the land".*

These clauses establish the principle of equal access to justice for all citizens without discrimination and excessive fees, and that the King would follow the legal procedure before His officials arrest, detain or punish a person.[8]*Magna Carta* explicitly protects, *inter alia,* the above rightsof the people and, hence, conceded to be the genesis of protection against arbitrariness of human rights of individuals.

2.2. The Petition of Rights, 1628

English Parliament refused to finance the King's unpopular foreign policy that had caused his government to exact forced loans and to quarter troops in subjects' houses as an economy measure. Arbitrary arrest and imprisonment for opposing these policies had produced a violent hostility in the Parliament against King Charles I and George Villiers, the Duke of Buckingham. In 1628, the Parliament sent the petition in the form of statement of civil liberties to King Charles I. Due to the inimical attitude of parliamentarians, the King had no option but to accept the Petition of Rights. The Petition of Rights is considered another mile stone in the history of development of human rights protection. The Petition of Rights initiated by Sir Edward Coke[9] had roots in the earlier statutes and charters including the *Magna Carta.* The Petition of Rights asserted that: (1) No subject may be imprisoned without cause shown;[10] (2) No soldiers may be quartered upon the citizenry; and (3) Martial law may not be used in time of

13

peace. This, in fact, is the origin of the concept that the arrested person shall be informed of the grounds of arrest. Thus, the Petition of Rights provided protection against arbitrary arrest and detention by affirming that no person may be imprisoned without showing a cause for the arrest and detention.

2.3. The Virginia Declaration of Rights 1776

The Virginia Declaration of Rights is a document drafted in 1776 to proclaim the inherent rights of men, including the right to rebel against "inadequate" government. It influenced a number of later documents, including the US Declaration of Independence (1776), and the French Declaration of the Rights of Man and of the Citizen (1789). Section 1of the Virginia Declaration provides: "all men are by nature equally free and independent, and have certain inherent rights, of which, when they enter into a state of society, they cannot, by any compact, deprive or divest their posterity; namely, the enjoyment of life and liberty, with the means of acquiring and possessing property, and pursuing and obtaining happiness and safety." Thus, the Virginia declaration affirms that all people have certain inherent rights such as right to life and liberty which they enjoy as human beings.

2.4. The American Declaration of Independence 1776

The American Declaration of Independence, 1776 is not remembered for giving independence to 13 colonies of America from the British King, George III,[11] but is remembered for its recognition, acceptance and respect for human dignity and human rights. The Declaration contains the progressive socio-legal-political language of human rights, *namely*: (a) the natural equality of man and certain inalienable rights of life, liberty and pursuit of human happiness; (b) the purpose of the government is to secure those inalienable rights, and (c) of man the

14

government gets the power; i.e. from the consent of the governed people.[12] The Declaration played a major role not only in the history of mankind, but in growth and development of the concept of the basics of human rights. The Declaration also inspired the French to undertake a similar revolt to achieve freedom in the pursuit of human happiness, which ultimately became the perambulatory language of the French Constitution and subsequently a guiding model for the constitutional democracy globally.

2.5. Declaration of the Rights of Man and of the Citizen

The Declaration of Rights of Man and of the Citizen, popularly known as "the French Declaration", was approved on August 26, 1789 by the National Assembly of France in consequence of the French Revolution.[13] The declaration, *inter alia*, stated that men are born free,[14] equal with the rights to liberty, property and security,[15] guaranteed equality before the law, [16] and granted of freedom from unlawful arrest or imprisonment.[17] The declaration also guarantees protection against unlawful arrest and detention.

2.6. UN Charter

The global system established after the Second World War had a number of underlying principles, ideals and motivations, including the need for an urgent response to atrocities against human beings that were taking place during the War. It was felt that these violations occur due to the lack of effective mechanisms to restrain such violations of human rights and human dignity at international level. Though the League of Nations came into existence after the First World War, it failed to address issues related with human rights and its violations.[18] The emerged extent of Nazi holocaust and atrocities against human beings during Second World War called for the definition of new crimes against humanity and human rights, and also, machineries to tackle with

15

such crimes effectively globally. While there were deliberations to outline a United Nations Charter[19] at Sans Francisco, there were also proposals to incorporate a Bill of Rights in the UN Charter, though not materialized for want of consensus among the Nations due to the factors such as Communist, Capitalist and Islamic religious blocks of countries.[20]Although there were no consensuses on the incorporation of Bill of Rights into the UN Charter, yet the Charter contains a number of important references to the promotion and protection of Human Rights, which are worth considering here.

The preamble of the UN Charter expresses the avowed faith of the Member Nations in furtherance of human rights and human dignity, and unequivocally declares:

> We the people of the United Nations determined...to reaffirm faith in fundamental human rights, in the dignity and worth of the human person, in the equal rights of men and women and of nations large and small, and...to promote social progress and better standards of life in larger freedom.[21]

The preamble, thus, discerns the UN's clearer vision and mission of its intention to uphold and protect human rights, human dignity and worth of the human personality.

More substantive provisions dealing with human rights under the UN Charter include Article 1(3) which expresses some of the broad purpose of the UN, including promotion and encouragement of human rights and fundamental freedoms without distinction as to race, sex, language or religion, Article 62(2) which enables Economic and Social Council to make recommendations to promote human rights based on studies or reports to be presented to the General Assembly, Member States, and specialized agencies, and Article 68 which empowers Economic and Social Council to set up commissions in the economic and social fields to promote human rights, and such other commissions as may be required for the performance of its functions.

16

In fact, there were no consensuses among the States for the incorporation of Bill of Rights into the UN Charter. However, the representatives of the States could reach an agreement to establish a Commission on Human Rights in order to provide protection of human rights at international level.[22] Thus, Article 68 was incorporated empowering the Economic and Social Council to establish Commissions for promoting human rights, and consequently, theCommission on Human Rights was established in 1946 to achieve the ends envisaged under the UN Charter related to human rights protection.[23]

It is submitted that the spirit envisioned in the preamble of the Charter in relation to upholding the human rights does not appear in the same vigor in the substantive provisions particularly in relation to the protection of civil and political rights. This could seem to be due to the flock of the communist countries led by Russia opposing to incorporate such civil and political rights in the body of the UN Charter, perhaps because of their obsession with respect to 'individual' human rights and human dignity.[24] However, one of the main objectives of the establishment of the UN was to avoid recurrence of atrocities against human beings by upholding human dignity and human rights. After the inception of the UN, the first main task was to initiate for a globally acceptable human rights document and this led to the birth of Universal Declaration of Human Rights.

2.7. Universal Declaration of Human Rights

Immediately after the coming into force of the UN Charter, the Economic and Social Council by the authority vested with it under Article 68 of the UN Charter established the Commission on Human Rights[25] in 1946 for the preparation of the International Bill of Rights.[26] The Commission on Human Rights headed by Eleanor Roosevelt[27] consisted of eighteen members.[28] The Human Rights Commission along with the Canadian human rights expert Dr.

John Peters Humphrey, the principal drafter, prepared a draft declaration and submitted it to the General Assembly through the Economic and Social Council.[29] The Declaration was adopted by General Assembly on 10 December 1948 at *Palais de Chaillot*, Paris and it became the historic Universal Declaration of Human Rights.[30] The Guinness Book of Records describes the Universal Declaration of Human Rights as the "Most Translated Document" in the world.[31] The Universal Declaration of Human Rights is the first ever international document produced with the term "human rights" in the title. It is, now, considered to be the soul of human rights and human dignity.

The Universal Declaration of Human Rights, however, is not an overnight product; but is a cumulative historic act of many pacts that had come into existence long before 1948 such as the *Magna Carta*, the Petition of Rights, Virginia Declaration of Rights, American declaration of Independence, French Declaration, *etc*. The historic words "all human beings are born free and equal in dignity and rights" that appear in Article 1 of Universal Declaration of Human Rights itself was taken from French Declaration which states that all "men are born, and always continue, free and equal in respect of their rights."[32] This shows that the drafters of the Universal Declaration of Human Rights relied on the previous historic humanistic declarations and covenants in drafting the Declaration.[33]

Endnotes

[1] G.S. Bajwa, *Human Rights in India: Implementation and Violations* (1995), p.27.

[2] Susan Ford Wiltshire, *Greece, Rome and the Bill of Rights* (1992), p.10.

[3] *Supran.1.at p.28.*

[4] *Ibid.*

[5]Yogesh K. Tyagi, *Third World Response to Human Rights*, I.J.L.I., Vol.21 (1981) pp.12021.

[6]*Ibid.*

[7]History, *Magna Carta*, also called *Magna Carta Libertatum* (Great Charter of Freedom), is an English legal Charter, originally issued in the year 1215 and was written in Latin.

[8]Though the term writ of 'Habeas Corpus does not appear in the body of Magna Carta, yet this provision is an oblique reference to it. The writ of '*Habeas Corpus ad subjiciendum*' is a legal action through which a person can seek relief from the unlawful detention of him or herself, or of another person. The practice and right of Habeas Corpus was settled practice and law at the time of Magna Carta and was thus a fundamental part of the unwritten common "law of the land" as was expressly recognized by *Magna Carta*.

[9] Sir Edward Coke was a prominent parliamentary adversary of the Crown, Speaker of the House of Commons, Attorney General, Chief Justice of the Court of Common Pleas and Chief Justice of the King's Bench.

[10]Petition of Rights 1628, Art. V.

[11] The intolerable Acts of the British Parliament by which the King restricted, among others, the natural and basic human rights of people in the colonies of America that cumulatively contributed to the American War of Independence during 1775-76.

[12]American Declaration of Independence was adopted by the Congress on July 4,1776.

[13] French Revolution is also called the revolution of 1789. French revolution took place between 1787 and 1789 and reached the peak in 1789 overthrowing the monarch in France.

[14]The Declaration of Rights of Man and of the Citizen, Art. 1.

[15]*Id.*, Art. 2 and 4.

[16]*Id.*, Art. 6.

[17]*Id.*, Art. 7.

[18]The Covenant of the League of Nations 1924 did not contain any provision effectively dealing with human rights.

[19]The Charter of the United Nations was signed on 26 June 1945, in San Francisco, at the conclusion of the United Nations Conference on International Organization, and came into force on 24 October 1945.

[20]Susan Waltz, *Who Wrote the Universal Declaration of Human Rights?*, e Journal, USA (2008), p. 219; It was Ricardo Alfaro, former president of Panama, who made the proposal of inclusion of a bill of human rights into the United Nations Charter. As Panama's representative to the United Nations' inaugural meeting in 1945, Alfaro brought with him a draft bill of international rights and formally proposed that it be incorporated into the U.N. Charter. *See* <www. Heinonline.org> accessed on 28-03-2010.

[21] UN Charter 1945, *Preamble*.

[22]*Ibid.*

[23] The functions of the Economic and Social Council included making 'recommendations for the purpose of promoting respect for, and observance of, human rights and fundamental freedoms for all'; See Mashood A. Bader in, *International Human Rights and Islamic Law* (2nd Ed., 2005), p. 19.

[24] Johannes Morsink, t*he Universal Declaration of Human Rights: Origins, Drafting and Intent* (1999), p. 17.

[25] The United Nations Commission on Human Rights has been replaced by the United Nations Human Rights Council as per United Nations General Assembly resolution A/RES/60/251 adopted on 15 March 2006. Thus, the Commission on Human Rights ceased to exist with effect from 16 June 2006.

[26] Amnesty International USA, *A Short History of Human Rights*, Human Rights Educators' Network, (1997) p. 19.

[27] The widow of former U.S. President Franklin Delano Roosevelt served as chair of the U.N. Human Rights Commission from 1946 to 1951.

[28] Eleanor Roosevelt, The Promise of Human Rights, in Allida M. Black (Ed.), What I Hope to Leave Behind: The Essential Essays of Eleanor Roosevelt (1995), p. 473; In the Economic and Social Council it was recommended by majority vote that since the Economic and Social Council consisted of representatives of governments, the members of the Commission on Human Rights should be elected by the Economic and Social Council from a list of nominees submitted by governments to serve in an individual capacity. The only dissenting opinion was from Union of Soviet Socialist Republic which insisted that they should be appointed as government representatives. Finally, the Council decided to leave it to the governments concerned to decide whether to appoint government officials or independent persons.

[29] The Commission on Human Rights headed by Eleanor Roosevelt assumed its first task of drafting of Bill of Rights in three parts, *viz.*, (i)a Declaration, (ii) a Convention containing legal rights and obligations, and (iii) measures of implementation — a system of international supervision and control. Canadian human rights expert Dr. John Peters Humphrey was called upon by the UN Secretary to work on the project and he later became the Declaration's principal drafter.

[30] Adopted by the UN General Assembly, Resolution 217 (III), with forty eight votes in favor, none against and eight abstentions; See *supra* n. 65 at 26.

[31] At present, there are 379 different translations of Universal Declaration of Human Rights.

[32] *Supra n. 10.*

[33] See for details infra Ch.4.

II

Chapter 3

HUMAN RIGHTS VIOLATIONS BY POLICE

The important function of the State in modern times is the protection of life, liberty and property of its citizens by maintaining law and order in the State. Rule of law comes to an end when the police who are bestowed with the authority to protect the common man turn out to be the violators of their human rights. There is no exaggeration in submitting that the police quite often violate the human rights of people in India. The magnitude and dimension of violation of human rights by the police in India are so painstaking that a common man or woman, whether as victim or witness would seldom approach the police for redressal of their grievance without the aid of a politician or a lawyer or a bureaucrat. The police in India are more known for their violations human rights than their protection. The main aim of this research study is to know the extent of human rights violations by the police in India generally, and in Kerala particularly. It becomes, therefore, necessary to analyse and comprehend the title terms "the human rights", "the police" and "the violation".

3.1. Meaning of the Term "Human Rights"

The encyclopedia Britannica defines the term "human rights" as "rights that belong to an individual as a consequence of being human."[1] Oxford advance learners dictionary defines it as "one of the basic rights that everyone has to be treated fairly and not in a cruel way, especially by their government".[2]Amnesty International defines human rights as "basic rights and freedoms that all people are entitled to regardless of nationality, sex, national or ethnic origin, race, religion, language, or other status".[3] The term came into wider use after the Second World War. As understood today human rights refers to a wide variety of values and capabilities reflecting the diversity of human circumstances and history. They are conceived as universal, applying to all human beings everywhere.[4] The definition "a human right is a universal moral right, something which all men, everywhere, at all times ought to have, something of which no one may be deprived without a grave affront to justice, something which is owing to every human simply because he is human"[5] clearly expresses the meaning of human rights in modern times.

3.1.1. Three Generation of Human Rights

A right is an entitlement to certain kinds of treatment; while positive rights grant people the ability to demand the performance of some action, as for example, ability to vote, negative rights entitle people to demand that others refrain from certain kinds of action, as for example, not being tortured.[6] Human rights exist as a basic moral rights that all human beings are entitled to and high priority moral reasons demanding decent treatment for such rights just by virtue its existence with human beings, and hence, cannot be denied on the basis of race, creed, ethnicity, or gender.[7] These rights are advanced as legal rights and protected by the rule of law. The Czech jurist Karel Vasak divides the human rights into three generations of rights. The first generation rights are basic human rights that protect individuals from slavery, torture, and arbitrary arrest, and ensure that they are free from arbitrary intrusions into their privacy.[8] Such rights include the rights set forth as civil and political rights, the most basic of which are the right to life, liberty, and personal security.[9] The second generation rights include the economic, social, and cultural rights to which all human beings are entitled.[10] The third generation provides solidarity rights

22

which include the right to a social and international order that allows for the exercise of fundamental freedoms.[11]

3.1.2. Definition under the Protection of Human Rights Act

The Section 2 (d) of the Protection of Human Rights Act, 1993 defines "human rights" as "the right relating to life, liberty, equality and dignity of individuals guaranteed by the Constitution or embodied in the International Covenants and enforceable by courts in India."But, before the 2006 Amendment to the Protection Human Rights Act, Section 2(c) provided that "international covenants" included only "the International Covenant on Civil and Political Rights" and "the International Covenant on Economic, Social and Cultural Rights".[12] This definition before 2006 Amendment was very restrictive one. This lacuna has been resolved by the 2006 Amendment which now includes all convention in which India is a party.

In Summary, today, the term human rights refers to a wide variety of values and capabilities reflecting the diversity of human circumstances and history and are conceived of as universal, applying to all human beings everywhere, and as fundamental, referring to basic human needs.[13] The definition "A human right is a universal moral right, something which all men, everywhere, at all times ought to have, something of which no one may be deprived without a grave affront to justice, something which is owing to every human simply because he is human" clearly expresses the meaning of human rights.[14] Thus, the human rights are the most fundamental of all rights enjoyed by human beings and are essential for the up keep of the dignity as human being.

3.2. Who are "Police"?

The term "police" have neither been defined in the Criminal Procedure Code nor in the Indian Police Act nor in any State laws including the Kerala Police Act. The Kerala Police Act, 2011 only states that there shall be a police force for the Kerala State.[15] Black's Law Dictionary defines "police" as (1) "the governmental department charged with the preservation of public order, the promotion of public safety, and the prevention and detection of crime" and (2) "the officers or members of this department."[16] The police force as an organized body came into being in England in the 1820s when Sir Robert Peel established London's first municipal force.[17] Before that, policing had either been done by volunteers or by soldiers in the military service.[18] The UN Code of Conduct for Law Enforcement Officials[19] defines "law enforcement official" as including all officials whether they are elected or appointed who exercise police powers, especially the powers of arrest or detention[20] and also include military personnel who exercise police powers whether they are clothed with police uniform or not, and personnel of State security forces whether they are named as police or not.[21] This definition seems to be wider in as much as it takes within its sweep all those who are exercising police powers. As per this definition the criteria to determine whether a personnel is a law enforcement official or not is to look for the nature of the power that is exercised by the personnel. Thus, the term "Police" can, simply, be defined as any person or body of persons created by the authority of the State, obligated and empowered to maintain law and order, prevention and investigation of crimes. For the purpose of this research study, the term 'police' is confined only to local police discharging police functions within the State such as police (law and order), reserve police aiding local police in the maintenance of law and order, crime branch, *etc.* Military, prison or forest officials are not included in the category of police for this study.

3.3. What does "Violation" mean?

Black's Law Dictionary defines violation as "an infraction or breach of laws; the contravention of a right or duty".[22]Literally, "violation" means the 'infringement; transgression; non-observance; as the violation of law or positive commands of covenants, promises etc'.[23] In the context of human rights, it can be any infringement on the rights which are guaranteed by relevant laws or the constitution of any particular country. Philosopher Immanuel Kant said that "human beings have an intrinsic value absent in inanimate objects; to violate a human right would, therefore, be a failure to recognize the worth of human life."[24] In the perspective of violations by the police it implies any encroachment or transgression by the police on the rights guaranteed by the Constitution of India, laws in India or International instruments such as Universal Declaration of Human Rights, International Covenant on Civil and Political Rights, *etc.*, to which India is a party. It also implies non-observance of duties or obligations connected with protection of human rights. Thus, any kind of transgression in compliance with the procedures prescribed by the Constitution or the laws or the directive set out by the Supreme Court or High Courts in the matters of investigation, interrogation, arrest or detention adversely affecting the rights of accused, victim or witnesses tantamount to violation of human rights by the police.

3.3.1. Torture

Torture is the most aggravated form of violation of human rights committed by the police. It varies from simple beating to causing death in custody. Police in India are generally blamed of employing the methods of torture for different reasons.

25

3.3.2. Reasons for Torture

The police department is entrusted with the task of investigation, and collection of evidences to prove the crime. The easiest method to collect evidence is to extract information from the accused himself. The police employ different methods of torture to collect evidences from the accused. These methods are popularly called as "third degree methods". But the evidence collected by torturing human beings is not justifiable from the human rights point of view, and often violates norms of human rights protection. Some police officers are rough and rude by nature and finds pleasure in torturing his fellow beings who are caught in their net. Pre-set offensive attitudinal behavioral pattern developed through training or years of experience by the police also results into the violations. Some Police officials have the false notion that they can keep their dignity and obtain respect from people only when they horrifies people by showing rude behavior or undignified attitudes towards accused or witnesses or even to general public. Corruption, political nexus or personal bias in particular cases under investigation may also cause violations of human rights by the police. Police also employ torture on individuals who stand against the police officer's abuse of power.

3.3.3. Death in police custody

The extreme form of torture in custody is causing death of a person by the police. In spite of the Constitutional guarantee, statutory protections, Supreme Court directives, and institutional supervision by the National Human Rights Commission and the State Human Rights Commissions, a considerable number of deaths occur in police custody all over India. The statement made in the LokSabha by Sri. Ajay Maken, Minister of State for Home Affairs[25] on

01-12-2009 shows the following data of death in police custody. (year 2000-2001 is taken as base year for calculating percentage increase):

Year	No. of deaths	% of increase
2000-2001	127	------
2001-2002	165	29.92%
2002-2003	183	44.09%
2003-2004	162	27.56%
2004-2005	136	7.09%
2005-2006	139	9.45%
2006-2007	119	-6.30%
2007-2008	187	47.24%
2008-2009	127	00
overall	------	19.88%

Source: Torture in India, 2010, Asian Commission for Human Rights

The statement of the Minister, Sri. Ajay Maken in the LokSabha on 1 December 2010 revealed that 127 cases of deaths in Police custody were registered by the National Human Rights Commission in 2008-2009 against 187 cases in 2007-2008 and 119 cases in 2006-2007.[26] It is also significant to note that the majority of complaints received by the National Human Rights Commission after its establishment in 1993 were against police personnel.[27]

As per the Crime in India Report 2008 of the National Crime Records Bureau, New Delhi under Home Ministry, Government of India, 253 cases of human rights violation by Police were reportedthroughout the country during 2008.[28] The reported violations pertains mainly to 'Illegal Detentions', 'Fake Encounters', 'Extortion', and 'Torture'. Out of the 253 cases reported, 14 Policemen were charge-sheeted and only 8 of them were convicted for human rights

27

violations during the year.[29] 59 out of 253 cases of 'Torture' were reported. 39 and 33 cases of 'Extortion' and 'Failure in taking action' respectively. 25 cases reported under the head of 'False implication'.[30] On the other hand, Asian Centre for Human Rights in its report "Torture in India 2009" states that in the last eight years (from April 2001 to March 2009), an estimated 1,184 persons were killed in police custody in India.[31] Most of the victims were killed as a result of torture within the first 48 hours of being taken into custody.[32]Since October 1993, in all, 2560 cases of police encounters have been brought into the notice of National Human Rights Commission. Of them 1224 cases have been found by the Commission to be fake encounters. It means that, roughly, every 2nd police encounter is a fake one in the country.From the above data it can easily be identified that there takes place a number of human rights violations by police through out the country.

3.4. Conclusion

Human rights, today, refers to a wide variety of values and capabilities reflecting the diversity of human circumstances. They are conceived as universal, applying to all human beings everywhere. These rights are inherent in every human being. Hence, State is under obligation to protect the human rights. However, the Police, chief organ of State in protecting life and liberty of people commit numerous violations of human rights. Torture is employed quite often by the police. Chiefly, the police employ torture to extract information from the accused. However, it is not a correct method to torture andextract information from the accused. The police official should not underestimate the rights of their fellow human beings. They should adopt scientific method to investigate the case rather than torturing. Extraction of evidence by torture reveals the inefficiency of the police.

Endnotes

[1] Britannica Ready Reference Encyclopedia, Vol.5 (2005), pp.82-83.

[2] Oxford Advanced Learners Dictionary, (2010).

[3] Amnesty International USA, *Basics of Human Rights, available at*: http://www.amnestyusa.org/research/human-rights-basics (Visited on May 22, 2011).

[4] See *supra* Ch.2. for details.

[5] Mridushi, *National Human Rights Commission – Role in Human Rights Protection, Legal Information to Knowledge,* Jurisonline (2010); *available at*: http://jurisonline.in/2010/03/national-human-rights-commission-%E2%80%93-role-in-human-rights-protection/ (Visited on June 3, 2011).

[6] *Supra* n. 21 at p. 17.

[7] *Id.,* p. 75.

[8] The United Nations Publication, *Human Rights Today: A United Nations Priority* (2000), p.3.

[9] Call Wellman, *Solidarity, the Individual and Human Rights,* Human Rights Quarterly, Vol. 22 (2000), p. 639.

[10] *Id.,* p. 641.

[11] *Id.,* p. 642.

[12] Adopted by the General Assembly resolution 2200A (XXI) of the 16th December, 1966.

[13] *Id., supra* n. 5.

[14] *Ibid.*

[15] Kerala Police Act 2011, S. 14.

[16] The Black's Law Dictionary, (8th Ed. 1999).

[17] David H. Bayley, *Police for the Future* (1994), p. 27.

[18] *Id.,* p. 27.

[19] The Code of Conduct for Law Enforcement Officials was adopted by the General Assembly by Resolution 34/169 of 17 December 1979.

[20] *See* The UN Code of Conduct for Law Enforcement Officials, Commentary (a) to Art. 1.

[21] *Id.,* Art. 1, Commentary (b).

[22] Black's Law Dictionary (8th Ed. 1999).

[23] Oxford Advanced Learner's Dictionary, (8th Ed. 2010).

[24] *Supra* n.5.

[25] Unstarred Question No.1890 answered by Mr. Ajay Maken, Minister of State for Home Affairs, on 1.12.2009 in the LokSabha.

[26] Asian Centre for Human Rights Report, *Torture in India 2010* (2010), p. 5.

[27] Joshi G.P, *Police Accountability in India: policing contaminated by politics,* Commonwealth Human Rights initiative (2005), available at: http://www.hrsolidarity.net/mainfile.php/2005vol15no05/2448/ (Visited on February 22, 2011).

[28] R.N. Mangoli and Ganapati M. Tarase, *A Study of Human Rights Violation by Police in India,* International Journal of Criminology and Sociological Theory, Vol. 3, No. 2, December 2010, p. 401.

[29] *Ibid.*

[30] *Id.,* p. 402.

[31] *Ibid.*

[32] *Ibid.*

Chapter 4

PROTECTION OF HUMAN RIGHTS FROM POLICE - INTERNATIONAL LEGAL FRAMEWORK

The protection of human rights has been a central issue for the UN ever since it had come into existence, as the main idea for the very inception of the UN was to restrain the recurrence of World War and of the vindictive acts of annihilation and carnage committed by Nazi Germany against human beings during the Second World War. Hence, the protection mechanisms afforded under the UN scheme assumes significance. An examination of the protection of human rights from the violation by the police at international level requires a systematic analysis of the provisions of the Universal Declaration of Human Rights (UDHR), the International Covenant on Civil and Political Rights, The Declaration Against Torture, the Convention Against Torture, *etc*. These International fundamental documents on human rights are critically analysed with a view to identify the international system, the scheme of protection, the enforceability and the effectiveness of the protection mechanism. Further, India's obligation towards such international instruments and the extent of commitment for the compliance of such instruments by the Indian Government is necessary to be evaluated here. This evaluation is made with a view to know how far the international legal framework is functional under the Indian context related with protection of human rights from the violation by the police. Systematic analyses of international instruments are made below.

4.1. Protection of Human Rights from the Police

The preamble of the Universal Declaration of Human Rights recognizes the inherent dignity and inalienable rights of all human beings which are the foundation of freedom, justice and peace. It also sets out the past experience of consequence of the disregard and contempt for human rights as the result of the barbarous acts which outraged the conscience of mankind during the Second World War.[1] The inclusion of "past experience" in the preamble seems to be a reminder that such events shall not be repeated, and regards and honours are essential for the enjoyment of human rights.

After the adoption of the Universal Declaration of Human Rights, the Human Rights Commission embarked on the preparation of a Convention that has the authority of enforcing the human rights contained therein against its violations.[2] This lead the General Assembly for the adoption of a separate document, the International Covenant on Civil and Political Rights, with a mechanism for enforceability of the rights contained therein.

Even after the adoption of the International Covenant on Civil and Political Rights, one of the major concerns of the UN was how to combat with the torture, and other cruel and inhuman practices that takes place within domestic jurisdictions of National States. Though the Universal Declaration of Human Rights and International Covenant on Civil and Political Rights contained specific provisions regarding the right against torture or other cruel, inhuman and degrading treatment or punishment, they did not provide a precise definition as to what amounts to torture and how to embark upon with such crimes effectively.[3] In order to have effective protection against torture, it was felt that there must be a separate instrument at least in the form of a declaration. This led to the birth of the Declaration against torture or other cruel, inhuman and degrading treatment or punishment in 1975[4], and subsequently to the Convention against

32

Torture or other Cruel, Inhuman and Degrading Treatment or Punishment in 1987 (Convention Against Torture).[5]Thus, the three documents, *viz.,* the Universal Declaration of Human Rights, International Covenant on Civil and Political Rights and Convention Against Torture, are the major international instruments which provide persons from safeguards against arbitrary arrest, illegal detention, torture, *etc.*

4.1.1.   *Protection from Arbitrary Arrest or Detention*

Arrest and detention by the police in the pre-trial stage procedure is controversial in almost every country as it inevitably affects the deprivation of liberty of a person. The police abuse the powers of arrest and detention against innocent persons, even at the instance of State machineries. Considering this situation, the Universal Declaration of Human Rights prohibits arbitrary arrests. Though the Universal Declaration of Human Rights dose not define the term "arrest", Article 9 declares that "no one shall be subjected to arbitrary arrest, detention or exile". Thus, the Universal Declaration of Human Rights provides a right against arbitrary arrest or illegal detention to any individual person.

Regarding arrest and detention, the International Covenant on Civil and Political Rights makes elaborate procedures that have to be followed on arrest by the police or other law enforcement agencies. Article 9 provides:

i.   No person shall be subjected to arbitrary arrest or detention;

ii.   No person shall be deprived of his liberty except on such grounds and in accordance with such procedure as are established by law.

iii.   Arrested person shall be informed of the reasons for his arrest at the time of arrest, and also, the charges levelled against him.[6]

33

iv.   Any person arrested or detained shall be brought before a judicial official and shall be entitled to trial within a reasonable time or to be released.[7]

v.   Anyone who is deprived of his liberty by arrest or detention shall be entitled to take proceedings before a court.

vi.   The court may decide, without delay, on the lawfulness of his detention, and order his release, if the detention is not lawful.[8]

vii.   Arrested or detained persons shall be treated with humanity and with respect for the inherent dignity of the human person.[9]

viii.   Accused persons shall be segregated from convicted persons and shall be subject to separate treatment appropriate to their status as un-convicted persons.[10]

The International Covenant on Civil and Political Rights is more elaborate than the Universal Declaration of Human Rights with regard to protection from arbitrary arrest and detention. A careful observation of the International Covenant on Civil and Political Rights shows that it has been drafted very carefully for the protection of persons from arbitrary arrest and detention by providing elaborate provisions. The Covenant also takes care of juvenile accused persons as well and it provides that they shall be separated from adults and brought as speedily as possible for adjudication.[11] If police arrest unlawfully or detain illegally, the victims shall have an enforceable right to compensation.[12] Thus, the International Covenant on Civil and Political Rights sets out broader protection from arbitrary and unlawful arrest and detention of persons than the Universal Declaration of Human Rights.

4.1.2. Protection from Arbitrary interrogation

Interrogation is the stage at which police questions persons acquainted with the facts of the crime, elicit facts and gather information for detecting the commission of crime and to prove the guilt of the accused before the court. The police officials may extract information of crime from the suspect by employing torture or other cruel and inhuman methods. Considering such circumstances the Universal Declaration of Human Rights included the presumption of innocence of the accused person as a matter of right. Article 11 of the in the Declaration reads:

> Every one charged with a penal offence has the right to be presumed innocent until proved guilty according to the law in a public trial at which he has had all the guarantees necessary for his defence.[13]

The UN High Commissioner for Human Rights stated that the presumption of innocence has an important implication for the investigative process that all persons under interrogation are to be treated as innocent people, whether they have been arrested or detained, or whether they remain at liberty during the investigation.[14]

The International Covenant on Civil and Political Rights also provides similar protection to a person accused of crime. Article 14 (2) provides that "Everyone charged with a criminal offence shall have the right to be presumed innocent until proved guilty according to law." Further, Article 14 (3) (g) prohibits a person to be compelled to testify against himself or to confess guilt. Article 14 (3) (g), in other words, sets out the accused person's right to remain silent in a crime.[15]Thus, the above guarantees under the Universal Declaration Human Rights and International Covenant on Civil and Political Rights are considered as significant control over the arbitrary interrogative process.

35

4.1.3. Protection from Torture

The Universal Declaration of Human Rights and the International Covenant on Civil and Political Rights categorically prohibits torture or other cruel, inhuman or degrading treatment or punishment. Article 5 of the Universal Declaration of Human Rights provides that "no one shall be subjected to torture or to cruel, inhuman or degrading treatment or punishment". The same wordings are used in Article 7 of the International Covenant on Civil and Political Rights also. Article 7 also provides "no one shall be subjected to torture or to cruel, inhuman or degrading treatment or punishment". Thus, both the documents unconditionally prohibit torture.

However, neither the Universal Declaration of Human Rights nor the International Covenant on Civil and Political Rights provide a definition for "torture". The Human Rights Committee constituted under International Covenant on Civil and Political Rights also does not define the term 'torture'. The Human Rights Committee in its General Comments[16] No. 20 which deals with torture expresses that the aim of the provisions of Article 7 of the International Covenant on Civil and Political Rights is to protect both the dignity and the physical and mental integrity of the individual and hence, it is the duty of the State party to afford everyone protection through legislative and other measures as may be necessary against the acts of torture or cruel, inhuman treatment or punishment.[17]

The Convention Against Torture in Article 1 defines torture as:

1. any act by which severe pain or suffering, whether physical or mental, is intentionally inflicted on a person for such purposes as obtaining from that person or a third person information or a confession; or

36

2. Punishing by a public official or other person acting in an official capacity on a person for an act she/he or a third person has committed or is suspected of having committed of; or

3. Intimidating or coercing him/her or a third person in connection with such commission or suspicious commission of the act; or

4. When such pain or suffering is inflicted by or at the instigation of or with the consent or acquiescence of a public official of or other person acting in an official capacity.

The definition suffers from clarity as to what the term 'severe pain' means or implies. It seems that the intent was to give room for determining severity of pain depending on the facts and circumstances of each case. The Working Group on Convention Against Torture interpreted the word "severe" to mean "prolonged coercive and abusive conduct which, in itself, is not severe but becomes so over a period of time".[18] Nevertheless, the definition seems providing wider import on the matters connected with torture inflicted by public officials. The definition takes within its sweep not only the actual torture inflicted by the public official but also, torture inflicted at the instigation of or with the consent or acquiescence of a public official or any person acting in an official capacity. Thus, it is not only the police official's direct acts but their indirect acts are also included within the purview of the definition.

The Convention Against Torture not only totally prohibits torture but makes it further clear that no exceptional circumstances what so ever can be invoked to justify torture and refoulement.[19] It also provides that the States must make torture a domestic and extraditable crime.[20] It directs the States to arrest suspects who committed torture against any individual[21]and to investigate suspicious circumstances of torture.[22] This provision is included cautiously as, many a time, the torture is committed by officials of the State, and the Government may favour the suspects rather than victims of torture. The Convention Against Torture also provides that interrogation methods, practices and rules must be kept under review by the State parties. It also directs State Parties to make arrangements for the custody and treatment of persons subjected to arrest, detention or imprisonment for preventing cases of torture.[23] In sum, it is submitted that mostly the provisions are in the form of directions, suggestions and recommendations towards State parties. Obviously the torture, generally, takes place within the domestic jurisdiction, and State parties have a significant role in curbing the barbarous acts of torture.

4.1.4. *Protection from Unlawful Search and Seizure*

Right to privacy is quite often invaded by the police during the course of investigation and it is inevitable during investigation. However, there must be transparency during such process and must be within the legal framework. The Universal Declaration of Human Rights protects the Right to privacy, honor and reputation. Article 12 of the Declaration reads:

> No one shall be subjected to arbitrary interference with his privacy, family, home or correspondence, nor to attacks upon his honour and reputation. Everyone has the right to the protection of the law against such interference or attacks.

Thus, the Universal Declaration of Human Rights provides protection against arbitrary search or seizure.

The International Covenant on Civil and Political Rights also provides a similar protection from arbitrary searches or seizures. Article 17 provides "no one shall be subjected to arbitrary or unlawful interference with his privacy, family, home or correspondence, nor to unlawful attacks on his honour and reputation". The Human Rights Committee under the

38

International Covenant on Civil and Political Rights in General Comment No. 16 has interpreted that no interference with privacy can take place "except in cases envisaged by the law....which itself must comply with the provisions, aims and objectives of the covenant" and "reasonable in particular circumstances". [24] Thus, the Universal Declaration of Human Rights and the International Covenant on Civil and Political Rights protects people from unlawful searches or seizures by the police and other law enforcement agencies.

Hence, it is submitted that the Universal Declaration of Human Rights and the International Covenant on Civil and Political Rights provides protection from torture, illegal arrest/detention, unlawful searches and seizures and arbitrary interrogation of any person. Though many of the protections are the same in both the documents, the International Covenant on Civil and Political Rights provides elaborate safeguards in the event of arrest and detention. It also provides for an enforceable right to compensation in the case of arbitrary arrest or detention. However, the crucial matter is how these rights are enforced in redressing the grievances of individuals.

4.2. Enforceability of the Rights under the UDHR

The Declaration is the first comprehensive instrument on International Human Rights which encompasses civil, political, economic, social and cultural rights in one document. However, as its name implies "the declaration", it was neither intended to impose legal obligations on States, nor does it establish any supervisory organ to enforce the rights. The major problem with Universal Declaration of Human Rights is that it does not possess a legally binding enforceability and as such cannot create any obligation on member States to enforce it. In other words, there are no mechanisms set forth for the implementation of the rights in the Universal

39

Declaration of Human Rights in cases of any violations. The Declaration is simply a statement of intent and principles, nothing more; because it is merely a Declaration, it is neither a Treaty nor a Covenant. As a result, some critics have questioned its significance.[25] Its defenders emphasis that since its unanimous adoption by the UN General Assembly without a dissenting vote reflects the international moral commitment of Member States to translate it through the mechanism of the language of respective State's Constitutional law.[26] In this way, the Universal Declaration of Human Rights imposes a moral obligation on the Member States not to ignore its effectuation. The operative part of the Preamble of Universal Declaration of Human Rights reads as follows:

> "The General Assembly proclaims this Universal Declaration of Human Rights as a common standard of achievement for all peoples and all nations, to the end that every individual and every organ of society, keeping this Declaration constantly in mind, shall strive by teaching and education to promote respect for these rights and freedoms and by progressive measures, national and international, to secure their universal and effective recognition and observance, both among the peoples of member states themselves and among the peoples of territories under their jurisdiction."

The Universal Declaration of Human Rights has attained significant recognition by the UN Member States by *jus receptum*.[27] It is true, the Universal Declaration of Human Rights has come out as an instrument of declaration and as such it did not contain any provision for its enforceability. But now, after 60 years, it is considered as a sacrosanct document setting the basic standards of human rights and human dignity, and over the years, it received greater recognition from all countries and has, now, acquired the status of customary international law.[28] However, as customary international law the Universal Declaration of Human Rights works on international sphere of human rights violations only, such as massacre, genocide, *etc*. It does not have the direct impact on the sporadic police atrocities unless the State is perpetrating the mass killings or tortures within the State. Nevertheless, it provides protection for people from illegal arrest, unlawful detention, torture, fair trial, *etc*. Although the Universal Declaration of Human Rights did not contain enforceability mechanism, it, indeed, has contributed a lot to the birth, growth and development of global and national human rights instruments. Owing to the major lacuna of enforceability that the Universal Declaration of Human Rights envisaged, there was felt that there ought to be a document which provides some kind of enforcement mechanism, at least in the areas of civil and political rights. In fact, this led the UN to adopt two separate documents, *namely,* International Covenant on Civil and Political Rights (ICCPR) and International Covenant on Economic, Social and Cultural Rights (ICESCR).

4.3. Enforcement Mechanisms under ICCPR

During the drafting process of the International Covenant on Civil and Political Rights, one of the controversial points was the mechanism of international remedy, control and supervision.[29] There were deliberations on the issues relating to inclusion of enforcement mechanisms in the International Covenant on Civil and Political Rights and, finally, a concurrence had been reached for the establishment of a Human Rights Committee.[30] Hence, International Covenant on Civil and Political Rights under Article 28 provides for the establishment of the Human Rights Committee which, thus, becomes the principal organ of implementation and enforcement of the International Covenant on Civil and Political Rights. The Human Rights Committee consists of eighteen Members from different State parties and the Members must have recognized competence in the field of Human Rights.[31] Article 28 (3) provides that the Members of the Committee shall serve in their personal capacity which implies that though they were nominated by State parties, once they are elected Members of the Human Rights Committee, they are not Government (State) representatives. This is intended to ensure their independence, autonomous and impartiality in discharging the duties entrusted to them under the Covenant.

The enforcement mechanism under International Covenant on Civil and Political Rights can be categorized as follows:

2.   State reporting

3.   Communications/Complaints

      i.   Inter-State (State-to State) communications/complaints

     ii.   Individual communications/complaints

4.3.1. State Reporting

As per the emergence of trans-national human rights jurisprudence, the States have the obligation to submit reports to treaty monitoring bodies at prescribed intervals.[32] The ICCPR adopted State reporting procedure as the principal means of implementation of the rights enshrined in it. Article 40 of the ICCPR imposes on States the duty to submit initial and periodic reports. The reports shall indicate:

a) the measures the Member States have adopted to give effect to the rights recognized in the ICCPR,

b) the progress made in the enjoyment of those rights, and

c) the factors and difficulties, if any, affecting the implementation of the ICCPR.

These reports are to be transmitted to the Secretary General of the United Nations for consideration. The reporting procedure, in general, is criticized as not effective in as much as that reports prepared by State (Government) officials would not naturally give the real human rights situation in their countries. France Viljoen says "Governments are likely to paint a relatively positive picture of the situation for which they bear responsibility. Some State Reports even blatantly distorts facts."[33] Besides, some States fail to submit reports properly and/or timely.[34] It can be stated that although these reporting systems by themselves do not constitute an effective measure of control, yet they open an opportunity for critical examination, for drawing attention to gaps or inaccuracies in the information provided, and for comparing official statements with other sources of information on the human rights situations in a State.

4.3.2. Communications

One of the mechanisms provided under the ICCPR for redressing the grievance of violation of human rights is communication procedure. This is a procedure by which one may submit communication of human rights violation to the Human Rights Committee with a view to obtain remedy from the appropriate organ alleging that a State party has not discharged its obligation in protecting the rights recognized in the ICCPR. In fact, the ICCPR doesn't use the word 'complaint' as the drafters seem to have deliberately avoided the use of the term at the instance of State parties. The State parties might have been sensitized by the fear of being accused for violation of human rights before an international organ as the 'complaint' requires some kind of remedy. The ICCPR rather uses 'communications' as a moderating term. It recognizes two types of communications, namely:

      (i)   Inter-state Communications; and

      (ii)   Individual communications

4.3.2.1.Inter-State Communications

The Inter-state communication is a process by which one State party directs a communication (complaint) to the Human Rights Committee against another State party in relation to the violation of human rights under ICCPR. The Committee examines communications only if (1) the State alleged to have committed violation of human rights has made a declaration recognizing the competence of the Human Rights Committee, and (2) the complaining State, the State that have submitted the communications, have made similar declaration.[35] When such communications are made, the first step is to enable the States concerned to resolve the matter themselves.[36] If the two States fail to solve the matter within six months, the matter may be referred to the Human Rights Committee by a notice.[37] The Committee, however, cannot pass its opinions on violations. It is to make its good offices available with a view to a friendly settlement, and if it is not possible, the Committee is required to submit a report to the UN setting out the facts, the steps taken by the Committee in resolving the matter, *etc.*[38] This mechanism is operative when there are mass violations of human rights at the instance of the State, and had gained international attention. This procedure is not applicable in the case of violation of human rights by the police in individual cases. Further, the solution by this process is conciliation, negotiations and settlements. The Human Rights Committee lacks authority for enforcement even if it finds violations of human rights. It is interesting to note that no interstate communication has been submitted under the UN human Rights treaties.[39] Thus, it is submitted that the mechanism is not an effective method in the case of violation of human rights by the police.

4.3.2.2. Individual Communication

Individual communication is a method by which individuals may submit communications directly to the Human Rights Committee with a view to obtain remedy, claiming that a State party has violated the rights recognized by the International Covenant on Civil and Political Rights. During the drafting process there were arguments for and against inclusion of a mechanism for enforcement of violation of human rights by individuals from the State Party.[40] However, it was difficult to reach a consensus when International Covenant on Civil and Political Rights was adopted in 1966 and hence, the provision for individual complaint mechanism was not included in the International Covenant on Civil and Political Rights. There were criticisms due to the lack of enforceability mechanism for individuals whose rights are violated within a domestic jurisdiction of a State party. It has been commented that the real test of the effectiveness of an international system for the protection of human rights lies on the fact that whether it permits an individual, who believes that his rights have been violated, to seek a remedy from an international institution."[41] Thus, the First Optional Protocol to International Covenant on Civil and Political Rights was adopted separately allowing individuals to make communications directly to Human Rights Committee.[42] Since it is a separate instrument, separate ratification by the State parties is essential for its operation in domestic jurisdictions.

There are stipulations for the admissibility of the Individual complaints. One of the stipulations is the rule of exhaustion which dictates that all domestic remedies must have been explored by the individual before approaching the Human Rights Committee.[43] Another stipulation is that communications which are anonymous, abusive or incompatible with the provisions of the ICCPR are not admissible.[44] Article 1 of the First Optional Protocol to ICCPR stipulates that a State party to the ICCPR that becomes a Party to the Protocol recognizes the competence of the Human Rights Committee to receive and consider communications from individuals who claim to be victims of violation by that State party of any of the rights set forth in ICCPR. The Human Rights Committee must communicate regarding the individual complaint to the State Party concerned, and the State party is required to submit written explanations or statements within six months clarifying the matter and the remedy, if any, that may have been taken by that State.[45] Article 5(4) provides that the Committee shall forward its views to the State Party concerned and to the individual.

ICCPR, no doubt, ensures a large number of human rights, particularly in relation to torture, custodial violence, arbitrary interrogation, arrest, detention, search and seizure, etc. However, it has only a weak mechanism for the enforceability of the rights in the event of violation of such rights. Even in the case of individual communication mechanism, after the conclusion of the complaint by the Human Rights Committee, it gives its opinion to the individual and the State concerned. The State may or may not comply with such opinion for lack of authority for enforcement by Human Rights Committee. State Reporting and Inter-State Communications have no much relevance as a mechanism for the enforceability of ICCPR rights. Hence, it is submitted that although the ICCPR guarantees a number of important rights for the protection of persons from police abuses, yet it suffers for want of effective enforceable mechanism.

4.4. Enforcement mechanism under Convention Against Torture

Part II of the Convention Against Torture provides for the establishment of a Committee Against Torture comprising a body of ten independent experts that monitors implementation of the Convention Against Torture.[46] Committee Against Torture is empowered to receive and consider communications for and on behalf of individuals who claim to be victims of torture by the State machineries, and the action or remedy given by the State is not satisfactory for the victim.[47] However, Committee Against Torture does not enjoy any authority to enforce its findings against any State. It is in the form of recommendation, suggestion or opinion only. To that extent, it is submitted that the enforcement mechanism under Convention Against Torture also suffers the same lacuna as the ICCPR mechanism of enforcement. It has alsobeenmade obligatory for the States parties to submit periodic reports to the Committee Against Torture indicating measures taken to fulfill their obligations under the Convention Against Torture.[48] The Committee Against Torture after examination of such reports, addresses its concerns and recommendations to the State party in the form of "concluding observations".[49] It may also conduct inquiries into the information of torture within a State Party jurisdiction and also consider inter-state complaints.[50] This way the UN makes the State parties responsible for torturous acts within their jurisdiction, and to deal with them separately as the acts of torture touch the very basis instinct of humanity and human dignity.

4.4.1. Monitoring under Optional Protocol to the Convention Against Torture

In order to provide protection from torture and to monitoring the commission of torture within the State jurisdictions, an Optional Protocol to the Convention Against Torture was adopted by the UN and it came into force in June 2006. Under the Optional Protocol to the Convention Against Torture, State Parties are obliged to establish an independent National Preventive Mechanisms for the prevention of torture at the domestic level and such National Preventive Mechanisms should have the mandate to inspect places of detention.[51] The Optional Protocol to the Convention Against Torture also creates the Sub-committee on Prevention of Torture at international level. [52] Sub-committee on Prevention of Torture makes recommendations to the State Parties regarding the working of National Preventive Mechanisms, and advice and assists the State Parties for the establishment of effective preventive mechanisms within their domestic jurisdictions.[53] Sub-committee on Prevention of Torture has an unrestricted access to all places of detention and to all relevant information to visit places where persons deprived of their liberties are kept within the jurisdiction of States parties.[54] Thus, the Sub-committee on Prevention of Torture can visit any places of detention including police stations, prisons, pre-trial detention centres, juvenile homes and any other places where people deprived of their liberty are kept within the jurisdiction of State Parties. However, the Sub-committee on Prevention of Torture has purely preventive mandate only. The mechanism provided for the Sub-committee on Prevention of Torture is only recommendations to the State Parties regarding the occurrence of torture, visits to places of detention and public reporting. The question that arises here is: Will those mechanisms be sufficient, or can be considered as efficient, to control the torture perpetrated by State police? The answer, surely, is negative. It happens, frequently, that State Governments tries to hush up torture in police custody. In such a situation there should be a super-national body which could investigate into and bring about action against the culprits.

4.5. India and the UN Declarations and Covenants

Indian Constitution does not explicitly provide for the incorporation of international convention and treaties into the domestic legal system. However, Article 51(c) of the Constitution provides that "the State shall endeavour to foster respect for international law and treaty obligations in the dealings of organized people with another." This shows that India follows the dualist pattern[55] pertaining to the implementation of the international declarations, treaties and covenants in the municipal legal system.[56] Hence, it is necessary for Indian Parliament to enact legislation incorporating the rights under such International covenants, declarations, *etc.*, for its implementation in Indian domestic jurisdiction. Constitution of India exclusively empowers the Parliament to implement international treaties and conventions in

48

India. Article 253 of the Constitution provides: "Parliament has power to make any law for the whole or any part of the territory of India for implementing any treaty, agreement or convention with any other country or countries or any decision made at any international conference, association or other body." Further, 'entry 14' of the Union List of the Seventh Schedule empowers Parliament to legislate in relation to "entering into treaties and agreement and implementing of treaties and agreement with foreign countries and implementing of treaties, agreements and conventions with foreign countries". Thus, in India, it is the Parliament which alone has the authority to implement the international treaties, covenants, declarations, *etc.*

4.5.1. *Supreme Court of India on UN Covenants*

The Supreme Court has reiterated this dualist approach by holding that an international treaty that India has signed do not become part of the *corpus juris* of India until Parliament makes implementing legislation incorporating those treaty provisions.[57] However, Supreme Court later has observed that non-conflicting treaties and covenants can be implemented into the domestic jurisdiction so long as they are not inconsistent with the sovereignty and integrity of India, and the supremacy of the legislative authority of the Parliament. The Supreme Court observed:

> "The comity of Nations requires that Rules of International Law may be accommodated in the Municipal Law even without express legislative sanction provided they do not run into conflict with Acts of Parliament. But when they do run into such conflict, the sovereignty and the integrity of the Republic and the supremacy of the constituted legislatures in making the laws may not be subjected to external rules except to the extent legitimately accepted by the constituted legislatures themselves. The doctrine of incorporation recognises the position that the rules of international law are incorporated into national law and considered to be part of the national law, unless they are in conflict with an Act of Parliament. Comity of nations or no, Municipal Law must prevail in case of conflict."[58]

Thus, the Supreme Court is demonstrating a harmonious construction between International treaties, declarations and conventions on the one hand and Indian laws on the other as long as there are no inconsistencies between them. It is only when there are inconsistencies that the domestic law shall prevail and requires an Act of Parliament for the implementation of such international treaties, covenants, declarations, *etc.*

However, in the case of implementation of rights guaranteed under the Universal Declaration of Human Rights and ICCPR, the Supreme Court has observed that those rights can be relied upon by courts and are enforceable in India even though implementing legislation has not been made by Parliament, since they are in tune with fundamental rights guaranteed by the Constitution. While dealing with handcuffing in *Prem Shankar Shukla* v.*Delhi Administration*[59] the Supreme Court reminded the relevance of the core principles of Article 5 of Universal Declaration of Human Rights and Article 10 of ICCPR which speaks for humane treatment in arresting and detaining a person.[60] In *People's Union of Civil Liberties* v. *Union of India*[61] taking the experience of Common Law system the Supreme Court differentiated the status of International Covenant on Civil and Political Rights and other multilateral treaties by observing that in the case of ICCPR, even in the absence of the Act of Parliament and though India entered a specific reservation[62] to Article 9 (5) of International Covenant on Civil and Political Rights when ratifying the Convention in 1979, rights guaranteed under International Covenant on Civil and Political Rights can operate into our legal system. Supreme Court observed:

"Apart from influencing the construction of a statute or subordinate legislation, an international convention may play a part in the development by the courts of the common law...it would suffice to State that the provisions of the covenant, which elucidate and go to effectuate the fundamental rights guaranteed by our

50

Constitution, can certainly be relied upon by courts as facets of those fundamental rights and hence, enforceable as such. So far as multi-lateral treaties are concerned, the law is, of course, different -and definite."[63]

Thus, it is now settled matter that the Universal Declaration of Human Rights and ICCPR are part of the Indian legal system, where as in the cases of multilateral treaties, it must get recognition from Indian Parliament.

In *Neelabati Behra* v. *State of Orissa*,[64] Supreme Court made a reference of Article 9 (5) of ICCPR which provides for an enforceable right to compensation for victims of unlawful arrest or detention, and observed "We may also refer to Article 9(5) of the International Covenant on Civil and Political Rights, 1966 which indicates that an enforceable right to compensation is not alien to the concept of enforcement of a guaranteed right *in India*."[65]Initially, the Supreme Court was also hesitant to provide compensation under Article 21 of the Constitution of India to victims of unlawful arrest, illegal detention or torture when it dealt with *Khatri.* *State of Bihar*[66], and *Veena Sethi* v. *State of Bihar*[67]. However, due to the continuous and unabated violation of human rights by the police and State machineries, the Supreme Court, taking the spirit from Article 9 of ICCPR, evolved the compensation jurisprudence inherent in Article 21. *RudalSha* v. *State of Bihar*[68] was the first case whereby the Supreme Court ordered to pay compensation of Rupees thirty five thousand for illegally detaining a person without legal justification for fourteen years. The Supreme Court thereby opened a new horizon in the Indian human rights jurisprudence by making the State accountable for the violation of human rights by State machineries. Thereafter, in a number of cases, the Supreme Court has awarded monetary compensation for the violation of human rights for illegal detention, unlawful arrest, torture, etc.[69] Thus, though the Constitution does not expressly provide an enforceable right to

51

compensation, taking the spirit from Article 9 (5) of ICCPR, now it has become a rule under Article 21 to provide compensation for the violation of human rights.

However, it is unfortunate to note that India has not ratified the First Optional Protocol to ICCPR which provide for individual communication mechanism for the individuals to directly approach the Human Rights Committee in connection with the violation of rights enshrined under the ICCPR where the complainant is not satisfied by the State action/remedy.[70] It is submitted that Government of India is not very serious about the enormous human rights violations that takes place in many quarters including violations by the police. Moreover, the system of individual complaint/communication mechanism is much more intrusive than the State Reporting mechanism into the affairs of domestic jurisdiction. Hence, it may be embarrassing for India among international community by the unequivocal findings of the Human Rights Committee. It is further submitted that considering the significance of human rights and values, India should have ratified the First Optional Protocol to ICCPR giving opportunities for individual citizens to redress their grievances, if the action/remedy of the State Institutions is not satisfying to the individuals.

4.5.2.   Adoption of Convention Against Torture in India

Regarding the Convention Against Torture, India was reluctant to adopt and ratify it ever since Convention Against Torture was passed by the UN General Assembly in 1984. After the establishment of National Human Rights Commission in 1993, one of the major tasks of the Commission was to persuade the Government of India to ratify the Convention Against Torture. The National Human Rights Commission, right from the beginning of its functioning, made a series of communications with the Prime Minister, Home Minister and External Affairs Minister for the adoption and ratification of the Convention Against Torture.[71] As a result of the relentless effort of the National Human Rights Commission, India has adopted the Convention Against Torture in 1997. Unfortunately, India has not ratified the Convention Against Torture so far. However, there is a move for the ratification of Convention Against Torture by India. In pursuance of this, the Central Government introduced the Bill against Torture in the LokSabha on April 26, 2010. The LokSabha passed it on May 6 and submitted to RajyaSabha. RajyaSabha adopted a motion on August 31,2010 referring the Bill to a Select Committee, comprising 13 of its members. The Select Committee has presented its report to RajyaSabha on December 6, 2010.[72] The Bill provides for punishment of torture inflicted by public servant or torture committed with the consent or acquiescence of a public servant. According to the Bill, "torture" means and includes any act that cause "grievous hurt "or "mental or physical danger to life, limb or health". There were criticisms about such a restrictive definition and, hence, the Select Committee consulted the Pre-Legislative Briefing Service, a group of legal experts, and obtained the advice from them. They suggested that the words "grievous hurt" and "danger to life, limb or health" be replaced with "severe pain or suffering" in line with Convention Against Torture.[73] The Select Committee has accepted its suggestion and recommended that the definition of torture be suitably enlarged so as not to exclude acts generally known to be committed on persons in custody which cause severe physical and mental injury, pain, trauma, agony, and so on.[74] The Bill provides for six months limitation period for making a complaint against torture. The Select Committee suggested that it should be extended for a period of two years from the date of alleged torture as this would give sufficient time to enable the victim of torture to initiate proceedings against those responsible for torture.[75] Another significant point to be noted is that the Clause 6 of the Bill provides for prior sanction from the Government in order to prosecute the public servant. It is submitted that this can be a bottleneck for the victim of torture in obtaining the prior sanction from the Government for taking action against erring Police officials. Police officials are already powerful and could influence the Government or even manipulate the case. However, it is provided in the Bill that if such sanction is not granted within three months, it would be deemed to have been granted. The Select Committee has recommended that sanction in blatant cases of torture should be the norm and where sanction to prosecute is declined, the said decision should be supported by reasons, and the decision must also be appealable.[76] It is hoped that India would ratify the Convention Against Torture sooner thereby upholding the rights against torture or cruel, inhuman treatment or punishment of the helpless individuals in the custody of police and other law enforcement agencies.

4.6. Conclusion

The Universal Declaration of Human Rights provides protection from torture, arbitrary arrest and illegal detention. However, the Universal Declaration of Human Rights was made as a declaration having neither the force of International law nor any mechanism to enforce the violations of the human rights. The so called 'Cold War' that existed between the two prominent veto powers of the Security Council of the UN, *namely*, USA and USSR, it was made further difficult to take concrete measures in protecting the human rights at international level and the status of the Universal Declaration of Human Rights remained more or less the same as a declaration. However, over the years, due to the popular recognition and acceptance, the Universal Declaration of Human Rights has attained the position of International customary law which implies that where ever and whenever there is violation of the rights contained in the Universal Declaration of Human Rights, UN can follow such procedure as are used in the case of violations of international law and can even use such force as is provided in the matters of

54

violations of any other international law to compel a State party to comply with it. However, the UN charter confirms by virtue of Article 2(7) by reassuring its Member States that it lacked the authority to intervene in matters that were "essentially within the domestic jurisdiction" of States. This prohibition was subject only to qualification relating to the overriding responsibility of the UN acting under Chapter VII of the Charter to maintain international peace and security.[77]Thus, it is submitted that though there is no specific mechanism provided in the Universal Declaration of Human Rights, UN Security Council can invoke its power to maintain international peace and security and compel any State to comply with the protection of the human rights under Universal Declaration of Human Rights and can also use such force as are necessary depending on the gravity of the offence committed by the State. However, such measures taken by the UN are only in cases of gross human rights violations such as genocide or mass killings at the instances of State. Individual human rights violations are not dealt with under such mechanism too. Hence, individual Police atrocities, which are outrageous in India, cannot be dealt with under this mechanism.

International Covenant on Civil and Political Rights gained significant credence over the years and it provides a number of protections in the cases of torture, arbitrary arrest, detention, search or seizure. However, the enforcement mechanisms provided such as State Reporting, Inter-State communication and Individual communication are not very effective in the event of violation of human rights by the police. Indian Supreme Court and High Courts which deal with enforceability of fundamental rights, tries to incorporate the spirit of Universal Declaration of Human Rights and International Covenant on Civil and Political Rights in its decisions, particularly in matters connected with unlawful arrest, illegal detention, torture, inhuman treatment, *etc.*, committed by the police and other law enforcement agencies. In many cases, irrespective of the fact that Indian Constitution does not expressly provide for enforceable right to compensation for the violation of fundamental rights, the Supreme Court relying on Article 9 (5) of International Covenant on Civil and Political Rights and by interpreting Article 21 of Constitution of India, has awarded monetary compensation for the violation of human rights of individuals. Thus, the Supreme Court, rely on Universal Declaration of Human Rights and International Covenant on Civil and Political Rights provisions for giving vivid interpretation to fundamental rights guaranteed by the Constitution of India.

However, it is unfortunate to note that India, the largest democratic country in the world, is not a signatory for the First Optional Protocol to ICCPR[78]which provides with a mechanism for individual communication. This way, the Government of India limits the opportunity of individuals to complain to a super-national body to redress their grievances related with violations of human rights. It may be positively seen as that the Courts in India, particularly the apex Court, are known for impartiality, autonomy and upholding the fundamental human rights by way of judicial activism, judicial interpretation and judicial review, and has widened the scope of impartial remedy to the aggrieved person whose rights are violated by State machinery. However, this cannot be a valid justification for not accepting the First Optional Protocol to ICCPR thereby restricting the right to effective remedy of an individual.

The message of United Nation is serious in relation to physical harm by torture or other cruel, degrading, inhuman treatment or punishment that such acts of barbarous nature must be curbed. The Convention Against Torture, in addition to defining what amounts to torture, also provide by the Optional Protocol to the Convention Against Torture an enforcement mechanism of individual communication. It is submitted that the enforcement mechanism cannot be considered as very effective in as much as there is no mechanism for punishing the wrongdoer.

56

However, Convention Against Torture categorically provides that any excuse for the torture employed by the State machineries will not be considered as a defense. India has adopted the Convention Against Torture in 1997, but has not ratified it so far. It is welcome that India is now taking positive steps to ratify Convention Against Torture.

Thus, in summary, it can be submitted that the Universal Declaration of Human Rights, International Covenant on Civil and Political Rights and Convention Against Torture provide effective international legal framework for the protection from being subjected to torture, arbitrary arrest, unlawful interrogation, illegal detention or unlawful search and seizure by the police. The International Covenant on Civil and Political Rights and the Convention Against Torture provides mechanism for enforceability of such rights. However, the mechanism suffers for its binding effect on the State Parties. This can be considered as a major defect of the International Covenant on Civil and Political Rights and the Convention Against Torture.

Endnotes

[1] *See* Preamble of the Universal Declaration of Human Rights.

[2] Rhona K.M. Smith, *Textbook on International Human Rights*(2007), p. 47; United States of America and some other Western Countries were of the view that there should be two separate documents where as the Union of Soviet Socialist Republics and the so called Communist bloc were of opinion that social, economic and cultural rights are of the same footing as that of civil and political rights.

[3] Universal Declaration of Human Rights, Art.5;International Covenant on Civil and Political Rights, Art. 7.

[4] G.A. Res. 3452 (XXX), passed on December 9, 1975; Hereinafter referred as "Declaration Against Torture"

[5] G.A. Res. 39/46, adopted by the General Assembly on December 10, 1984 and entered into force on June 26, 1987; Hereinafter referred as "Convention against Torture".

[6] International Covenant on Civil and Political Rights, Art.10, Sub-Art. (1).

7   *Id.,* Sub-Art. (3).

8   *Id.,* Sub-Art. (4).

9   *Id.,* Art. 10, Sub-Art. (1).

10 *Id.,* Sub-Art. (2)(a).

11 *Id.,* Sub-Art. (2)(b).

12 *Id.,* Art. 9, Sub-Art. (5).

13 The same presumption is provided under International Covenant on Civil and Political Rights, Article 14, paragraph 2; the European Convention on Human Rights, Article 6, paragraph 2; the American Convention on Human Rights, Article 8, paragraph 2; the African Charter on Human and People's Rights, Article 7 paragraph1(b);*See also* High Commissioner for Human Rights, *Human Rights and Law Enforcement: Manual on Human Rights Training for the Police*, Professional Training Series No.5, Center for Human rights, Geneva, p.59.

14 High Commissioner for Human Rights, *Human Rights and Law Enforcement: Manual on Human Rights Training for the Police*, Professional Training Series No.5, Center for Human rights, Geneva P.59.

15 See*infra*Ch.6 for details regarding 'right to remain silent'.

16 Human Rights Committee constituted under the International Covenant on Civil and Political Rights publishes its interpretation of the content of human rights provisions in Covenant in the form of General Comments and it is considered to be an authoritative interpretation.

17 Human Rights Committee, General Comments, No. 20, Para 2.

18 V. Venkatesan, "Redefining Torture", *The Frontline*, January 29, 2011.

19 Sending or extraditing to a State where torture is likely to occur.

20 *See* Convention against Torture and other Cruel, Inhuman or degrading treatment or punishment (herein after referred as "Convention Against Torture"), Art. 5 and 8.

21 *Id.,* Art. 6.

22 *Id.,* Art. 12.

23 *Id.,* Art. 11.

24 Mashood A.Baderin, *International Human Rights and Islamic Law* (2003), p.114.

25 Richard A. Falk, *Human Rights Horizons: The Pursuit of Justice in a Globalizing World* (2000), p.38.

26 With abstentions from the Byelorussia, Czechoslovakia, Poland, Saudi Arabia, South Africa, the Soviet Union, the Ukrainian, and Yugoslavia.

27 Foreign laws are additions to a particular nation' domestic laws and in that respect are called *jus receptum, See* Black's Law Dictionary, (1990), p. 647.

28 See *supra* n. 86 at pp.37-40; As long as international human rights treaties do not enjoy universal ratification, the treaties will be an incomplete means of attaining the goal of universal respect for human rights. Customary International Law fills the gap, as it fills those states not party to the treaty-provided that the relevant norm has become a rule of customary international law. A norm

attains that status if it is a 'general practice accepted as law'. This means that the existence of such a rule has to be proven by demonstrating two elements, viz; state practice and *opinion juris; See* Frans Viljoen, *International Human Rights Law in Africa* (2007), p. 27.

[29] *Supra* n. 24, at p.114.

[30] Michael J. Dennis, *Human Rights in 2002: The Annual Session of the UN Commission on Human Rights and the Economic and Social Council,* American Journal of International Law, Vol. 97, 2 (2003) p.377.

[31] International Covenant on Civil and Political Rights, Art. 28.

[32] Communication 869/1999, *Piandiong and Others v. The Philipines*, UN Doc a/56/40, Vol II, 19 October, 2000; See *also* Frans Viljoen, *International Human Rights Law in Africa* (2007) p.37.

[33] FransViljoen, *International Human Rights Law in Africa* (2007), p.38.

[34] *Id.,* p.38.

[35] *See* International Covenant on Civil and Political Rights, Art. 41 (1).

[36] *Id.,* Art. 41, Sub-Art. (1) (a) and (b).

[37] *Id.,* Sub-Art. (1) (b)

[38] *Id.,* Art. 41.

[39] *Supra* n.33, at p.35.

[40] Michael J. Dennis and David P. Stewart, Justiciability of Economic, Social, and Cultural Rights: Should There be an International Complaints Mechanism to Adjudicate the Rights to Food, Water, Housing, and Health?, 98 A.J.I.L. (2004), p. 462.

[41]Steven R. Ratner and Jason S Abrams, *Accountability for Human Rights Atrocities In International Law: Beyond the Nuremberg Legacy,* (2nd Ed., 2001), p.46.

[42] First Optional Protocol was adopted separately but in the same year in 1976 when the International Covenant on Civil and Political Rights entered in to force.

[43] First Optional Protocol to International Covenant on Civil and Political Rights, Art. 2.

Id., Art. 3.

'., Art. 4(2).

t Optional Protocol to International Covenant on Civil and Political Rights, Art. 17.

rt. 22.

19.

ional Protocol to International Covenant on Civil and Political Rights, Art.19 (2).

ᐟ (2).

ᐟtocol to International Covenant on Civil and Political Rights, Art.11 (1) (a).

54   *Id.,* Art. 11 (1) (a) and 12.

55'Dualist pattern' is one system whereby the international treaties, covenants etc. becomes part of the Municipal law by the act of Legislature in the State, on the other hand 'Monolist pattern' is one whereby the international treaties, covenants etc. becomes part of the Municipal law with out any act of the Legislature in the State.

56   *State of Madras* v.*G.G. Menon,* A.I.R. 1954 S.C. 517.

57   *Jolly George* v. *Bank of Cochin,* A.I.R. 1980 S.C. 470; *See also* Reenu Paul, *National Human Rights Commission-An evaluation* (2003),Unpublished Master's Thesis, London School of Economics, London, P.24.

58   *Gramophone Co. of India Ltd* v.*BirendraBahadurPandey*A.I.R. 1984 S.C. 667, p. 671.

59   1980 S.C.R. (3) 855.

60   1980 S.C.R. (3) 855, p. 864.

61   A.I.R. 1997 S.C. 1203.

62   India entered a specific reservation regarding Article 9(5) of the International Covenant on Civil and Political Rights at the time of ratification in 1979.

63   *Supra* n. 149, at 1206; *See also Visakhav.State of Rajasthan,* A.I.R. 1997 S.C. 3011.

64   1993 S.C.R. (2) 581.

65   *Id.,* p. 604; emphasis added.

66   A.I.R. 1981 S.C. 928; *See also* R. VenkataRao, *Custodial Violence and Judicial Response,* Vol. 7, Journal of the National Human Rights Commission, India, (2008) P. 88.

67   A.I.R. 1983 S.C. 339.

68   A.I.R. 1983 S.C. 1086.

69   *Sebastian M. Hongray* v. *Union of India,* A.I.R. 1984 S.C. 1026, where Supreme Court awarded Rupees One lakh each as exemplary cost for the wives of two person who were not been produced even after the writ issued by the Supreme Court ; *Bheem Singh* v. *State of Jammu & Kashmir,* A.I.R. 1986 S.C. 494, where SC awarded Rupees fifty thousand for illegal arrest and detention; *Supreme Court legal Aid Committee* v. *State of Bihar,* (1990) 3 S.C.C. 482, where Supreme Court awarded Rupees twenty thousand for not providing medical treatment while in custody; *Peoples' Union for Democratic Rights* v. *State of Bihar,* A.I.R. 1987 S.C. 355, where the Supreme Court awarded Rupees twenty thousand each to the dependants of deceased and rupees five thousand to the injured in a brutal police firing; *Saheli* v. *Commissioner of Police,* (1990) 1 S.C.C. 422, where Supreme Court awarded compensation of Rupees twenty five thousand to the mother of the deceased who was tortured to death by police; *Neelabati Behera* v. *State of Orissa,* (1993) 2 S.C.C. 746, where Supreme Court awarded Rupees one lakh fifty thousand to the mother for the torture to death of her son.

70   International Covenant on Civil and Political Rights has two optional Protocols; while the First Optional Protocol deals with allowing individual communication, the Second Optional Protocol is meant for abolition of death penalty in State Jurisdictions.

·   National Human Rights Commission, Annual Report, 1994-95 and 1995-96.

[72] *Supra* n. 18.

[73] Article 1 of Convention Against Torture provides definition of "torture".

[74] *Supra* n.18.

[75] Clause 5 of Convention Against Torture Bill.

[76] *Supra* n.18..

[77] *Supra* n. 25

[78] Christof Heyna and Frans Viljoen, *The Impact of the United Nations Human Rights Treaties on the Domestic Level*, Kluwer Law International(2002), p. 323.

Chapter 5

PROTECTION OF HUMAN RIGHTS FROM POLICE UNDER THE INDIAN CONSTITUTION

The Universal Declaration of Human Rights provides for a number of minimum guarantees that must be complied with under all circumstances during arrest, detention and interrogation of a person. The Constitution of India came into operation just two years after the adoption of Universal Declaration of Human Rights by the UN General Assembly in 1948. This had a great bearing on Part III of the Constitution of India which elaborates fundamental rights and freedoms. The Framers of the Indian Constitution had a crucial concern about the protection of rights of accused, arrested and detained persons from the false inculpation, arbitrary arrest, unlawful detention and vexatious prosecution in criminal cases of the underprivileged, illiterate and ignorant masses by the State colonial police. This had, *inter alia*, influenced the framers to include provisions such as Article 20 dealing with protection from double jeopardy and self incrimination; Article 21 dealing with right to life and personal liberty; and Article 22 dealing with rights of arrested and accused persons in criminal cases. Basically, these provisions are the constitutional safeguards available to any person as accused or arrested or detained by the police. Indeed, the areas of accusation, arrest and detention are the most controversial areas in connection with the police action on the one hand and the rights of arrested or detained persons on the other.

5.1. Fundamental Rights under the Indian Constitution

The Constituent Assembly which first met on December 9, 1946 deliberated to uphold the civil liberties of the people as a significant matter. The demand for a declaration arose from four factors (i) lack of civil liberties in India during the British rule, (ii) Deplorable socio-economic conditions particularly affecting the untouchables and women, (iii) Existence of different religious, linguistic and ethnic groups encouraged and exploited by the British, and (iv) Exploitation of the tenants by the landlords.[1] Considering these aspects the founding fathers of the Constitution gave a significant place for fundamental rights in the Constitution as an embodiment of the aspirations of the people for the Constitutional recognition of civil rights. The Fundamental Rights, in Indian Constitution have been grouped under seven heads as follows:

i. Right to Equality comprising Art. 14 to 18.

ii. Right to Freedom comprising Art. 19 to 22 which guarantee several freedoms such as freedom of speech and expression, right to life and personal liberty, freedom from arbitrary arrest and detention, etc.

iii. Right against Exploitation consists of Art. 23 and 24.

iv. Right to Freedom of Religion is guaranteed by Art. 25 to 28.

v. Cultural and Educational Rights are guaranteed by Art. 29 and 30.

vi. Right to Property is now very much diluted and is secured to some extent by Art. 31-A, 31-B, 31- C.

vii. Right to Constitutional Remedies is secured by Art. 32 to 35.

It is guaranteed under the Indian Constitution that these rights are available irrespective of race, place of birth, religion, caste, creed or gender. The Fundamental Rights are enforceable though court of law and hence, the concept of Fundamental Rights protects individuals against excesses of the State and constitutes by and large, a limitation on the govt.[2] In *A. K. Gopalan* v. *The State of Madras,*[3] Sastri J., said:

"It is true to say that, in a sense, the people delegated to the legislative, executive and judicial organs of the State their respective powers while reserving powers to themselves the fundamental rights which they made paramount by providing that the State shall not make any law which takes away or abridges the rights conferred by that Part".[4]

Thus, the Indian Constitution provides the fundamental rights of the people and safeguards from the arbitrary encroachment or abuse or abridgment of those rights by the State machineries.

5.2. Fundamental Rights are Human Rights

The Part III of the Constitution of India sets out a number of civil, political and cultural rights as fundamental rights. The rights provided in this part are made enforceable thought court of law. Fundamental rights differ from ordinary rights in the sense that the former are inviolable. No law, ordinance, custom, usage, or administrative order can abridge or take them away. Any law, which is violative of any of the fundamental right, is void to the extent of its inconsistency. In *A.D.M. Jabalpur* v. *Shiv Kant Shukla*,[5] Jusitce Beg observed "the object of making certain general aspects of rights fundamental is to guarantee them against illegal invasion of these rights by executive, legislative, or judicial organ of the State".[6] Earlier, Chief Justice Subba Rao in *Golak Nath* v. *State of Punjab*[7] had also observed that the fundamental rights are the modern name for what have been traditionally known as natural rights.[8]

The Supreme Court recognised these fundamental rights as "Natural Rights" or "Human Rights" while dealing with different cases. The Chief Justice Patanjali Shastri in *State of West Bengal* v. *Subodh Gopal Bose*[9] referred fundamental rights as those great and basis rights, which are recognized and guaranteed as the natural rights inherent in the status of a citizen of a free country.[10] Referring to the fundamental rights contained in Part III of the constitution, Sikri the then Chief Justice of India in *Keshavananda Bharathi* v. *State of Kerala*, [11] observed , "I am unable to hold these provisions to show that rights are not natural or inalienable rights. As a matter of fact India was a party to the Universal Declaration of Human Rights... and that Declaration describes some fundamental rights as inalienable."[12] Thus, Fundamental rights under the Indian Constitution are nothing but a synonym of human rights and natural rights.

5.3. Procedural Safeguards against Arrest and Detention

When Indian Constitution came into force in 1950, it provided three clear provisions in relation to rights of liberties and security of person, *namely,* Articles 20, 21 and 22. These provisions stand as pillars against the Governmental arbitrariness affecting life, liberty and security of persons. Article 20 of the Constitution of India provides three safeguards in respect of conviction of offences to a person accused of crimes, *namely, Ex post facto law* (clause 1), Double jeopardy (clause 2) and Prohibition against self-incrimination (clause 3). Since Clauses 1 and 2 of Article 20 are matters connected with conviction by a court, these provisions are not the subjects of study here. Since the Clause (3) of Article 20 deals with prohibition against self-incrimination, it affects a person ever since he is arrested because of the guarantee of 'right to remain silent' of an accused in a criminal case. Article 21 of the Constitution of India guarantees right to life and personal liberty, and Article 22 provides safeguards against arbitrary arrest and detention. Supreme Court of India played a vital role in elaborating the protection and safeguards implied in these rights. A brief account of the protection afforded by these provisions is made below.

5.3.1. Right to remain Silent

India follows adversarial system [13] of trial proceedings in which accused person is presumed to be innocent until the guilt is proved before the court beyond reasonable doubt. As the burden, in this system, lies on the Prosecutions and in turn, on the police to prove the case before the court to such an extent to remove the shadow of doubt, the police who follow colonial system of unscientific investigation import torture, threat, assault, harassment etc. as methods to elicit confessions, facts and information from accused and witnesses of crimes. The right to self-incrimination is a privilege given to a person accused of crime as he is the one who has to fight against the mighty State and its machineries, and this right ensures that encroachment shall not be made against a person to extract facts from him if he is not willing to provide it.[14] By this privilege the accused can remain silent and, more importantly, it is an obligation of the police official interrogating the accused to inform him that he has a right to remain silent.

The Fifth Amendment to the US Constitution, 1791 protects persons from compelling to be witness against himself.[15] In *Miranda* v. *Arizona*[16], a landmark case decided by the United States Supreme Court, the Court ruled that when a suspect is taken into police custody, prior to any interrogation by the police, the suspect must be informed of the rights available to him as per the Constitution of the US secured through the 1st, 5th and 6th Amendments to the US Constitution. These rights are often called as "Miranda Rights" or "Miranda Warning." The Miranda rights as laid down by the US Supreme Court include:

(i)   The accused have a right to remain silent,

66

(ii). It is the duty of the interrogating police official to inform the accused that

    a. as accused, he is not bound to say any thing, but if he says anything it will be used against him during the trial before a court of law"

    b. as accused, he has a right to consult his lawyer, and

    c. If he is not able to afford a lawyer, one will be appointed for him.

In the US, failure to advise the suspect of these rights by police results in the rejection of the statements made by the suspect as evidence and can not be used at the trial. Under the US Constitution the protection is available even to witnesses where as in India the protection is available only to the accused. From this, it can be seen that the position in India is much narrower than the US Constitution.

However, the right to remain silent is not expressly provided under Indian Constitution. Article 20 (3) protects persons from self-incrimination thereby avoiding to be witness against himself in a crime. By judicial interpretation of the Supreme Court, the right to remain silent is implied under Article 20 (3) which reads: "No person accused of any offence shall be compelled to be a witness against himself". Since the term used in Article 20 (3) "to be a witness", the question before the Supreme Court was that whether Article 20 (3) is applicable only during a trial before a court of law or is it available even before a trial when a person is arrested by the police as an accused. The Supreme Court dealt with the question in *M.P. Sharma* v. *Satish Chandra*[17] by holding that a person, whose name was mentioned as an accused in the First Information Report and an investigation was conducted by the police on the basis of that Report, could claim the protection as 'accused of an offence' under Article 20(3). The Supreme Court explained the meaning of the phrase "to be a witness" in this case as not only covering oral evidence but documentary and testimonial evidences also.

5.3.1.1. "To be a Witness" and "Furnishing Evidence"

The wider definition given by the Supreme Court for the phrase "to be a witness" created a lot of practical difficulties and confusions in applying provisions such as Section 27 of the Indian Evidence Act. However, the Supreme Court in *State of Bombay* v. *Kathi Kalu*[18] held that the interpretation given in *M.P.Sharma's* case for the phrase "to be a witness" was too broad and 'to be a witness" is not equivalent to "furnishing evidence".[19] The Court observed:

> "To be a witness" may be equivalent to "furnishing evidence" in the sense of making oral or written statements, but not in the larger sense of the expression so as to include giving of thumb impression or impression of palm or foot or fingers or specimen writing or exposing a part of the body by an accused person for purpose of identification. "Furnishing evidence" in the latter sense could not have been within the contemplation of the Constitution-makers for the simple reason that-though they may have intended to protect an accused person from the hazards of self- incrimination, in the light of the English Law on the subject-they could not have intended to put obstacles in the way of efficient and effective investigation into crime and of bringing criminals to justice.[20]

The Court, thus, held that self-incrimination can only mean conveying information based upon personal knowledge of the person giving information and cannot include merely the mechanical process of producing documents in court which may throw light on any point in controversy, but which does not contain any statement of the accused based on his personal knowledge.[21] Thus, when a person gives his finger impression or specimen writing or signature, though, it may amount to furnishing evidence in the large sense, the same is not included within the expression "to be a witness". In these cases, he is not giving any personal testimony. What is forbidden under Article 20 (3) is to compel a person to say something from his personal

68

knowledge relating to the charge against him. However, the Court reiterated that "to be a witness" is not merely in respect of testimonial compulsion in the court room but may well extend to compelled testimony previously obtained from him. The Supreme Court observed:

> "As was pointed out in Sharma's Case (1) the phrase used in Art. 20(3) is "to be a witness" and not "to appear as a witness". That by itself justifies the conclusion "that the protection afforded to an accused in so far as it is related to the phrase "to be a witness" is not merely in respect of testimonial compulsion in the court room but may well extend to compelled testimony previously obtained from him". If the protection was intended to be confined to being a witness in Court then really it would have been an idle protection. It would be completely defeated by compelling a person to give all the evidence outside court and then, having what he was so compelled to do, proved in court through other witnesses. An interpretation which so completely defeats the constitutional guarantee cannot, of course, be correct. The contention that the protection afforded by Art. 20(3) is limited to the stage of trial must therefore be rejected."[22]

Thus, the Supreme Court limited the scope and application of the phrase "to be a witness" in this case to the personal knowledge of the accused and not to extent to the documentary evidence or material objects or body parts. Nevertheless, the Court confirmed that so far as personal knowledge of the accused is concerned, the protection extends not to only to testimonial compulsion in the court proceedings but may well extend to the testimony obtained previously by compelling the accused even before a court proceeding. It means that the protection is available even during police investigation and interrogation. However, it must be noted that the Article 20(3) is operative as long as there is compulsion and if there is no compulsion and the person is providing information voluntarily, the information can be considered as valid.

5.3.1.2.   Physical and Psychological Coercion

In *Nandini Satpathy* v. *P.L. Dani*[23] the Supreme Court has reiterated the protection afforded under Article 20 (3) by unequivocally declaring that the protection afforded under

69

Article 20 (3) is not only for the trial stage but it should start from the time the investigation is initiated by the police against a person accused of an offence. The Court has widened the scope of Article 20 (3) by holding that the compulsion does not only mean physical torture or coercion but it also extends to psychic torture, atmospheric pressure, environmental coercion, tiring interrogatives, prolixity, overbearing and intimidatory methods and the like.[24] In this case, charges of corruption were levelled against the former Chief Minister of Orissa, Smt. Nandini Satpathi. In the course of investigation the appellant, a former Chief Minister of Orissa and one time Minister at the National level was directed to appear at the Vigilance Police Station, Cuttack, in September, 1977 for being examined in connection with the case registered against her by the Deputy Superintendent of Police, Vigilance, Cuttack under Section 5 (2) read with Section 5 (1) (d) and (e) of the Prevention of Corruption Act and under Sections 161, 165, 120-B and 109 Indian Penal Code. She was asked to answer written questions in connection with the corruption allegations and she refused to answer the questions invoking the protection afforded under Article 20(3). As a result a complaint was filed by the Deputy Superintendent of Police, Vigilance (Directorate of Vigilance) Cuttack, against the appellant, under Section 179 Indian Penal Code Justice V R Krishna Iyer held in summary the following:

a) Section 161 of Criminal Procedure Code enables the police to examine the accused during investigation;

(b) The prohibitive sweep of Art. 20(3) extend not only to the proceedings before a court but it extend to the stage of police interrogation also;

(c) The ban on self-accusation and the right to silence, while an investigation or trial is under way, goes beyond that case and protects the accused in regard to other

70

offences pending or imminent, which may deter him from voluntary disclosure of incriminatory matter.

(d) A police officer is clearly a person in authority. Insistence on answering is a form of pressure especially in the atmosphere of the police station unless certain safe guards erasing duress are adhered to.

(e) "Self incrimination or tendency to expose oneself to a criminal charge is less than 'relevant' and more than 'confessional'. Irrelevance is impermissible; while relevance is licit if the relevant questions are loaded with guilty inference in the event of an answer being supplied the tendency to incriminate springs into existence."

(f) The accused person cannot be forced to answer questions, merely because the answers thereto are not implicative when viewed in isolation and confined to that particular case. He is entitled to keep his mouth shut if the answer sought has a reasonable prospect of exposing him to guilt in some other accusation actual or imminent, even though the investigation under way is not with reference to that.[25]

From the above, the right to remain silent is implicit in Article 20(3) and the protection is available not only during the trial before a court but also during interrogation by police. This right also extends not only with regard to the offence pending but with other offences pending or imminent which may deter him from voluntary disclosure of incriminatory matter.

5.3.1.3.   Narco-analysis and Right to Remain Silent

Narco-analysis,[26] Poligraph,[27] Brain Mapping[28] are the tests that have been used by the police against the accused in certain crimes as an alternative to the third degree methods with a view to extract information. The investigative agencies have been using these tests even without the consent of the accused. In 2010, in a land mark judgment in *Selvi* v. *State of Karnataka*[29] the Supreme Court held that narco-analysis, brain mapping and polygraph tests carried out on the suspects by the investigative agencies for the interrogation was unconstitutional. A bench headed by Chief Justice K. G. Balakrishnan held that these tests are violation of the fundamental rights under Article 20(3) of the Constitution. The Court observed that forcing a person to undergo narco-analysis, brain-mapping, or polygraph tests itself amounted to the requisite compulsion, regardless of the lack of physical harm done to administer the test or the nature of the answers given during the tests.[30]Further,since the answers given during the test are not consciously and voluntarily given, and an individual does not have the ability to decide whether or not to answer a given question, the results from these tests amount to the requisite compelled testimony to violate Article 20(3).[31]

The court further observed that the results of these tests are not absolutely foolproof and hence, not completely reliable, and may not be admissible in court as evidence. In a narco test, the accused is injected with 'truth serums' that cause the person to become uninhibited and talkative. It is still possible for people to lie under the influence of truth serums, so it is not altogether reliable.[32] The Supreme Court comprising Chief Justice K.G. Balakrishnan, and Justices R.V. Raveendran and J.M. Panchal observed:

> We hold that no individual should be forcibly subjected to any of the techniques in question, whether in the context of investigation in criminal cases or otherwise. Doing so would amount to an unwarranted intrusion into personal liberty.[33]

The Court held that compelling public interest cannot justify the dilution of constitutional rights such as the "right against self-incrimination". Further, the Court observed that "compulsory administration of any of these techniques is an unjustified intrusion into the mental privacy of an individual. It would also amount to 'cruel, inhuman or degrading treatment' with

72

regard to the language of evolving international human rights norms."[34] The judgment of the Supreme Court is appreciable as this decision prohibits the violation of right against self-incrimination, and consequently, right to remain silent of the accused which were violated by the investigative agencies under the pretext of narco-analysis, brain mapping and polygraph tests. However, the question is how far the judgment be respected by the police and investigating officials.

5.3.1.4. Justice Mallimath Committee on the Right to Silence

Since the accused is presumed to be innocent in adversarial legal systems, the accused has a right to remain silent and the burden is always on the prosecution. Hence, the police have to gather facts and information from other sources than the accused to support the prosecution to prove the case before the court of law. The Mallimath Committee on Criminal Justice Reforms[35] states that the accused is a valuable source of information.[36] Since India follows adversarial system of investigation and trial proceedings, the accused remains silent or even if he provides information to police during investigation, later he may disown it before the court of law. Hence, Mallimath Committee recommended that India should adopt a system which also appreciates the investigation by the police being supervised by a Magistrate as in the case of inquisitorial system that is prevalent in continental countries such as France, Germany etc. This system will have the advantage of proving the statement of accused as valuable piece of evidence during trial, and hence, the proceeding would be more effective.[37] The Committee considered the right to remain silent available to the accused, but recommended that since the accused is the best source of correct information, without any kind of coercion such information must be gathered under the supervision of the Magistrate, and the Magistrate shall have the authority to question the accused and gather relevant information related with the crime.

However, the Law Commission has refused to accept the recommendations on the ground that the acceptance of such procedure under Indian legal system would adversely affect the rights and liberties enshrined to the Individuals under the Constitution of India and hence, the Law Commission in its 180th report recommended that there is no need to dilute the existing right to remain silent.[38] It is submitted that the view of the Law Commission is acceptable as India follows predominantly a democratic system which is not fully trustworthy as against developed civil law systems and, hence, in India persons in authority can easily be influenced and evidences can be easily tampered, the innocent persons may be put in peril. Considering the nature and attitude of the police from top to bottom towards accused, the right to remain silent must be protected in all cases.

5.3.2. *Right to Life and Personal Liberty*

Article 21 which provides "right to life and personal liberty" is the most significant provision under the Indian Constitution in relation to protection of human rights. It provides that "No person shall be deprived of his life or liberty except according to procedure established by law." Article 21 of the Indian Constitution is equivalent to the 'due process' clause of US Constitution.[39]Article 21 clearly provides two concepts, namely, the right to life and personal liberty.

5.3.2.1. Concept of "Right to Life"

The 'right to life' is the most fundamental of all rights that a person holds since without life there is no meaning of other rights. It is the natural right and is the basic human right. All other rights are supplemental to the right to life. 'Life' in Article 21 of the Constitution is not merely the physical act of breathing.[40] Judicial magnanimity of Supreme Court of India gave a heavenly interpretation to Article 21 by holding that the right to life does not connote mere animal existence.[41] The Court relied on the meaning given to the term 'life' by the US Supreme Court in *Munn* v.*Illinois*,[42] in which Field J held that the term 'life' meant something more than mere animal existence and the prohibition against its deprivation extended to all those limbs and faculties by which the life was enjoyed. It has a much wider meaning which includes right to live with human dignity.[43] Right to life is fundamental to our very existence without which we cannot live as human being and includes all those aspects of life which go to make a man's life meaningful, complete and worth living.[44] After the wider interpretation given to Article 21 by the Supreme Court in *Maneka Gandhi* v. *Union of India*,[45] a large number of human rights have been recognized under the umbrella of Article 21.

5.3.2.2.   Concept of "Personal Liberty"

Individual freedoms and liberties has been a subject for struggle for long in the world as liberty is as important as life to an individual. The *Magna Carta*[46] in England, knows as the greater Charter of Fundamental Rights, as back as 1215 provided that "No freeman shall be taken or imprisoned... but... by the law of the land." Article 21 has the greatest significance of providing the concept of liberty under the Constitution of India. The personal liberty under Article 21 has received a far more expansive interpretation at the hands of Supreme Court of India. The Supreme Court in A.K.*Gopalan* v. *State of Madras*[47] held that the liberty denotes merely freedom from bodily restraint. But in *Maneka Gandhi's* case[48], the Supreme Court has rejected this view and held that it encompasses those rights and privileges which have long been

75

recognized as being essential to the orderly pursuit of happiness by free men.[49] Thus, 'right to life and personal liberty' under Article 21 means to live with human dignity and enjoyable as a free man.

Article 21 has always been central for judicial scrutiny and interpretation after the adoption of the Constitution in 1950. Immediately after the coming into operation of Constitution of India, crucial questions of right to life and personal liberty of persons arose in *A.K. Gopalan* v. *State of Madras*[50] and the Supreme Court interpreted the provisions of Article 21 in a restrictive way. In this case, India's first preventive detention law, the Preventive Detention Act 1950, was challenged as violative of article 21 of the Constitution. A.K. Gopalan, a Communist leader, was detained under the Act and he challenged the Act mainly on the ground that the 'procedure' prescribed in the Act violated article 21 by infringing upon the personal liberty of him. The Supreme Court , 6-Judges Bench headed by Chief Justice Kania held that the impugned Act is not violative of the Article 21of the Constitution. The Court held that whatever may be the generally accepted connotation of the expression "personal liberty', it is used in Article 21 in a sense which excludes the freedom of movement dealt with in Article 19. Thus, the personal liberty in the context of part III of the constitution is something distinct from the freedom to move freely throughout the territory of India.[51]

Justice B.K. Mukherjee concurring majority opinion observed that 'personal liberty' in Article 21 is the antithesis of physical restraint or coercion, and it means a personal right not to be subjected to imprisonment, arrest or other physical coercion in any manner that does not admit legal justification.[52]

76

Justice Murtaza Fazal Ali, delivering minority judgment, observed that the expression personal liberty and personal freedom have wider meaning and also a narrower meaning. In the wider sense, they include not only immunity from arrest and detention, but also freedom of speech, freedom of association, *etc*. In the narrower sense, they mean immunity from arrest and detention. He further observed that when these words are used in the sense of immunity from arrest, the juristic conception of personal liberty is that it consists in freedom of movement and locomotion.[53]

Thus, the majority judges in the Supreme Court gave a narrower interpretation to the concept of personal liberty. Four Judges, *namely*, Kania, CJ, Patanjali Shashtri, B.K. Mukherjee and Dass JJ held that "procedure prescribed by law' means procedure prescribed by the law of the State. According to them, these words are to be taken to refer to a procedure which has a statutory origin, for no procedure is known or can be said to have been established by such vague and uncertain concepts as "the immutable and universal principles of natural justice".[54] Hence, the majority rejected the connection of Article 21 with natural justice principles.

However, Justice Fazal Ali gave the minority judgment which attained far reaching consequences in later years in the concept of personal liberty and which ultimately proved correct.[55] In his dissenting opinion, Justice Fazal Ali had opined that 'law' in Article 21 means a valid law and 'procedure' means certain definite rules of proceedings and not something which is a mere pretence for procedure.[56]

Thus, where the majority rejected the presence of the principles of natural justice in Article 21, the minority observed that the 'procedure' in Article 21 is meant a fair and just procedure.[57] This view was partially supported by the Supreme Court in *Kharak*

77

*Singh's*case[58]and held that the right of personal liberty in Art. 21 as a right of an individual to be free from restrictions or encroachments on his person, whether those restrictions or encroachments are directly imposed or indirectly brought about by calculated measures.[59] However, the minority view has been fully accepted in terms and in spirit by the Supreme Court after twenty eight years in *Maneka Gandhi* v. *Union of India.*[60]

5.3.2.3. "Right to Life and Personal Liberty" and Violations by the Police

Justice Bhagwati in *Maneka Gandhi's* case overruled the authority of *A.K.Gopalan's* case. In *Maneka Gandhi's* case, Supreme Court gave a dynamic interpretation to Article 21 and held that the law which deprives the life and liberty of the people must be "fair, just and reasonable" and not "arbitrary, oppressive and fanciful". The Supreme Court observed:

> The mere prescription of some kind of procedure cannot even meet the mandate of Article 21. The procedure prescribed by law has to be fair, just and reasonable, not fanciful, oppressive or arbitrary. The question whether the procedure prescribed by law which curtails or takes away the personal liberty guaranteed by Art. 21 is reasonable or not has to be considered not in the abstract or on hypothetical considerations like the provision for a full-dressed hearing as in a court room trial but in the contest, primarily, of the purpose which the Act is intended to achieve and of urgent situations which those who are charged with the duty of administering the Act may be called upon to deal with. Secondly, even the fullest compliance with the requirements of Art. 21 is not the journey's end because a law which prescribes fair and reasonable procedure for curtailing or taking away the personal liberty granted by Art. 21 has still to meet a possible challenge under the other provisions of the Constitution.[61]

Justice V. R. Krishna Iyer, speaking in *Sunil Batra* v. *Delhi Administaration*[62] has said that though our Constitution has no due process clause as available under the US Constitution, but after Maneka Gandhi's case the consequence is the same, and as much as such Article 21 may be treated as counterpart of the due process clause which requires fair and reasonable procedure for depriving liberty under American Constitution.[63] The dynamic interpretation that has been given to Article 21 in *Maneka Gandhi*'s case has widened the horizons of human rights jurisprudence in India and the Supreme Court has brought many rights under the umbrella of Article 21 such as right to live with human dignity,[64] right against delayed execution of death sentence,[65] right against inhuman treatment,[66] right against smoking in public places,[67] right to free legal aid,[68] right to lively hood,[69] right to privacy,[70] right against solitary confinement[71] right to speedy trial,[72] right against hand cuffing,[73] etc. Thus, the *ratio* 'just, fair and reasonable' feature of law for depriving the liberty of a person in *Maneka Gandhi*'s case has widened the scope and ambit of "right to life and personal liberty" under Article 21 and the Supreme Court has opened new vistas for the growth and development of human rights protection in India including in the areas of protection of human rights from being violated by the police. The areas where the Supreme Court has acted for the protection of human rights from being violated by the police are discussed below.

i)   **Investigation**

Police investigations are the basic method of collection of evidences in order to establish the guilt of the accused person before a court of law. Many a time, the manner of collection of evidence during investigation, the methods of interrogation, arrest and detention detrimentally affect the decency and dignity of persons; thereby infringing the human rights of individuals by police. The Supreme Court of India, time and again, has assumed the mantle of saviours of innocent or accused persons from the hands of mighty police and has issued directives and guidelines that must be observed by the police during the course of investigation, interrogation, arrest or detention.[74] Delaying the investigation process is one of the tactics of the police in order to harass the party disfavoured by police. Since the investigation is an integral part in the process of trial, delaying the investigation adversely affects speedy trial. Supreme Court has held in many cases that speedy trial is implicit in Article 21.[75] In *Abdul Rehman Antulay* v. *R.S. Nayak*[76] *(A.R. Antulay's* case*)* the Supreme Court emphasized that the "fair, just and reasonable"[77] procedure implicit in Article 21 of the Constitution creates a right in the accused to be tried speedily and that the right to speedy trial flowing from Article 21 encompasses all the stages, namely, the stage of investigation, inquiry, trial, appeal, revision and retrial. Thus, speedy investigation is a prerequisite for speedy trial and hence within the purview of Article 21. Again, in *Vakil Prasad Singh* v. *State of Bihar*[78] the Supreme Court reiterated the same view and held that the right to speedy trial in all criminal prosecutions is an inalienable right under Article 21 of the Constitution and this right is applicable not only to the actual proceedings in court but also includes within its sweep the preceding police investigations as well. There was an unreasonable delay of 17 years for investigating this case. In *Nirmal Singh Kahlon* v. *State of Punjab*[79] the Court had to consider the case of fairness of the investigation. The Court held that fair trial includes fair investigation and fair investigation is essential for the preservation of fundamental right of an accused under article 21. Again in *Babubhai* v. *State Of Gujarat*[80] *(Babubhai's case)* the Supreme Court reiterated that not only fair trial but fair investigation is also a part of constitutional rights guaranteed under Articles 20 and 21 of the Constitution of India. Thus, from *AR Anthulay's* case to *Babubhai's* case the Supreme Court affirmed categorically that speedy investigation is an integral part of speedy trial, and hence, delaying investigation process by the police is against constitutional right of the accused. Otherwise the very purpose of Constitutional right of speedy trial would be meaningless.

ii)   Arrest

Arrest of a person by the police is yet another controversial area in the criminal justice process as a result of the wide discretionary powers enjoyed by the police and the practical misuse of those powers by them. According to the National Police Commission's Third Report, the power of arrest is one of the chief sources of corruption by the police and around 60 % of the arrests made by the police are unnecessary and unjustified.[81] There lies the point of misuse of power to arrest by the police. Even when arrest is necessary, the police do not comply with the procedural requirement provided by the Constitution of India and Criminal Procedure Code 1973. This had come to the notice of the Supreme Court in different cases and the Court has been obsessive in the matters connected with unlawful arrest, illegal detention and non-compliance of the procedural requirements while effecting arrest and detention. In *Bhim Singh* v. *State of Jammu & Kashmir*[82] the petitioner, an MLA, was arrested and detained in Police custody and deliberately prevented from attending the session of the legislative assembly. The Supreme Court held that the police officials acted deliberately and hence, the court awarded compensation to the petitioner.

In *Joginder Kumar* v. *State of UP*[83]the Supreme Court has laid down guidelines governing arrest of a person during investigation. This has been done with a view to strike a balance between the needs of police on the one hand and the protection of human rights of citizens from oppression and injustice at the hands of law enforcing agencies, on the other hand.[84] The court has held in *Joginder's case* that the police officer arresting a person must be able to justify the arrest apart from his power to do so. Arrest and detention in police lock-up of a person can cause incalculable harm to the reputation and self-esteem of a person.[85] A person is not to be arrested merely on the suspicion of complicity in an offence, but there must be reasonable justification in the opinion of the police officer effecting the arrest that such arrest was necessary and justified.[86] For effective enforcement of these fundamental rights, the Supreme Court has laid down that (i) an arrested person being held in custody is, entitled to have one friend, relative or other person, informed, as far as is practicable, that such person has been arrested and where he is being detained; (ii) the police officer shall inform the arrested person when he is brought to the police station of this right; and (iii) an entry shall be required to be made in the diary as to who was informed of the arrest. The Court observed that these protections from power must be held to flow from Articles 21 and 22(1) of the Constitution of India and must be enforced strictly. In fact, the guidelines of the Supreme Court in *Joginder's* case were a foot step towards judicial activism of Supreme Court in the protection of human rights of persons from the hands of police. *Joginder* case has paved the way for Supreme Court to give judicial standing directives in *D.K. Basu's* case to police and law enforcement officials.

The judgment of Supreme Court in *D.K Basu* v. *State of West Bengal*[87] is a milestone in matters of arrest, detention and interrogation by police as in this case the Court gave a pragmatic as well as realistic approach to procedural requirement of arrest and detention. The Supreme Court laid down eleven directives to the Police and law enforcement officials to be followed in all cases of arrest and/ detention. The directives, as directed by the Supreme Court, must be complied with in all cases of arrest or detention till legal provisions are made in that behalf as preventive measures. The directives are:

(1) The police personnel carrying out the arrest and handling the interrogation of the arrestee should bear accurate, visible and clear identification and name tags with their designations. The particulars of all such police personnel who handle interrogation of the arrestee must be recorded in a register.

(2) The police officer carrying out the arrest of the arrestee shall prepare a memo of arrest at the time of arrest and such memo shall be attested by atleast one witness, who may be either a member of the family of the arrestee or a respectable person of the locality from where the arrest is made. It shall also be counter signed by the arrestee and shall contain the time and date of arrest.

(3) A person who has been arrested or detained and is being held in custody in a police station or interrogation centre or other lock-up, shall be entitled to have one friend or relative or other person known to him or having interest in his welfare being informed, as soon as practicable, that he has been arrested and is being detained at the particular place, unless the attesting witness of the memo of arrest is himself such a friend or a relative of the arrestee.

(4) The time, place of arrest and venue of custody of an arrestee must be notified by the police where the next friend or relative of the arrestee lives outside the district or town through the Legal Aid Organization in the District and the police station of the area concerned telegraphically within a period of eight to twelve hours after the arrest.

(5) The person arrested must be made aware of this right to have someone informed of his arrest or detention as soon as he is put under arrest or is detained.

(6) An entry must be made in the diary at the place of detention regarding the arrest of the person which shall also disclose the name of the next friend of the person who has been informed of the arrest and the names and particulars of the police officials in whose custody the arrestee is.

(7) The arrestee should, where he so requests, be also examined at the time of his arrest and major and minor injuries, if any present on his/her body, must be recorded at that time. The "Inspection Memo" must be signed both by the arrestee and the police officer effecting the arrest and its copy provided to the arrestee.

(8) The arrestee should be subjected to medical examination by a trained doctor every 48 hours during his detention in custody by a doctor on the panel of approved doctors appointed by Director, Health Services of the concerned State or Union Territory. Director, Health Services should prepare such a penal for all *Tehsils* and Districts as well.

(9) Copies of all the documents including the memo of arrest, referred to above, should be sent to the *illaka* (local) Magistrate for his record.

(10) The arrestee may be permitted to meet his lawyer during interrogation, though not throughout the interrogation.

(11) A police control room should be provided at all district and State Headquarters, where information regarding the arrest and the place of custody of the arrestee shall be communicated by the officer causing the arrest, within 12 hours of effecting the arrest and at the police control room it should be displayed on conspicuous notice board.[88]

The Supreme Court made it clear that these requirements are in addition to the constitutional and statutory safeguards and do not detract from various other directions given by the courts from time to time in connection with the safeguarding of the rights and dignity of arrestee.[89]

In effect, *D.K. Basu*'s case is a drive far ahead of *Joginder Kumar*'s casein relation to arrest, detention and interrogation by police officials. *D.K. Basu*'s case is significant in as much as it is almost a legislation made by the Supreme Court. The judgment in *D.K. Basu*'s case is landmark as it was the need of the hour and the Government was not positive enough to formulate legislation to this effect despite growing atrocities of the police.

It is significant to note that in this case the Court, after setting out the directives, made it clear that failure to comply with such directives will not only attract the departmental action but also the Contempt of Court proceedings. *D.K. Basu*'s case occupied the field in the absence of clear legislation related with arrest and detention of persons. The Parliament has amended the Code of Criminal Procedure thrice (in 2005, 2008 and 2010) after *D.K. Basu*'s case in order to incorporate the directives into the Code of Criminal Procedure.[90] However, *D.K. Basu*'s case is a clear illustration of judicial activism in the protection of human rights of arrested persons.

iii.) Handcuffing

The Police, at large, believe that handcuffing is a necessity in effecting the arrest and they, quiet often, do not take into consideration the humiliation and embarrassment suffered by the handcuffed person and the disrepute of his family. At times, they do it intentionally in order to tarnish the image, esteem and dignity of the arrestee or the family of the arrestee even though there is no danger of accused escaping from custody. In the landmark case of *Sunil Batra* v. *Delhi Administration*[91] the Supreme Court pronounced that fetters should be shunned as violative of human dignity under Article 21and that the indiscriminate use of handcuffs is illegal. The Court observed:

85

Where an under trial has a credible tendency for violence and escape a humanely graduated degree of 'iron' restraint is permissible if only if-other disciplinary alternatives are unworkable. The burden of proof of the ground is on the custodian. And if he fails, he will be liable in law.[92]

This decision has influenced subsequent judgments on the use of handcuffs and has been heavily relied on. In *Prem Shankar* v. *Delhi administration*[93] the Supreme Court held that hand cuffing is *prima facie* inhuman, unreasonable and over harsh, and it is permitted only in exceptional circumstances where there is a reasonable apprehension of escape of the detainee.[94] The court observed:

Handcuffing is *prima facie* inhuman and, therefore, unreasonable, is over harsh and at the first blush, arbitrary. Absent fair procedure and objective monitoring to inflict "irons" is to resort to zoological strategies repugnant to Article 21.Surely, the competing claims of securing the prisoner from fleeing and protecting his personality from barbarity have to be harmonized. To prevent the escape of an under-trial is in public interest, reasonable, just and cannot, by itself be castigated. But to bind a man hand and foot, fetter his limbs with hoops of steel, shuffle him along in the streets and stand him for hours in the courts is to torture him, defile his dignity, vulgarise society and foul the soul of our Constitutional culture.

In *State of Maharshtra* v. *Ravikant S. patil*[95] a detainee was handcuffed and paraded on streets. The Bombay High Court held that hand cuffing and parading was violative of article 21 and directed the police official who was responsible for hand cuffing and parading to pay Rs 10,000 by way of compensation and directed that this act of violation of Article 21 should also be entered in his service record. Although the Supreme Court upheld the judgment of the High Court, directing a payment of compensation yet held that the police officer was not personally liable as he acted as an official in the discharge of his official function. It is submitted that the decision of the High Court must be accepted as the police official was acting in excess of his authority and hence, he must be made personally liable.

Though the Supreme Court gave verdict that the hand cuffing could genuinely be used only in extreme cases of danger of escape of detainee, police may not follow it because they are either unaware of it or just ignore it. In one such case, *Citizen for democracy* v. *State of Assam*[96] the Supreme Court expressed its great concern when the police officials hand cuffed undertrial prisoners ignoring the Supreme Court guideline in *Prem Shankar Shukla's* case. Supreme Court gave direction to the State Government that stringent measures are taken against erring police officials. This itself shows the intolerance of the Supreme Court against such acts of disgrace as it viewed the same as a very grave and offending act of demeaning a person *sans* dignity.

iv.   Torture and Death in Police Custody

The Indian Constitution does not contain an express prohibition of torture. However, the Supreme Court has construed Article 21 of the Constitution as including a prohibition of torture. The Supreme Court in *Fancis Coralie Mullin* v. *Union Territory of Delhi*[97] held:

> "Now obviously, any form of torture or cruel, inhuman or degrading treatment would be offensive to human dignity and constitute an inroad into this right to live and it would, on this view, be prohibited by Article 21 unless it is in accordance with procedure prescribed by law, but no law which authorizes and no procedure which leads to such torture or cruel, inhuman or degrading treatment can ever stand the test of reasonableness and non-arbitrariness: it would plainly be unconstitutional and void as being violative of Articles 14 and 21."[98]

"Third degree" methods are the barbarous weapon in the hands of police for various purposes such as eliciting hidden facts, to compel a person to falsely admit guilt, to retaliate favouring the other party, to coerce a person in custody, *etc*. In a land mark judgment, *Kishore Singh* v. *State of Rajasthan*[99] the Supreme Court held that the use of "third degree" method by police is violative of Article 21. In this case the detainees were brought before the Court as per the direction of the

Court. While they were brought, in transit, violence had been used by the escort police on the person of one of the petitioners resulting in deep wounds on his person. The Court observed "Article 21 would become dysfunctional unless the agencies of the law in the police and prison establishments have sympathy for the humanist creed of that Article."[100] The Court in this case directed the State to re-educate the police and inculcate a respect for the human person and to punish the escort police who misconducted with the prisoner. Precisely, a human rights course has been prescribed for police in Police Academies in the country to impart training on human rights.

In *Sheela Barse* v. *State of Maharashtra,* [101] the petitioner, a journalist, in her letter addressed to the Supreme Court stated that five women prisoners interviewed by her in the Bombay Central Jail alleged that they had been assaulted by the police in the police lock up and two of them in particular alleged that they had been assaulted and tortured in the lock up. The Supreme Court gave detailed instructions to the concerned authorities for providing security and safety in police lockup, particularly to women suspects and the Court directed that the female suspect should be kept in separate police lockups and not in the same in which male accused are detained and should be guarded by female constables.[102]

Custodial violence and atrocities portray the extent of flagrant violation of human rights and brutal attitude of police. There are many instances of custodial death and violence by police. *In Nilabati Behera@ Lalita Behera* v. *State of Orissa*[103] petitioner's son was arrested and taken in custody from his home by the Assistant Sub-Inspector of Police in connection with the investigation of a theft and the petitioner came to know that the dead body of her son was found on the railway track. There were multiple injuries on the body and his death was unnatural, caused by those injuries. The Supreme Court directed the District Judge to hold an inquiry into the matter and to submit a report to the Supreme Court. The District Judge found that petitioner's son died on account of multiple injuries inflicted to him while he was in police custody. The Supreme Court awarded compensation of Rs. 1, 50,000 to the mother of the deceased and directed the State government to take appropriate action against each erring police personnel. While awarding the compensation the Court observed:

> Article 21which guarantees the right to life and liberty will be denuded of its significant content if the power of this Court were limited to passing orders to release from illegal detention. One of the telling ways in which the violation of that right can reasonably be prevented and due compliance with the mandate of Article 21 secured, is to mulct its violators in the payment of monetary compensation.[104]

The Court further observed that the violation of fundamental rights attracts strict liability for which the Supreme Court or High Court has the authority to compensate the victim or dependents of the victim.[105]

In *Smt. Shakila Abdul Gafar Khan* v. *Vasant Raghunath Dhoble*[106] the complainant's husband was taken in custody by the police and was beaten up in public for more than an hour in front of the complainant (wife), deceased's mother and sister with hockey sticks. Later, he was released from the custody and admitted in a hospital where he died. The Supreme Court ordered for compensation of Rs. 100,000/- to the mother and children of the deceased and expressed great concern over the defect of the present criminal law due to which the police atrocities and custodial crimes go unpunished. The Apex Court further directed the State Government to conduct a detailed enquiry to find out who are the police personnel responsible for the injuries caused on the body of the deceased and to take appropriate action against the culprit. In yet another glaring example of police atrocities, in *Peoples' Union for Democratic Rights* v. *Police*

89

Commissioner, Delhi Head Quarter[107] where a labourer who was engaged to work for police for wages when demanded his wages was beaten to death. The Supreme Court awarded compensation of Rs.75,000/- to the family of the deceased. In *Saheli* v. *Commissioner of Police*[108] a 9 year old child was beaten up by the police and later succumbed to injuries inflicted on him by the police. The Supreme Court awarded compensation of Rs 75,000/- to the mother.

How cruel and barbaric are our police can be found in *C.B.I.* v. *Kishore Singh*[109] where a police constable chopped off the genital organ of a person due to the suspected illicit relationship with the wife of the relative of the police constable. The Supreme Court observed that the case reveals how some policemen in our country have not got over their old colonial mentality and are still persisting in barbaric acts in a free country which claims to be run by a democratic Constitution and the rule of law. The Court held that the policemen who commit such acts of criminal nature deserve harsher punishment than other persons who commit such acts, because it is the duty of the policemen to protect the people, and not break the law themselves.

Custodial violence against women very often includes rape and other forms of sexual violence such as threats of rape, touching, virginity testing, being stripped naked, invasive body searches, insults and humiliations of a sexual nature, etc. *Tukaram* v. *State of Maharashtra*,[110] notoriously known as *Mathura rape case* where a 16 year old girl was raped in a police station. The Session Judge acquitted the accused but the High Court, on appeal, convicted the accused but Supreme Court reversed the conviction of the High Court saying that there was no mark of injury on her body and there was no stiff resistance on the part of the girl in custody. This judgment attracted much criticism and public outcry for the amendment of the rape laws. The most important factor in this case was in relation to consensual sex and rape. In this case the Supreme Court did not take into consideration a girl of 16 years during night in the hands of dreadful intoxicated police where she would fearfully submit herself for whatever they demand from her. This decision, however, made way for making amendments in the Indian Evidence Act and the Indian Penal Code. The Indian Evidence Act was amended by inserting Sec.114-A drawing a conclusive presumption as to the absence of consent of the woman in the case of prosecution of rape under Sec 376(2) clauses (a) to (g), the Indian Penal Code was amended shifting the burden of proof of innocence on the accused. The Criminal Law (Amendment) Act 1983, incorporated custodial rape as a new offence by including Sections 376-B to D to the Indian Penal Code making custodial rape by police as an aggravating offence. *Ram Kumar* v. *State of Himachal Pradesh*[111] is yet another glaring instance of custodial rape and the Supreme Court upheld the sentence awarded by the State High Court to the two policemen in this case with seven years and two years rigorous imprisonment.

v.   Fake Encounter

"Fake Encounter" is another area where the police commit glaring human rights violations by way of atrocities and arbitrary killings against persons. In *People's Union for Civil Liberties* v. *Union of India*[112] the Supreme Court held that killing of two people in fake encounter by Imphal Police was clear violation of right to life guaranteed by Article 21 of the Constitution of India and defence of sovereign immunity does not apply in such cases. The Court awarded Rs.1, 00, 000/- as compensation for each deceased. People's Union for Civil Liberties, an NGO committed for protecting human rights, demanded for Central Bureau of Investigation enquiry on all encounters that took place in Chattisgarh since 2005.[113] Mangoli and Ganapati, Criminologists, study reveals that every 2nd police encounter in the country is fake.[114] Thus, fake encounter is enormous in many parts of India either under the pretext of terrorist or Maoist or Naxalite or dacoit killing and flagrantly violating the human rights of individuals by police.

5.3.3. *Protection against Arbitrary Arrest and Detention*

In the Constituent Assembly, there had been a heated discussion about the exception clause of Article 15 (now Article 21) which ends with the proviso "except according to law". The discussion centered on the issue that Parliament could take away the life and liberty by a mere Act of Parliament due to the reason that Article 15 gives very wide powers to the Parliament to restrain the right to life and personal liberty by making a simple law.[115] It was, therefore, felt necessary to limit the authority of the Parliament from taking away such rights unless there are exceptional circumstances so warrants. This led to the incorporation of another Article 15-A (now Article 22). Thus, Article 22 was "brought in as a compensation" to provide extra safeguard to the proviso "procedure established by law" in Article 21.[116] The Framers had taken the experience of colonial feudalism that persisted in a wide spread abuse of power in the case of arrest and detention of persons arbitrarily without proper investigation and trial.[117] Article 22 in Sub-articles (1) and (2) expressly provides the rights and protections of the arrested and detained persons. The Article 22 (1) reads, "no person who is arrested shall be detained in custody without being informed, as soon as may be, of the grounds for such arrest nor shall he be denied the right to consult, and to be defended by, a legal practitioner of his choice." Article 22 (2) further provides:

> Every person who is arrested and detained in custody shall be produced before the nearest Magistrate within a period of twenty-four hours of such arrest excluding the time necessary for the journey from the place of arrest to the court of the Magistrate and no such person shall be detained in custody beyond the said period without the authority of a Magistrate.

Thus, the Constitution has guaranteed certain rights to the arrested and detained persons such as: (i) the right to be informed of the ground of arrest 'as soon as possible'; (ii) the right to consult a lawyer and to be defended by a lawyer of his choice; (iii) the right to be produced before a Magistrate within twenty four hours; and (iv) the right to be released from custody beyond the period of twenty four hours if not produced before a Magistrate.

5.3.3.1.   Right to Know the Grounds of Arrest

It is important for an arrested person to know the grounds of depriving his liberty immediately on arrest so that he can assess whether the arrest is arbitrary or not, and, he can prepare for his defence. The Article 22 requires the arresting officials to disclose the grounds of arrest "as soon as may be" to the arrested person. In *re Madhu Limaye,*[118] the Supreme Court held that the requirements of Article 22(1) are meant to afford the earliest opportunity to the arrested person to remove any mistake, misapprehension or misunderstanding on the part of the authorities who made the arrest.[119] The provision is essential so that the arrested person may know the accusations that have been levelled against him before hand and will not take it as a surprise.[120] He also gets opportunity to prepare himself and to engage a lawyer to defend his side before a court of law. Thus, article 22(1) embodies the fundamental safeguards of the personal liberty of an arrested person.

Since the words used in Article 22(1) are "as soon as may be", the question arises as to what exactly the term "as soon as may be" implies. In *D.P Ghosh* v. *State of West Bengal*[121] the Supreme Court held that while the object of communicating the grounds of arrest is to enable the concerned person to make a representation against the arrest, communicating the grounds of arrest ' as soon as may be' must be interpreted in the correct context. The Court held that it implies that the ground of arrest must be conveyed as early as practicable and without delay.[122]

The question, at times, arises is as to whether oral communication is sufficient or written communication is mandatory. In *Ajith kumar* v. *State of Assam*[123] the Supreme Court held that the details of particulars of the offence must be communicated in a way understandable by the arrested person and should also be in a language understandable by him. [124] Thus, the communication may be oral or written, but what is important is that it must be understood by the arrested person regarding the grounds of his arrest. In *Joginder Kumar*'s case[125] and *D.K. Basu's* case[126] the Supreme Court has laid down detailed procedures to be complied with in making the arrest such as to inform about the arrest to a friend, relative or other person who is known to him or likely to take an interest in his welfare as far as is practicable that he has been arrested and where he is being detained. Further, it has been obligation to the arresting officer to inform the arrested person about this right.

The Criminal Procedure Code contains analogous provision in Section 50 (1) which provides that "Every police officer or other person arresting any person without warrant shall forthwith communicate to him full particulars of the offence for which he is arrested or other grounds for such arrest." The Supreme Court In *re Madhu Limaye*[127] explained the reasons of analogous provisions under the Code of Criminal Procedure and under the provisions of the Constitution as that the Constitution-makers were anxious to make these safeguards an integral part of fundamental rights. The Supreme Court observed that Dr. B. R. Ambedkar said while moving for insertion of Article 15-A (as numbered in the Draft Bill of the Constitution) which corresponded to present Article 22:

"Article 15-A merely lifts from the provisions of the Criminal Procedure Code two of the most fundamental principles which every civilised country follows as principles of international justice. It is quite true that these two provisions contained in clause (1) and clause (2) are already to be found in the Criminal Procedure Code and thereby probably it might be said that we are really not making any very fundamental change. But we are, as I contend, making a fundamental change because what we are doing by the introduction of Article 15-A is to put a limitation upon the authority both of Parliament as well as of the Provincial Legislature not to abrogate the two provisions, because they are now introduced in our Constitution itself."

Further, in *Govind Prasad* v. *State of West Bengal*[128] the Supreme Court held that the provisions of Section 50 of the Code of Criminal Procedure are material and cannot be overlooked as it brings the law in conformity with Article 22(1) of the Indian Constitution.[129] The Court further observed that this Section confers a valuable right to the arrested person and non-conformity with its mandatory provision would lead to non-conformity with the "procedure established by law" in article 21.[130]

Hence, the Article 22(1) of the Constitution provides safeguards against arbitrary arrest. A duty is caste on the arresting official to make known the arrested person the grounds of arrest at the earliest possible time. If the arresting official is not complying with this mandate, he would be liable for unlawful arrest of the person.

5.3.3.2.   Right to Consult a Lawyer

The right to consult a lawyer is a constitutional safeguard guaranteed to an arrested person by the Constitution under Article 22 (1). In fact, the Original Draft Constitution initially contained only a right to "consult" lawyer. In the Constituent Assembly, there was a strong argument for the incorporation of "to be defended" by a legal practitioner of his choice in Article

15-A. Dr. B.R. Ambedkar[131] was of the opinion that the words "to consult" included also the right to be defended because he observed that 'consultation' would be utterly purposeless if it was not for the purpose of defense.[132] However, in order to provide clarity and remove any ambiguity he added the words "and be defended by a legal practitioner" after the words "to consult".[133] The Supreme Court in *Nandini Satpathy*'s case[134] made a clear departure from its earlier decisions[135] and held that Article 22 (1) does not mean that persons who are not strictly under arrest or custody can be denied the right to counsel. The Supreme Court widened the scope of the right "to consult" to include right to counsel to any accused person coming within the purview of interrogation by a police official.[136] The Supreme Court went further in *Joginder Kumar's* case[137] and took a pulsating approach in relation to right "to consult" by holding that right to consult implies right to consult *privately* with his lawyer.[138] The Supreme Court in *D.K. Basu's case* issued directives that in the event of arrest, the arrestee can ask the police to allow him to consult his lawyer. It provides that "the arrestee may be permitted to meet his lawyer during interrogation though not throughout the interrogation".[139]

In a recent case, the Supreme Court affirmed its position once again. In *Shukur Ali* v. *State of Assam*[140] the Supreme Court held that the "right to consult and to be defended by a lawyer of choice" should be given widest possible construction to effectuate the intention of the Founding Fathers of the Indian Constitution. The Supreme Court observed:

> The Founding Fathers of our Constitution were themselves freedom fighters
> who had seen civil liberties of our people trampled under foreign rule, and
> who had themselves been incarcerated for long period under the formula "*Na
> vakeel, na daleel, na appeal*" (No lawyer, no hearing, no appeal). Many of
> them were lawyers by profession, and knew the importance of counsel,

particularly in criminal cases. It was for this reason that they provided for assistance by counsel under Article 22 (1), and that provision must be given the widest construction to effectuate the intention of the Founding Fathers.[141]

It is worth noting that a similar provision to Article 22(1) can be found under Article 303 of the Criminal Procedure Code. Section 303 of Code reads "any person accused of an offence before a Criminal Court, or against whom proceedings are instituted under this Code, may of right be defended by a pleader of his choice". While it may seem superfluous to have the same provision in the Constitution as well as in the Code of Criminal Procedure, Dr. B. R. Ambedkar stated that by introducing this provision in the constitution, there would be a limitation upon the authority of the Parliament as well as the Provincial Legislatures not to abrogate the rights guarantee under this provision.[142]

5.3.3.3.   Right to be Produced Before a Magistrate

After the arrest of a person by the police officer, judicial recourse is important to determine the legality of the arrest and detention. Article 22 (2) provides that the arrested person must be produced before a Magistrate within twenty four hours. Within the period of twenty four hours, the investigation has to be completed by the investigating officer. Even if the investigation cannot be completed, arrested person must be produced before the Magistrate immediately. Right to be brought before a Magistrate within twenty-four hours of arrest has been provided under the Constitution so that the arrest and detention are not carried out for extracting confessions or compelling information by means of duress or terror.[143] Supreme Court in *State of Punjab* v. *Ajaib Singh*[144] held that the arrests without warrants require more protection than those with warrants. The Court observed:

"...arrests without warrants issued by a court call for greater protection than do arrests under such warrants. The provision that the arrested person should within 24 hours be produced before the nearest Magistrate is particularly desirable in the case of arrest otherwise than under a warrant issued by the court, for it ensures the immediate application of a judicial mind to the legal authority of the person making the arrest and the regularity of the procedure adopted by him. In the case of, arrest under a warrant issued by a court, the judicial mind had already been applied to the case when the warrant was issued and, therefore, there is less reason for making such production in that case a matter of a substantive fundamental right."[145]

Thus, the provision for compulsorily producing the arrested person within twenty-four hours before a Magistrate ensures the immediate application of a judicial mind to the legal authority of the person making the arrest and legality of the arrest made by him.

The twenty four hours time excludes the time taken for travel to bring the arrestee before the magistrate. Failure to comply with the requirement will attract the police officer liable under section 340 of the Indian Penal Code for wrongful detention.[146] In the case of *Khatri (II) v. State of Bihar*[147] the Supreme Court observed that the State and its police authorities must see that this constitutional and legal requirement to produce an arrested person before a Judicial Magistrate within 24 hours of the arrest must be scrupulously observed.[148] The Court further observed that "the provision inhibiting detention without remand is a very healthy provision which enables the Magistrates to keep check over the police investigation and it is necessary that the Magistrates should try to enforce this requirement and where it is found to be disobeyed, come down heavily upon the police".[149] A question arose was whether the protection is available to the arrests made on the order of legislative bodies. In *Gunupati Keshavram v. Nafisul Hasan*[150] it was held that the protection conferred by clauses (1) and (2) of Article 22 extends to arrest and detention in pursuance of an order of the Speaker of a Legislature on a charge of breach of privilege.

Thus, the right to be produced before the Magistrate is a safeguard available to the arrested person under Article 22(2), even if the investigation cannot be completed within twenty-four hours. It is illegal for the police to keep a person in custody beyond the period of twenty-four hours without producing before a Magistrate. Though the Constitutional mandate is like this, but in reality there is always hue and cry of illegal arrest and detention by the police.

5.3.4. Preventive Detention

Detentions can be broadly divided into punitive and preventive detentions. While the former is applicable when a person is alleged to have committed an act in due disregard of law, the latter is aimed at preventing a person from doing anything that may be detrimental to the public order or national security. Though preventive detention is a curse to rule of law, it is a necessary evil to maintain public order and safety. Since it is a repugnance to human rights and liberty of common man, the principle is that the preventive detention is to be used sparingly when there is an imminent danger of public order and safety. However, the wielders of power frequently and grossly misuse preventive detention to suppress the opponents who stand against them. The danger of preventive detention lies on the fact that it is an administrative order and hence, the scope of judicial review is limited. In other words, the court will have the power only to the extent of examining the legality of the decision-making process and not to the legality of the order *per se*. As the phrase "preventive detention" suggests, it is meant for preventing the commission of crimes and hence, this measure cannot be considered as a punitive measure. Article 22 (3) (b) provides that nothing in sub Article (1) and (2) shall apply to any person who is arrested or detained under any law providing for preventive detention. Thus, preventive detention is exempted from the purview of the operation of Article 22 (1) and (2). However, clauses (4) to (7) of Article 22 provides procedures that have to be followed in the event of the arrest and detention under preventive detention laws.

Article 22 was inevitably included in the constitution due to the anxiety of the exception clause under article 21 which provides "except according to the procedure established by law". Thus, there was an apprehension during the constituent Assembly debate that the liberty can be deprived of by any arbitrary law in accordance with the whims and fancies of the ruling government. This led to the incorporation of additional Article 15-A (now Article 22) providing certain procedural requirements and safeguards to the accused and arrested persons under Clause (1) and (2). Article 22 (3) dealing with preventive detention denies the safeguards provided under Clause (1) and (2). The reason for denying such safeguards for the preventively detained persons were explained by Dr. B.R. Ambedkar as the then prevailing circumstances of aftermath of partition of the country that led to the turmoil and communal violence resulting in huge loss to life and property.[151] This shows that the Framers of the Constitution had in their mind the emergence of untoward disturbances to public order and safety and thought of having some guiding principles that could possibly prevent the commission of such disturbances and communal violence before its occurrence. Dr. B.R. Ambedkar argued that in such a state of situation the Parliament must be able to pass laws arming the Executive with adequate powers to check these forces of violence, anarchy and disorder.[152] He contended that the interest of the State is of paramount importance over the individual liberty. Nevertheless, he explained that this power of preventive detention had been enclosed in by two limitations : (i) power is limited by three months period of time for detaining a person and if further extension of period is inevitable, the Government must obtain positive report from the Advisory Board constituted for this purpose justifying the continuing the detention; and (ii) in other cases, the three months period can be extendable for more than three months period only by Parliament by making a legislation in this regards.[153]

5.3.4.1.   Protection against Arbitrary Detention

Article 22 (4) provides that no preventive law shall authorizes a person to be detained for more than three months. However, exception to this general prohibition also is provided under Clause (4). The exceptional situations for exceeding detentions for more than three months are (i) obtaining an opinion from an advisory body consisting of Judges of High Court; or (ii) such person is detained in accordance with the provisions of any law made by Parliament under sub-clauses (a) and (b) of clause (7).[154] It is also made clear that the advisory body shall, in no case, authorize the detention of any person beyond the maximum period prescribed by any law made by Parliament under sub-clause (b) of clause (7).

Though Clause (1) and (2) of the Article 22 is exempted from the purview of preventive detention , Clause (5) of Article 22 provides certain safeguards even in the case of preventive detention. Article 20 (5) which reads:

> When any person is detained in pursuance of an Order made under any law providing for preventive detention, the authority making the Order shall, as soon as may be, communicate to such person the grounds on which the Order has been made and shall afford him the earliest opportunity of making a representation against the Order.

Thus, Article 22(5) of the Constitution provides two categories of protection, namely, (i) the grounds on which the detention Order is passed must be communicated to the detenue as soon as possible; and (ii) earliest opportunity of making representation against the detention Order shall be provided.

A person who has been detained under preventive detention law shall have a right to be supplied copies of all documents, statements and other materials relied upon in the grounds of detention without any delay. The predominant object of communicating the grounds of detention is to enable the detenue at the earliest opportunity to make effective representation against his

detention. In *Dr. Ram Krishan Bhardwaj* v. *State of Delhi*[155], the Supreme Court while

interpreting Clause (5) held that "preventive detention is a serious invasion of personal liberty

and such meager safeguards as the Constitution has provided against the improper exercise of the

power must be jealously watched and enforced by the Court".[156] In *Shalini Soni* v. *Union of*

India[157] the Supreme Court considered the significance of 'communication' and 'representation'

in the event of preventive detention of a person. The Court observed:

> Article 22(5) has two facets: (i) communication of the grounds on which the order
> of detention has been made; (ii) opportunity of making a representation against
> the order of detention. Communication of the grounds pre-supposes the
> formulation of the grounds and formulation of the grounds requires and ensures
> the application of the mind of the detaining authority to the facts and materials
> before it, that is to say, to pertinent and proximate matters in regard to each
> individual case and excludes the elements of arbitrariness and automatism.[158]

While in *Shalini Soni's* case the Supreme Court was explaining the significance of the

right to communication and representation in the case of preventive detention, in *Vijay Kumar* v.

State of J& K[159] the supreme Court has elaborated the words used as "earliest opportunity" and

held:

> The word "earliest" which qualifies the term "opportunity" must equally qualify
> the corresponding obligation of the State to deal with the representation if and
> when made as expeditiously as possible. The jail authorities who are merely a
> communicating channel have to move with promptitude so that sufficient
> guarantee of affording earliest opportunity of making the representation and the
> same reaching the Government is translated into action. The corresponding
> obligation of the State to consider the representation cannot be whittled down by
> merely saying that time was lost in transit.[160]

The Supreme Court in this case has reminded of the obligation of the State in affording the

earliest opportunity for a person detained under the preventive detention law for making his

representation in a court of law.

Thus, the Constitution provides certain safeguards for protecting persons from preventive detention laws. When a preventive detention law authorizes to detain a person, the Constitution provides two important safeguards to the detenue, i.e., (i) the right to know grounds of detention and (ii) right to make representation. The Supreme Court has also been cautious to extent the safeguards provided under Article 22 relating to preventive detention in protecting the interest of detained persons.

5.4. Conclusion

The Constitutional safeguards that are provided for the arrested or detained persons are set out under the provisions of Articles 20 (3), 21 and 22. Article 20 (3) provides the right against self- incrimination which implies the right to remain silent also. The crucial question before the Supreme Court was whether these rights are available to an accused only during trial before a court or it was available from the stage of investigation by the police. The Supreme Court settled the matter by affirming that these rights are available to the accused from the time the First Information Report is registered by the police.[161] The Supreme Court has further broadened the scope of this right in *Nadini Satpathy's* case by holding that this right is available to an accused even when the investigation is initiated by the police. In a very recent casethe Supreme Court held that narco analysis, polygraph and brain mapping tests are violative of Artic 20(3) as the information are obtained without the consent of the accused and are not conclusively reliable.[162] Mallimath Committee on Criminal Justice Reform recommended that the accused person is a valuable source of information in a crime, and hence, India should adopt a system where in the statement made to the higher ranking police officer or under the supervision of a Magistrate shall be made valid. However, the law commission of India rejected the recommendation of Mallimath Committee as dilution of 'right to remain silent' jeopardizes the accused persons.[163]

Right to life and personal liberty is an important safeguard provided under the Indian Constitution. Article 21 of the Constitution of India provides that right to life and personal liberty shall not be curtailed to any person except according to the procedure established by law. Initially, in *A.K Gopalan's* case[164] the Supreme Court interpreted the provision narrowly and held that the liberty denotes merely freedom from bodily restraint, any law passed by parliament can take away the personal liberty as provided under Article 21. However, Fazal Ali J delivering minority judgment ruled that 'law' which curtails the liberty must be valid and the 'procedure' that take away the liberty must be fair. The Supreme Court has overruled A.K. *Gopalan* decision in *Maneka Gandhi's* case,[165] and held that the law which takes away or abridges the liberty must be "just, fair and reasonable" and not "arbitrary, oppressive and fanciful". The Court observed that Article 21 encompasses those rights and privileges which have long been recognized as being essential to the orderly pursuit of happiness by free men. The *ratio* in *Maneka Gandhi's* case has played a vital role in the growth and development of human rights in India including the protection of human rights from being violated by the police.

Article 22 provides safeguards against arbitrary arrest and detention. Article 22 (1) an (2) provides that the arrested person has a right to know the grounds of arrest, to consult and to be defended by a lawyer, to be produced before a Magistrate within twenty-four hours. Clauses (4) to (7) of Article 22 provides procedures that have to be followed in the event of the arrest and detention under preventive detention laws. The Article 22(5) of the Constitution provides two categories of protection in the event of preventive detention, namely, (i) the grounds on which the detention order is passed must be communicated to the detenue as soon as possible; and (ii) earliest opportunity of making representation against the detention order shall be provided. The

Supreme Court held that preventive detention is a serious invasion of personal liberty and such meager safeguards as the Constitution has provided against the improper exercise of the power must be jealously watched and enforced by the Court.

Thus, the analysis above clearly reveals that the Constitution of India provides a number of safeguards against arbitrary arrest and illegal detention. The interpretations of Article 20 (3), 21 and 22 by the Supreme Court has added strength and meaning to these safeguards of the rights of arrested and detained persons. However, there have always been hue and cries about human rights violations by police.

---

[1]   Sunil Deshta and Kiran Deshta, *Philosopjhy of Right to life: A Movement from Rigidity to Flexibility*, Civil and Military Law Journal, Vol.31, No.3 (1995), p.102.

[2]   M. P. Jain, *Indian Constitutional Law* (2006), p. 6.

[3]   A.I.R. 1950 SC 27.

[4]   H. M. Seervai, *Constitutional Law of India: A Critical Commentary*, vol. 1 (1991), p. 369.

[5]A.I.R.1976 S.C. 1207.

[6]   *Id.,* p. 1293.

[7]   A.I.R.1967 S.C. 1643.

[8]   *Id.,* p. 1656.

[9]   A.I.R.1954 S.C. 92.

[10] *Id.,* p. 96.

[11] A.I.R.1973 S.C. 1461.

[12] *Id.,* p. 1536.

[13] Criminal trials involve the risk of life and liberty of persons who may not have committed the crime and by the two known trial systems viz., Adversarial system (also known as accusatorial or the Common Law system) and the Inquisitorial system (also known as Continental or the Civil Law system) culprits are punished and innocents are set free. In adversarial system each side, acting in its self-interest, is expected to present facts and interpretations of the law in a way most favorable to its interests before an impartial tribunal and the Inquisitorial system, is characterized by a continuing investigation conducted initially by police and then more extensively by an impartial examining magistrate. The adversarial approach presumes that the accused is innocent (*See* Lord Sankey LC in *Woolmington v. DPP,* (1935) AC462), and the burden of proving guilt rests with the prosecution. The Inquisitorial system assumes that an accurate verdict is most likely to arise from an exhaustive investigation and the examining magistrate serves also as investigator who directs the fact-gathering process by questioning witnesses, interrogating the suspect, and collecting other

evidence. Due to the different operating styles of these two systems, there are differences in the role of the accused in the trial proceedings *viz.*, in adversarial proceedings the accused has great role in defending his case and in inquisitorial trials he has only limited role in defending his case.

14   John H Langbien, *The Privilege and Common Law Criminal Procedure:The Sixteenth to the Eighteenth Centuries* in Helmholz R.H. et al, *The Privilege against Self-Incrimination: Its Origins and Development* (1997), pp.83-84.

15   The Fifth Amendment to US Constitution provides "No person shall be........compelled in any criminal case to be a witness against himself, nor be deprived of life, liberty, or property, without due process of law; nor shall private property be taken for public use, without just compensation."

16   384 U.S. 436 (1966).

17   1954 S.C.R. 1077; (hereinafter referred as "*M.P. Sharma's* case").

18   1962 S.C.R. (3) 10.

19   *Id.,* p. 29.

20   *Ibid.*

21   *Id.,* p. 30.

22   *Id.,* p. 40.

23   1978 S.C.R. (3) 608; (hereinafter referred as "*Nandini Satpathy's* case").

24   *Id.,* p. 644.

25   *Id.,* pp. 609-610.

26   Narco-analysis is conducted by intravenously injecting Sodium Pentothal into the bloodstream; it is an ultrafast-acting anesthetic and acts within 45 seconds of being injected. There are 4 stages to this process of anesthesia. The aim in narco analysis is to keep the person in the second stage where an appropriate dose of the chemical is maintained where the person is partly conscious and loses his inbuilt inhibitions which could allow him to lie successfully. Therefore, under the effect of this chemical, the person is not only induced into a trance like state, but is also induced into speaking the truth. This is based on the fundamental assumption that the cortical portion of the brain is responsible for our ability to lie and Sodium Pentothal affects this portion thus successfully impairing the ability to lie; this assumption however, has no concrete scientific basis. The effects of the second stage are reversible; an overdose of the chemical form this stage could lead the victim to be unconscious and send him into the 3rd or 4th stage of anesthesia, the latter being irreversible and leading to a coma or death.

27   This is also known as Lie detector. In this, the Polygraphic machine records Blood Pressure, nerves, breathing speed, skin sensation at the time when continuous questioning is done on the suspect. Firstly, such questions are asked where suspect can't lie. During this, by polygraphic machine his blood pressure, heart beats, breathing speed and skin sensation is recorded. After that such questions asked, which investigators wanted to know. Actually, during right answer and wrong answer body language changes. Based on this results truth and lies are detected.

28   Brain Mapping is a test that maps the brain to reveal 'guilty knowledge'. The brain-mapping test is done to interpret the behaviour of the suspect and corroborate the investigating officers'

observation and the suspect's statements. During the tests, forensic experts apply unique technologies to find out if a suspect's brain recognizes things from the crime scene that an innocent suspect would have no knowledge of.

[29] Criminal Appeal Nos. 54, 55, 56-57, 58-59 of 2005, 1199 of 2006, 1471 of 2007, and 990 of 2010 (Arising out of SLP (Crl.) Nos. 10 of 2006 and 6711 of 2007), Supreme Court of India, available at: http://www.indiankanoon.org/doc/338008/(Visited on May 25, 2011).

[30] *Id.* at paras 158, 165.

[31] *Id.* at paras 161, 165.

[32] *Id.* at para 28.

[33] *Id.* at para 223.

[34] *Id.* at para 218.

[35] The Ministry of Home Affairs, Govt. of India constituted Justice V.S Mallimath Committee on Reforms of Criminal Justice System (hereinafter referred as "Mallimath Committee") to make a comprehensive examination of all the functionaries of the Criminal Justice System, the fundamental principles and the relevant laws. The Committee, having given its utmost consideration to the grave problems facing the country, has made its recommendations in its final report in 2003.

[36] Government of India, Report: *Justice V.S. Mallimath Committee on Criminal Justice Reform* (Ministry of Home Affairs, 2003), p.39.

[37] Mallimath Committee Report recommends for giving authority to Judges to supervise the investigating and prosecuting officials to gather evidences to make the criminal justice system effective in bringing the truth.

[38] Government of India, Law Commission of India, 180th Report (2002), p. 2.

[39] Fifth Amendment to the US Constitution provides "No person shall.....be deprived of life, liberty, or property, without due process of law".

[40] P.M. Bakshi, *The Constitution of India* (2010), p.55.

[41] Kharak sigh v. State of U.P, 1964 S.C.R. (1) 332 at p.345.

[42] 94 U.S. 113 (1877).

[43] *Maneka Gandhi* v. *Union of India,*1978 SCR (2) 621.

[44] *Id.,* at 662.

[45] *Id.,* at p. 696.

[46] See *supra*Ch.2 n.4.

[47] (1950) S.C.R. 88. AIR 1950 SC 27; (hereinafter referred as " the *A.K. Gopalan's* case").Here, the Supreme Court gave a narrow interpretation holding that the Article 21 must be seen by the letter of the Article and principle of natural justice has no place under it.

[48] 1978 S.C.R. (2) 621.

[49] See *supra* n. 43 at p. 696.

[50] *Supra n 47.*

[51] *Id.*, p.195.

[52] *Id.*, p. 262.

[53] *Id.*, p. 150.

[54] Dr. G.B. Reddy, *Judicial Activism in India (1997)*, pp. 164-165.

[55] Id. at pp.164-165.

[56] 1950 S.C.R. 88 at p.169.

[57] *Id.*, pp. 165-166.

[58] 1964 S.C.R. (1) 332.

[59] *Id.*, p. 360.

[60] *Supra n.43.*

[61] See *supra n.43* at p.626.

[62] 1979 S.C.R. (1) 392.

[63] *Id.*, at 428.

[64] *Francis Coralie* v. *Union Territory of Delhi*, A.I.R. 1981 S.C. 746

[65] *Sher Singh* v. *State of Punjab*, A.I.R. 1981 S.C. 625.

[66] *Kishore Singh* v. *State of Rajasthan*, A.I.R. 1986 S.C. 180.

[67] *Murli S. Deora* v. *Union of India*, A.I.R. 2000 S.C. 40.

[68] *M.H. Hoskot* v. *State of Maharashtra*, A.I.R. 1978, S.C. 1548.

[69] *Olga Tellis* v. *Bombay Municipal Corporation,* A.I.R. 1986 S.C. 180.

[70] *R. Rajagopal* v. *State of Tamil Nadu*, (1985) 2 S.C.C. 431.

[71] *Sunial Batra (No.1)* v. *Delhi Administration*, A.I.R. 1978 S.C. 1575.

[72] *Hussainara Khatoon (No.1)* v. *Home Secretary, State of Bihar*, A.I.R. 1979 S.C. 1360.

[73] *Premshankar* v. *Delhi Administration*, A.I.R. 1980 S.C. 1535.

[74] *D.K. Basu v State of West Bengal*, A.I.R. 1997 S.C. 610; *Joginder Singh v State of UP*, (1994) 4 S.C.C. 260; *Arvind Singh Bagga v State of U.P.*, AIR 1985 S.C. 117; *Prem Shankar Shukla v Delhi Administration*, (1980) Cr L J 930; *Sunil Batra v Delhi Administration*, (1978) 4 S.C.C. 494.

[75] Supreme Court held in *Hussainara Khatoon (No.1) v. Home Secretary, State of Bihar*, A.I.R. 1979 S.C. 1360, that 'right to speedy trial is implicit in Article 21; In *Hussainara Khatoon (No.2) v. Home Secretary, State of Bihar*, A.I.R. 1979 S.C. 1369, and *Hussainara Khatoon (No.3) v. Home Secretary, State of Bihar*, A.I.R. 1979 S.C. 1377 the Court reiterated the same view.

[76] A.I.R.1992 S.C. 1630.

[77] See *supra* n. 43.

[78] A.I.R.2009 S.C. 1822.

[79] A.I.R.2009 S.C. 984.

[80] Supreme Court, Judgment delivered on 26 August, 2010.

[81] *Joginder Kumar v. State of U.P.*, (1994) 4 S.C.C. 260, at.para 12.

[82] (1985) 4 S.C.C. 730.

[83] (1994) 4 S.C.C. 260.

[84] See supra n.23. at p.1032.

[85] *Ibid.*

[86] *Ibid.*

[87] AIR 1997 S.C. 610.

[88] *Id.*, para 36.

[89] *Id.*, para 39.

[90] See *supra*CH.5 for details.

[91] 1979 S.C.R. (1) 392.

[92] *Id.*, p. 489.

[93] 1980 S.C.R. (3) 855.

[94] *Id.*, p. 859.

[95] (1991) 2 S.C.C. 373.

[96] (1995) 3 S.C.C. 743.

[97] 1981 S.C.R. (2) 516.

[98] *Id.*, p. 539.

[99] 1981 S.C.R. (1) 995.

[100] *Id.*, p. 999.

[101] 1983 S.C.R. (2) 337.

[102] *Id.*, p. 345.

[103] 1993 S.C.R. (2) 581.

[104] *Id.*, p. 597.

[105] *Id.*, p. 596

[106] A.I.R. 2003 S.C. 4567.

[107] (1989) 4 S.C.C. 730.

[108] A.I.R. 1990 S.C. 513.

[109] S.L.P. (Criminal) Nos. 8485-87 of 2009, Supreme Court Judgment delivered on 25 October, 2010, available at: http://www.indiankanoon.org/doc/1473938/(Visited on January 7, 2011).

[110](1979) 2 S.C.C. 143.

[111]A.I.R. 1995 S.C. 1965.

[112]A.I.R. 1990 S.C. 513.

[113] Press Release, People's Union for Civil Liberties, 9th May 2007.

[114] See *supra* Ch.3 n.28 pp. 401-418.

[115] Constituent Assembly of India, Volume IX, 15 September, 1949. Available at <http://parliamentofindia.nic.in/ls/debates/vol9p35a.htm>accessed on 17th December 2010.

[116]*Ibid.*

[117] Kolsky, E, *Codification And The Rule Of Colonial Difference: Criminal Procedure In British India*, (2005), 23 law & hist. rev. p. 631; See also Kalhan. A et al, *Colonial Continuities: Human Rights, Terrorism, And Security Laws in India*, (2006), 20 Colum. J. Asian L. 93, fall 2006.

[118]1969 Cri.L.J. 1440.

[119]*Id.*, p. 1452.

[120] P. Ramanatha Aiyer, *Code of Criminal Procedure* (1999), p.262.

[121](1972) 2 S.C.C. 656.

[122]*Id.*, at 662.

[123]1976 Cri.L.J. 1303.

[124]*Id.*, p. 1316.

[125]1994 S.C.C. (4) 260, at p. 268.

[126] See *supra* n.74.

[127]*Supra* n. 118 at 1018.

[128]1975 Cri.L.J. 1249.

[129]*Id.*, at 1261.

[130]*Ibid.*

[131]Chairman, The Drafting Committee for Constitution of India after its independence in 1947.

[132] See *supra* n. 16 September, 1949. (Constituent Assembly Debate, Volume IX).

[133]*Ibid.*

[134] See *supra*n.23.

[135]The Supreme Court in *Janardhan Reddi v. State of Hyderabad,* A.I.R. 1951 S.C. 217, held that "the right to be defended by a legal practitioner of his choice" could only mean a right of the accused to have the opportunity to engage a lawyer and does not guarantee an absolute right to be supplied with a lawyer by the State. This in fact is a literal interpretation of Article 22 (1).

[136]*Supra* n. 5.

[137]1994 S.C.C. (4) 260.

[138]*Id.*, p. 268.

[139]*Supra* n.74, para 10.

[140](2011) INSC 195 (24 February 2011); In the Supreme Court, Crl. App. No. 546 of 2011 (arising out of S.L.P. (CRL.) No(s).679 of 2011) , available at:http://www.indiankanoon.org/doc/1470346/ (Visited on May 22, 2011.).

[141]*Ibid.*

[142]*Supra* n.118 at 1018.

[143] R.V. Kelkar, *Criminal Procedure* (1998), p.53.

[144]1953 S.C.R. 254.

[145]*Id.*, p. 268.

[146] D.D. Basu, *Crimial Procedure Code* (1973), p.143.

[147]1981 S.C.R. (2) 408.

[148]*Id.*, p. 414.

[149]*Ibid.*

[150]A.I.R. 1954 S.C. 636.

[151]See *supra* n.115, Constituent Assembly Debate, 15 September, 1949.

[152]*Ibid.*

[153]*Ibid.*

[154] Article 22, Clause (7) provides that the Parliament may by law prescribe-(a) the circumstances under which, and the class or classes of cases in which, a person may be detained for a period longer than three months under any law providing for preventive detention without obtaining the opinion of an Advisory Board in accordance with the provisions of sub-clause (a) of clause (4);(b) the maximum period for which any person may in any class or classes of cases be detained under any law providing for preventive detention.

[155]1953 S.C.R. 708.

[156]*Id.*, p.713.

[157]1981 S.C.R. (1) 962.

[158]*Id.*, p. 966.

[159]1982 S.C.R. (3) 522.

[160]*Id.*, p. 523.

[161] See *supra* n. 17.

[162] See *supra* n. 29.

[163]Law Commission of India, 180th Report on Article 20(3) of the Constitution of India and the Right to Silence (2002), p.2.

[164] See *supra* n. 47.

[165] See *supra* n. 43.

Chapter 6

STATUTORY PROTECTION OF HUMAN RIGHTS FROM POLICE IN INDIA

Apart from the Constitutional safeguards, the Indian legal frame work provides elaborate provisions in relation to the protection of human rights of accused, arrested or detained persons and the procedural formalities that are to be complied with in the event of arrest, detention or interrogations. These provisions can be found primarily in the Code of Criminal Procedure, 1973, Code of Criminal Procedure (Amendment) Act 2008, Code of Criminal Procedure (Amendment) Act, 2010, Indian Evidence Act, 1872, Indian Penal Code. In addition to these laws, Indian Police Act, 1861 and Kerala Police Act, 2010 provide organization and structure of police force in India and Kerala respectively. Protection of Human rights Act, 1993 is a special Act which was enacted to create institutions such as National Human Rights Commission and State Human Rights Commissions for the protection of human rights of the people from various spheres including from the police. The legislature intended to make such laws with a view to avoid arbitrary interrogation, arrest and detention by police and unnecessary intrusion into the privacy of persons. Though the legal framework envisions protecting the innocent and accused persons from the high handedness of police, yet there takes place many violations of human rights of people by police. Illegal arrest, arbitrary interrogation, unlawful detention, torture, custodial violence, false implication, fake encounters, extortions, etc., are the chief violations of human rights perpetrated by police. An analysis of these provisions would enlighten how far and to what extent they could protect the human rights of people, and the merits and demerits of following such provisions.

6.1. Criminal Procedure Code, 1973

Procedural aspect of arrest, detention, searches and seizures by police affect liberty, dignity and human rights of individuals. It is essential to provide effective procedural requirements and proper control of exercise of power by police in making arrest, detention, searches and seizures for effective administration of criminal justice in any country. Code of Criminal Procedure in India provides a large number of provisions in order to control arbitrary arrest, capricious interrogation, Illegal detention, illegal search and seizure, etc.

6.1.1. Arrest and Detention

Arrest and Detention are the procedures by which an offender is taken into custody thereby depriving his liberties. It becomes essential for either the prevention of commission of crime or the continuance of commission of crime, or enabling investigation to be carried out without interruption, or producing the evading offender before the judicial or other authorities. It, then, becomes indispensable to empower the police with ample powers to arrest and detain a person and in case of resistance from the offender, even to use force or firearms in appropriate cases. Vesting of such discretionary powers with the police is justified in any democratic set up of the country for the safety and security of the members of the society. However, arrest and detention are that areas which attract much criticism due to the abuse of power by the police on the one hand and it necessarily effect the deprivation of liberty of persons on the other hand.

114

6.1.1.1. Report of Police and other Commissions on Arrest and Detention

Irrespective of procedural requirements for carrying out arrest, there takes place large number of arbitrary arrests and illegal detentions. The National Police Commission in its Third Report, referring to the quality of arrest by the police in India had reported that the power of arrest was one of the chief sources of corruption in the police. The report suggested that by and large nearly 60% of the arrests were either unnecessary or unjustified and that such unjustified police actions accounted for 43.2% of the expenditure of the prison department.[1] Thus, the National Police Commission recommended for reducing the arresting and detaining power of the police.

Generally, the police making the arrest and detention do not take into consideration of the personal and psychological aspects of the arrestee. How the arrest affects the people psychologically, physically and personally, and the attitude of the police making arrest are depicted by the Mallimath Committee in the following words:

> Power of arrest is often misused. The person arrested apart from suffering considerable inconvenience, also suffers by loss of his image in the society. Even if ultimately he is found to be innocent that damage done to the arrested person can not be undone. There is an erroneous impression in the minds of the police that the first thing for him to do is to arrest the suspected person even without making any inquiry. It may be necessary to arrest the person when the offence involved is fairly serious and the accused is likely to abscond or evade the process of law or there is reasonable apprehension of the accused committing offences or when he would be a serious threat to the victim, or witnesses, or is likely to tamper the evidence, or when it is necessary in the circumstances to restore a sense of security in the locality and similar other considerations as pointed out by the Law Commission in its 154th report.[2]

The Law Commission of India in its 152nd report made recommendations to make the arrest more transparent by intimating relatives or friends by the police officer arresting the person.[3] Further, in its 154th report the Law Commission recommended that when an arrest of women is to be made, it shall be done by a female police officer only, and if male officer is making arrest, he shall not touch the body of the woman.[4]

Arrest is a major area where police commit breach of human rights violations in total disregard of the arrestee's personal, physiological, physical conditions and status. Different Commissions and Committees recommended for the reform of the arrest and detention laws and procedures. Recently, Code of Criminal Procedure has been amended in 2005, 2008 and 2010 to incorporate many of the recommendations and also the directions of the Supreme Court in different cases such as *Sheela Barse*,[5] *Joginder Kumar*[6] and *D.K Baus*'s[7] cases on arrest and detention.

6.1.1.2.   Protection from Arbitrary Arrest and Detention

The Code of Criminal Procedure does not define the term "arrest", though Section 46 details "arrest how made". Arrest ordinarily coveys the meaning of depriving of the liberty by virtue of legal authority. Thus, if the arrest is not made under a legal authority or misuse the legal authority for making arrest, it cannot be considered as an "arrest" in the legal sense. It can only be considered as illegal confinement in accordance with the provisions of Indian Penal Code or as a subject matter of tort. Sections 41-50, 53-60, 76, 89, and 151 deal with powers to arrest a person and the procedure to be complied with in the event of making an arrest of a person.

The Code Criminal Procedure (Amendment) Act, 2010 [8] has made substantial amendments in Section 41 of the Criminal Procedure Code relating to the power of police to arrest without warrant. The Amendment intended that the powers of arrest conferred upon the police officer must be exercised after reasonable care and justification. The major change that is

116

made in relation to arrest is in sections 41, 41-A, 41-B, 41-C and 41-D. One of the important changes is that it is now compulsory for the police to record the reasons both for making as well as for not making an arrest on the basis of a complaint or information or reasonable suspicion in respect of a cognizable offence for which the maximum punishment prescribed is 7 years or less. Hence, no person can be arrested for a complaint or suspicion of involvement in such an offence without a warrant. However, there are certain exceptions to this rule where in the police officer can arrest a person without a warrant and they are:

a) When a person commits a cognizable offence in the presence of a police officer; or the police officer has reason to believe that such person has committed the offence and is satisfied that such arrest is necessary,

    i. to prevent such person from committing any further offence;   or

    ii. for proper investigation of the offence; or

    iii. to prevent such person from causing the evidence of the offence to disappear or tampering ;

    iv. to prevent such person from making any inducement , threat or promise to any person acquainted with the facts of the case; or

    v. to ensure his presence before the court as and when required.

b) The Amendment provides that the reasons for arrest should be sound and recorded in writing by the police officer.

c) In all cases where the arrest of a person is not required, the police officer shall record the reasons in writing for not making the arrest.

d) In all cases where the arrest of a person is not required under the provisions of sub section 1 of section 41, the police officer shall, issue a notice directing the person to appear before him and to comply with the terms of notice. He can be arrested if such person fails to comply with such direction. No arrest will be made in a non-cognizable offence except under a warrant or order of a magistrate.

e) The police officer while making the arrest shall-(a) bear an accurate, visible and clear identification of his name for easy identification, (b) prepare a memorandum of arrest which shall be attested by at least one witness and counter signed by the person arrested, (c) inform the person arrested that he has a right to have a relative or a friend named by him to be informed of his arrest.

f) When any person is arrested for any offence and interrogated by the police, he shall be entitled to meet an advocate of his choice during interrogation, though not through out the interrogation.

In fact, the new Amendment loosens the power of arrest by police in crimes carrying upto seven years imprisonment; but it can be misused over its discretionary powers to shield the culprits by the police department as well as politicians and could give a free hand to gangsters, anti-socials and habitual offenders without any fear of being arrested. It would remove the fear or deterrence from the minds of criminals, who will misuse the provisions under the cover of personal liberty. However, it must be appreciated that the Amendments aim at reducing arbitrary arrests and illegal detentions by the police. The Amendment is expected to reduce corruption and extortions in police stations and will also decrease the number of false complaints.

As per Section 46, a police officer is empowered to use all means necessary to effect the arrest in case of a person forcibly resists the arrest of him, or attempts to evade the arrest. In the event of arrest, Section 50 of the Code of Criminal Procedure casts a duty on police officer making arrest to inform the arrestee of the ground of his arrest and of the right to be released on bail on arrest if the case is one of bailable offence. Similarly, Section 56 of the Code of Criminal

Procedure expressly provides that on arrest, a person shall be produced before the nearest Magistrate within 24 hours of his arrest, excluding time taken for journey in bringing him before the Judicial Magistrate.[9] This provision corresponds to Article 22 (2) of the Constitution of India. Section 49 further casts a responsibility on the police that the arrested person shall not be subjected to more restraint than what is necessary to prevent his escape.

Section 167 provides safeguards to accused person when investigation cannot be completed within twenty four hours. It provides that whenever the investigation cannot be completed in twenty-four hours and there is reasonable ground for believing that the accusations are well founded, the accused person shall be brought to the Magistrate and the Magistrate, if necessary, may authorize to keep the accused person in custody under detention. This provides a judicial control over the rights of arrested person where the investigation is prolonged beyond twenty-four hours.

6.1.1.3.   Special Procedure for Arrest and Detention of Woman

Code of Criminal Procedures provides that every woman who is a suspect and is required to be searched shall be searched by a female only and in strict regard to decency.[10]The Code of Criminal Procedure (Amendment) Act, 2005 and 2008 provides a number of safeguards and special treatments that have to be made in arresting or detaining women. After the Amendment in 2005, Section 46 of the Code of Criminal Procedure provides that no woman shall be arrested after sunset and before sunrise. If such exceptional circumstances exist to arrest a woman during this period, the woman police officer shall, by making a written report, obtain the prior permission of the Judicial First Class Magistrate within whose local jurisdiction the offence is committed or the arrest is to be made. Section 46 further provides that where a woman is to be

119

arrested, unless the circumstances indicate to the contrary, her submission to custody on an oral intimation of arrest shall be presumed. The provision prohibits the touching of the body of the women by a male police officer in making an arrest, unless the circumstances otherwise require. This provision has been incorporated on the basis of the recommendations of the 154th Report of the Law Commission of India. Further, Section 167 now provides that in case of arrest of a woman under eighteen years of age, the detention shall be authorized to be in the custody of a remand home or recognized social institution. The new Amendment also incorporates the Supreme Court guidelines in *Sheela Barse v. State of Maharashtra*[11] in arresting and detaining women. Thus, the new Amendments to the Code of Criminal Procedure provide various safeguards to the women in the event of arrest and detention.

Thus, the Criminal Procedure Code, now, after the amendments provides elaborate safeguards in relation to arrest and detention. It provides special treatment and precautions to women in the event of being arrested by the police. It is submitted that after the Amendments, the Code of Criminal Procedure makes the arrest and detention more transparent and tries to avoid arbitrary arrest and illegal detention. It makes the police officials more accountable in the making of arrest and detention.

6.2. Juvenile Justice (Care and Protection of Children) Act

The Juvenile Justice (Care and Protection of Children) Act, 2000 (Act 56 of 2000)[12] was made repealing the earlier Juvenile Justice Act of 1986. The Act was made in compliance with the UN Convention on the Rights of the Child 1989. The Act provides for a special approach towards the prevention and treatment of juvenile delinquency and affords a framework for the protection, treatment and rehabilitation of children in the purview of the juvenile justice system.

The Juvenile Justice (Care and Protection of Children) Act, 2000 was amended in 2006.[13]In the case of arrest and detention of juveniles, normal criminal procedures of arrest and detention are not applicable. Special procedures are laid down in the Juvenile Justice (Care and Protection of Children) Act.

Section 18 of the Juvenile Justice (Care and Protection of Children) Act specifically provides that no child shall be kept in police lock-up or jail, what ever may be the crime committed by the child. Children shall be dealt with by specially trained Juvenile Police officer only.[14] The Act further provides that when any juvenile is accused of a bailable or non- bailable offence and is arrested by a police officer, the police officer arresting the juvenile shall produce him immediately to the Magistrate.[15] If it is not possible for the police officer to bring the juvenile to the Magistrate immediately, the police officer shall cause him to be kept in an observation home or a place of safety until he can be brought before a Juvenile Court.[16] The juvenile shall not be kept in police station or jail in any circumstances. Section 19 states that where a juvenile is arrested, the officer-in-charge of the police station to which the juvenile is brought shall, as soon as may be after the arrest, inform – (a) The parent or guardian of the juvenile, if he can be found, of such arrest and direct him to be present at the Juvenile Court before which the juvenile will appear; and (b) The probation officer of such arrest in order to enable him to obtain information regarding the antecedents and family history of the juvenile and other material circumstances likely to be of assistance of the Juvenile Court for making the inquiry. However, there are number of incidences violating the procedure of handling of juveniles by the Police. Though the law is as above, many a times, the police officer making the arrest of juvenile, while preparing First Information Report, may bring the age of juvenile into adult.

6.3. Indian Penal Code, 1860

The Indian Penal Code does not explicitly provide provisions for criminal offence of arbitrary arrest or illegal detention or torture committed by police officers. However, the Indian Penal Code contains many criminal provisions that could be utilized against police in the case of illegal arrest, unlawful detention, torture, assault etc. The Indian Penal Code provides certain provisions that might have relevance in taking criminal action against the police who commit violation of human rights and these provisions are:

i. Public servant concealing design to commit offence which it is his duty to prevent. (Section 119)[17]

ii. Public servant disobeying law, with intent to cause injury to any person.(Section 166)[18]

iii. Fabricating false evidence. (Section 192)[19]

iv. If the policeman causes death of a person in custody, it may amount to either Culpable homicide (Section 299);[20] or, Murder (Section 302)[21] or Causing death by negligence (Section 304-A)[22],

v. Voluntarily causing "hurt" (Section 323)[23]

vi. Voluntarily causing "grievous hurt" (Section 324)[24]

vii. Voluntarily causing "hurt" to extort confession or to compel restoration of property (Section 330)[25]

viii. Voluntarily causing "grievous hurt" to extort confession or to compel restoration of property (Section 331).[26]

ix. Wrongful confinement (Section 340)[27]

x. Wrongful confinement to extort confession, or compel restoration of property (Section 348)[28]

xi. Criminal force (Section 350) [29]

xii. Assault (Section 351)[30].

122

xiii. Assault or criminal force in attempt to wrongfully confine a person (Section 357)[31].

xiv. Assault or criminal use of force with intent to dishonour a person (Section 356)[32].

xv. Rape Committed in police custody. (Section 376 (2) (a))[33].

xvi. Assault or criminal force to woman with intent to outrage her modesty.(Section 354)[34].

6.3.1. The Punishments for the Offences

The above Penal Code provisions are generally applicable in the cases connected with illegal arrest, unlawful detention, assault, torture, causing death, rape in custody by the police, *etc.* The punishments prescribed for public servant concealing design to commit offence which it is his duty to prevent under Section 119 of the Indian Penal Code are classified into three categories, namely, (i) if the offence is committed, the offender public servant shall be punished with imprisonment of any description provided for the offence, for a term which may extend to one-half of the longest term of such imprisonment, or with such fine as is provided for that offence, or with both; or (ii) if the offence be punishable with death or imprisonment for life, the offender public servant shall be punished with imprisonment for a term which may extend to ten years; or (iii) if the offence is not committed, the offender public servant shall be punished with imprisonment of any description provided for the offence for a term which may extend to one-fourth part of the longest term of such imprisonment or with such fine as is provided for the offence, or with both.[35] Similarly, public servant disobeying law with intent to cause injury to any person is punished with simple imprisonment for a term which may extend to one year and/or with fine.[36]The punishment prescribed for voluntarily causing hurt to extort confession or to compel restoration of property is seven years and with fine.[37] If the hurt caused is grievous one to extort confession or to compel restoration of property, the maximum punishment is ten years imprisonment and fine.[38] Wrongful confinement to extort confession or compel restoration of property carries a maximum punishment of three years imprisonment and liability to pay a fine.[39]

The police officers are generally known for using assault or criminal use of force to intimidate the accused or witnesses to elicit information. Assault or criminal force is attempted wrongfully to confine a person carries imprisonment for a term which may extend to one year and/or with fine which may extend to one thousand rupees.[40] Assault or criminal force with intent to dishonour a person under section 356 prescribes punishment with imprisonment for a term which may extend to two years and/ or fine. Culpable homicide, depending on the circumstances, carries punishment ranging from various terms of imprisonment up to imprisonment for life and fine.[41] Murder which covers acts where the offender intended to cause death or inflicted bodily injury or committed other acts sufficient or likely to cause death is punishable with death or life imprisonment and a fine.[42] However, culpable homicide is not murder if the offender, being a public servant or aiding a public servant acting for the advancement of public justice, exceeds the powers given to him by law, and causes death by committing an act which he, in good faith, believes to be lawful and necessary for the due discharge of his duty.[43] If death is caused by negligence, the maximum punishment is imprisonment of two years and/or a fine.[44]

6.3.1.1.   Punishment for Custodial Violence against Woman

Assault or criminal force to a woman with intent to outrage her modesty is punishable with imprisonment which may extend to two years and /or with fine.[45] Rape carries a punishment ranging from seven years to life imprisonment.[46] After the controversial *Mathurarape* case,[47] an amendment was brought about in Sec. 376 of the Indian Penal Code. Sec. 376(2) (a) now

124

penalizes custodial rape committed by police officers. This has been made after a hue and cry raised by public aftermath of acquittal of police officials who committed rape on a 16 year old girl named Mathura in police custody taking the advantage of police authority. After the amendment, rape in custody is considered to be an aggravating circumstance carrying a heavier punishment. The new amendments of Code of Criminal Procedure, 2005 incorporated into it the recommendations of the National Police Commission (Fourth Report) and the amendment to Section 176 now provides for mandatory judicial inquiries in all incidences of custodial rapes.

It is submitted that the provisions in the Indian Penal Code which specifically deal with police atrocities and human rights violations committed by police in custody are very few. The general provisions dealing with hurt, murder, culpable homicide, assault, wrongful confinement *etc.*, is used for the purpose of prosecuting the erring police personnel. This, some times, creates anomaly due to the fact that the police generally commit atrocities in the custody where there are no independent witnesses. When the normal provisions are made applicable, it may not be easily proved before a court of law and the police will always be in an advantageous position due to the lack of witnesses and evidences. Hence, there requires special procedural law to tackle the situations of human rights violations committed by police.

6.4. The Indian Evidence Act, 1872

The areas that come in touch with the Indian Evidence Act, 1872 and human rights violations by the police are 'confessions' made to police and 'presumptions' in the case of custodial violence. Custodial confessions are always controversial, though presumption as to consent of the woman sparingly comes for decision. The Indian Evidence Act does not define the term 'Confession". Nevertheless, the Act provides generally that the confession made under threat, promise or undue influence as inadmissible.[48] Further, the confession made to a police officer is altogether made inadmissible. Section 25 provides: "confession made to a police officer is not admissible in evidence". It is also provided by the Act that confession made to any person while in the custody of the police is also not admissible.[49] However, any recovery made on the basis of information given by the accused is proved in trial against him.[50] Thus, in India, the confessions made to a police officer or to any other person while in the police custody, are inadmissible. But this is not the position in other parts of the World. Singapore, which virtually follows the same system as ours, has empowered the Sergeant-level officers to record confessional statements.[51] Indian legal system does not admit the validity of confession made to police due to the apprehension that police may use force, threat or torture to extract confession.

However, confessions made to certain law enforcement agencies are made admissible in evidence in India such as (i) Section 9 of the Railway Property (Unlawful Possession) Act, 1996;[52] (ii) Section 108 of Customs Act, 1962;[53] and (iii) Section 32 of POTA, 2002.[54]

6.4.1. Supreme Court on Admissibility of Confession to the Police

Terrorist and Disruptive Activities (Prevention) Act, 1987 (TADA)[55] also contained provisions for the admissibility of the confession, but TADA expired on May 23, 1995. However, it is worth noting that section 18 of the TADA provided for the admissibility of confessional statements made to police officers. The constitutionality of section 18 was challenged in *Kartar Singh* v. *State of Punjab*.[56] The Supreme Court while upholding the validity of section 18 laid down guidelines so as to ensure that the confession obtained in the pre-indictment interrogation by a police officer not lower in rank than a Superintendent of Police is not tainted with any vice but is in strict conformity of the well recognized and accepted aesthetic principles and fundamental fairness. The guidelines laid down by the Supreme Court are:

i. The confession should be recorded in a free atmosphere in the same language in which the person is examined and as narrated by him;

ii. The person from whom a confession has been recorded under section 15(1) of the Act, should be produced before the Chief Metropolitan Magistrate or the Chief Judicial Magistrate to whom the confession is required to be sent under Rule 15(5) along with the original statement of confession, written or recorded on mechanical device without unreasonable delay;

iii. The Chief Metropolitan Magistrate or the Chief Judicial Magistrate should scrupulously record the statement, if any, made by the accused so produced and get his signature, and in case of any complaint of torture, the person should be directed to be produced for medical examination before a Medical Officer not lower in rank than of an Assistant Civil Surgeon;

iv. Notwithstanding anything contained in the Code of Criminal Procedure, 1973, no police officer below the rank of an Assistant Commissioner of Police in the Metropolitan cities and elsewhere of a Deputy Superintendent of Police or a Police Officer of equivalent rank, should investigate any offence punishable under this Act of 1987;

v. In case, the person, taken for interrogation, on receipt of the statutory warning that he is not bound to make a confession and that if he does so, the said statement may be used against him as evidence, asserts his right to silence, the police must respect his right of assertion without making any compulsion to give a statement of disclosure.[57]

Thus, the Supreme Court favoured for admitting the statement made to higher ranking police officers in certain cases of complex nature, but, at the same, the Court insisted that the right to silence of the accused should be respected and the police should make sure that there was no compulsion to make the statement. This view has been taken due to the growing organized terrorist and disruptive acts that take place frequently in the country.

6.4.2. Law Commission on Confession to the Police

The Law Commission in its 48th Report had recommended that the confession recorded by a Superintendent of Police or a higher ranking Officer should be admissible in evidence subject to the condition that the accused is informed of his right to remain silent and to consult a legal practitioner.[58] Justice Mallimath Committee has also made recommendation in its Report that officers of the level of Superintendents of Police or higher level officers shall be entrusted to record confessions fairly and without subjecting the accused to duress or inducement. If the confession is audio/video recorded, it would lend further assurance that the accused was not subjected to any form of compulsion. Hence, Mallimath Committee recommended that section 25 of the Indian Evidence Act may suitably be substituted by a provision rendering the confessions made before a Police Officer of the rank of Superintendent of Police and above as admissible. It also recommended that provisions should also be made to enable audio/video recording of statements made to police as admissible in evidence. However, the Law Commission of India in its 180th Report changed its earlier stand in 48th Report and rejected the recommendation of Mallimath Committee that confession made to high ranking police officer should be made admissible on the ground that it adversely affect the accused person's civil liberties.

It is submitted that Mallimath Committee, it seems, did not give due consideration of the fact that in India, even higher police officials are also not absolutely free from corruption or the secret political nexus. If the recommendation of Mallimath Committee is accepted, police may use the power for trapping innocent persons. Though the custodial torture is not expressly prohibited by law in India, the evidence collected by illegal means such as extraction of confession by torture, threat, *etc.*, is not accepted and is not admissible. At the same time, judicial confessions are admissible and considered as a valid piece of evidence. It seems the existing position is better from the point of view of human rights of accused, arrested or detained persons.

6.5. Torture and Criminal Law

Police use torture for various purposes such as extraction of confession, means of retaliation, bribery by the opposite party, political influence by the opposite party, etc. Since Police notoriously use torture as a means to extract confession, the Indian Evidence Act makes the confessions made to police as inadmissible.[59] The Indian Penal Code does not contain a definition of "torture' nor uses the term "torture". However, the Indian Penal Code contains provisions such as hurt,[60] grievous hurt,[61] hurt or grievous hurt to extract confession,[62] a public servant disobeying the law with intent to cause injury,[63] assault,[64] etc., as amounting to torture and can be used against a police official who import torture against a person. The Supreme Court has, though not defined the term torture, but attempted to provide in general phrase the impact of torture on human beings. Justice Dr. A.S. Anand quoting Adriana P. Bartow in *D.K. Basu* observed:

129

"Torture" has not been defined in the Constitution or in other penal laws. "Torture" of a human being by another human being is essentially an instrument to impose the will of the 'strong' over the 'weak' by suffering. The word *torture* today has become synonymous with the darker side of human civilization. "Torture" is a wound in the soul so painful that sometimes you can almost touch it, but it is also so intangible that there is no way to heal it. Torture is anguish squeezing in your chest, cold as ice and heavy as a stone paralyzing as steep and dark as the abyss. Torture is despair and fear and rage and hate. It is a desire to kill and destroy including yourself."- Adriana P. Bartow."[65]

Sections 46 and 49 of the Criminal procedure Code protect persons under custody from torture who are not attempting to evade lawful arrest or not accused of an offence punishable with death or imprisonment for life.[66] After the new Amendment of Criminal Procedure Code in 2008, the police officer is required to make the accused person medically examined immediately after the arrest. Section 54 (1) now provides:

When any person is arrested, he shall be examined by a medical officer in the service of Central or State Governments and in case the medical officer is not available by a registered medical practitioner soon after the arrest is made: Provided that where the arrested person is a female, the examination of the body shall be made only by or under the supervision of a female medical officer, and in case the female medical officer is not available, by a female registered medical practitioner.

This indicates that in the event of torture by police in custody, the medical examination can prove it and the Magistrate shall verify the record of the result of the examination. It affords an opportunity to the arrestee or detainee to bring to the attention of the Magistrate's notice of any torture or assault committed against him during the custody. But in practice, the police may intimidate the arrestee not to disclose to the Magistrate, if he was tortured in custody. Further, Section 176 of the Criminal Procedure Code expressly provides inquiry by a Magistrate into the cause of death in custody. It provides that when any person dies while in the custody of the police, the nearest Magistrate empowered to hold inquest shall conduct inquiry into the cause of death. Thus, in the case of death in police custody, an immediate magisterial inquiry is provided under the provisions of Criminal Procedure Code to determine the cause and circumstances of death.

In summary, the Indian Penal Code does not use the term "torture" nor does it prescribe punishment for torture as such, though it contain provisions which can operate for criminalizing police official who commit torture. The Criminal Procedure Code takes certain measures under sections 46, 49, 50, 56 and 167 to ensure that torture is not committed against arrested or detained persons. Guidelines are given by the Supreme Court in *D.K. Basu* case with respect to procedure to be followed when a person is arrested or under detention. The significant one in connection with torture being the arrestee should be subjected to medical examination every 48 hours during his detention by a doctor from the approved panel of doctors and copies of all prescribed documents should be sent to the concerned Magistrate. This directive is now incorporated into the Criminal Procedure Code by the Amendment in 2008. This provision is intended to assess the health condition of arrested or detained person and to ensure that torture is not employed on him by the police.

6.6. Indian Police Act, 1861

Indian police Act, 1861 was enacted during the colonial period of British rule and there has always been criticism about following such a colonial Act which was made for the purpose of suppressing the people by force and intimidation during British rule. Many States in India are also following the colonial Police Acts. Mallimath Committee on Criminal Justice Reform stated the need for reform of Police Act in the following words:

> The police system in the Country is functioning under the archaic Indian Police Act which was enacted in 1861 for the perpetuation of the British Empire. The police now have an obligation and duty to function according to the requirements of the Constitution, law and democratic aspirations of the people. Further, the

police is required to be a professional and service-oriented organization, free from undue extraneous influences and yet be accountable to the people. Besides, it is necessary to have the police force which is professionally controlled and is politically neutral, non-authoritarian, people friendly and professionally efficient. The National Police Commission had recommended enactment of a new Police Act for achieving the above objectives about two decades back. The Central Govt., however, has not taken any action. The Committee strongly feels that a new Police Act may be enacted by the Central Govt. on the pattern of the draft prepared by the National Police Commission.[67]

Sections 7 and 29 of the Act provide for dismissal, penalty or suspension of police officers who are negligent in the discharge of their duties or unfit to perform the same. Apart from the general provision of negligence, the Act is silent about the atrocious acts committed by police on people and an impartial mechanism to redress the grievance against police atrocities. Even after the Mallimath Committee Report in 2003, the Government of India did not come forward to reform the Police Act. Hence in 2006, considering the growing atrocities and police excesses, the Supreme Court in *Prakash Singh* v.*Union of India*[68] came forward directing the reform of Police Acts both at the Centre and the States in India. The Supreme Court observed that there has been no reform of archaic police Acts even after many Committee's and Commission's Reports. The Supreme Court further observed the need for giving directives in the following words:

> Having regard to (i) the gravity of the problem; (ii) the urgent need for preservation and strengthening of Rule of Law; (iii) pendency of even this petition for last over ten years; (iv) the fact that various Commissions and Committees have made recommendations on similar lines for introducing reforms in the police set-up in the country; and (v) total uncertainty as to when police reforms would be introduced, we think that there cannot be any further wait, and the stage has come for issue of appropriate directions for immediate compliance so as to be operative till such time a new model Police Act is prepared by the Central Government and/or the State Governments pass the requisite legislations.[69]

The Supreme Court has observed that the time was already over for police reform in Central and State Governments and issued seven directives that may be considered for police reform by Central and State governments such as:

(i)   constituting a State Security Commission,

(ii)   ensuring that the Director General of Police is appointed through merit based transparent process,

(iii)   ensuring that police officers on operational duties are provided a minimum tenure of two years,

(iv)   separating the investigation and law and order functions of the police,

(v)   setting up a Police Establishment Board to decide transfers, postings, promotions and other service related matters of police officers,

(vi)   setting up a Police Complaints Authority at State level and District level to inquire into public complaints against police officers, and

(vii)   setting up a National Security Commission at the Union level to prepare a panel for selection and placement of Chiefs of the Central Police Organizations.

It is submitted that the direction of the Supreme Court to the Central and State Government is a very welcome step for reforming traditional Police Acts. Significance of the guidelines lies in the fact that the Central and State Governments, sooner or later, will have new Police Acts which would insulate the police from external pressure, enable it to secure to all citizens their rights under the Constitution, ensure Rule of Law and equality for everyone.

6.7. Kerala Police Act, 2011

As per the Seventh Schedule of the Indian Constitution, the "police" is a subject coming under both the State List and the Concurrent list. Therefore, the States as well as the Central Government can maintain police force. Strictly speaking, maintenance of law and order in India is a matter concerned with State responsibility and hence, maintenance of police force within a State jurisdiction is primarily the responsibility of the concerned State. Kerala Police Act was passed in 1968 following the foot steps of the colonial Indian Police Act. In the backdrop of Supreme Court directives in *Prakash Sing*'s case to reform the Police Acts in Union and States, and considering the growing cry of the general public, new Kerala Police Act has been enacted for the State of Kerala in 2011. One of the most significant aspects to be noted in the new Act is that it expressly incorporates, *inter alia,* the protection human rights and dignity of all persons as the function of the police.[70]The Act introduces several changes with a view to protect the human rights of people from being violated by the police.

6.7.1.   *Reception at the Police Station*

The Act ensures that all citizens shall have the right to efficient police services from any Police Station.[71] It provides for peaceful entry and reception at any time at any Police Station and to receive lawful services as a matter of right of the public.[72]It is submitted that this provision intents to remove the dreadful image of the police and police stations in the State. It also provides for facility for women to submit complaints with privacy and in the presence of women police. The general trend in police stations is not to give any receipt of the complaint. The new Kerala Police Act now makes it as a matter of the right of the complainant to receive mandatorily a receipt acknowledging the complaint given by him, and also to know the stage of the police action or investigation in respect of the complaint.[73]

Another significant aspect is the provision relating to the whereabouts of detained person is Section 8 (6) which provides that 'any citizen shall have the right to know whether any particular person is in custody at the police station'. It is submitted that this has been made with a view to reduce illegal detentions in police custody, and as a matter of right any citizen can require the police to give information about a person in custody. Section 13 provides that all Chairpersons and Members of the State Human Rights Commission or the State Women's Commission or the State Scheduled Caste/Scheduled Tribe Commission or the State or District Police Complaints Authorities may enter in a Police Station and directly verify the entries in any General Diary and also the condition of any person kept in custody. It further provides that any such person visiting the police station shall make a contemporaneous record of his visit in the diary, and also communicate to the District Police Chief the summary of his observations. The District Police Chief shall take, as soon as possible, further actions as may be necessary on such observations. It is submitted that this measure can provide effective supervision and control mechanism on the situation of the police stations and also on the police.

6.7.2.   Behaviour of the Police

There have always been grumblings and controversies regarding the police behaviour and use of abusive language of police towards accused, victims or witnesses of crime. Section 26 of the new Kerala Police Act bans such indecent behaviour and use of filthy languages of the police. It provides:

135

(i) All Police officers on duty, in their dealings with the public, shall exhibit courtesy, propriety and compassion appropriate to the occasion and use polite and decent language.

(ii) The police officers shall not use force against anybody or threaten that force be will used, or any adverse police or legal action will be taken unless it is necessary to carry out any lawful purpose.

(iii) The police officers shall exhibit special sympathy in their dealings with the victims of crimes and give due consideration to the special needs of women, children, senior citizens and the disabled.

(iv) The police officer shall give up unnecessary show of aggression and avoid intemperate behaviour even on provocation.

(v) The police officer shall not misbehave or use indecent language to anyone in their care or custody.

Where any person is arrested and kept in the custody of the Police, he shall be permitted to wear the dress which is decent and appropriate under the circumstances and which he is used to wear.[74] Regarding handcuffing, the Act makes the general rule that handcuffs shall not be used on an arrested person. However, in exceptional circumstances where the Police Officer arresting the person has sufficient ground to believe that the arrested person shall escape from custody or injure himself or others if not handcuffed.[75]

Thus, the Kerala Police Act attempts to change the behavioural pattern and use of language of the police. It is submitted that only the time can determine how far, by law, the behaviour and attitude of the police can be changed. However, the move of the Government for the incorporation of such a provision in the Act must be appreciated.

6.7.3. Audio, Video or Other Electronic Records

The Act, as part of making the police actions transparent and non-arbitrary, provides certain measures such as that the police may make and keep audio or video or electronic records of any activity performed by them during the discharge of their duties and such records may be used in any proceedings in which the correctness of police action is called in question.[76] Further, no Police Officer shall prevent any member of the public from lawfully making any audio or video or electronic record of any police action or activity carried out in a public or private place.[77]

6.7.4. Injury due to the Use of Force

Section 50 casts a duty on the police officer concerned when a person who is physically injured due to the use of force by a police officer complaints about his physical injury or the matter of sustaining injury comes to the notice of the police officer to take such person before the nearest qualified medical practitioner. The medical practitioner shall seek and understand about the injury and the manner of its causation and record the same and shall render necessary treatment. The section further provides that if such person is medically fit to be taken before a Magistrate, he shall be produced by the Station House Officer before the Judicial Magistrate having jurisdiction or before an Executive Magistrate if it is outside the jurisdiction of such Judicial Magistrate. The Magistrate shall seek and understand details of the injured in respect of the matter in which the injury was caused. However, if the injured is not in a condition to be produced before a Magistrate, the details of the incident and circumstances shall be furnished forthwith by the Station House Officer to such Magistrate and a copy of the said report shall be given to the medical officer and the injured and proper acknowledgement shall be obtained from them in writing. This provision is significant in relation to prevention of torture in police custody.

Again, Section 96 is significant as it makes every police officer liable to report directly to Deputy Superintendent of Police or the District Police Chief regarding the occurrence of torture of any person with the intention of admitting the commission of an offence or creating evidence. The Kerala Police Act also attempts to create confidence in police officers who has information about the torture to report to higher police officers by providing that no such report of the police official shall attract any disciplinary action.[78] But, it is made clear that the failure to report such matter shall attract departmental disciplinary proceedings.[79] Thus, the new Act contains specific provision to prevent torture. Thus, the Act every police officer bound to inform such acts of torture to higher police officials.

6.7.5. *Vexatious Arrest, Search, Seizure, Violence, etc.*

The Act also makes vexatious arrest, search, seizure, violence, *etc.*, as offences punishable with three year imprisonment and /or with fine. Section 116 provides:

Whoever, being a police officer,—
  (a) enters into or conducts unnecessary searches or causes to be searched without lawful authority or reasons in any building, vessel, tent or place for causing annoyance; or
  (b) seizes the property of any person or detains a person in custody or conducts search or arrests any person illegally for causing annoyance and without reasonable cause; or
  (c) deliberately subjects, any person in custody or with whom he comes into contact in the course of his duties, to torture or any kind of inhuman or unlawful personal violence or grave misconduct; or
  (d) deliberately, knowingly and maliciously with intent to implicate an innocent person in a criminal offence records a false statement or make a forged document or raises a false allegation of attack on the police ; or
  (e) deliberately and directly aids or abets for the commission of an offence which, as a police officer, he is bound to prevent, shall on conviction, be

138

punished with imprisonment for a term which may extend to three years or fine or with both.

Thus, the Act punishes the acts of arbitrary arrest, search, seizure, violence, *etc.*, committed by the police. At the same time, the Act does not restrict the operation of any other laws for punishing offender, if the same matter is an offence under the provisions of that law.

6.7.6.   *State Security Commission*

Section24 of the Kerala Police Act provides for the establishment of State Security Commission. The Act provides that the State Security Commission shall consist of members, namely, (i)   the Minister in-charge of Home Department who shall be the Chairman; (ii)   the Minister in-charge of Law; (iii) the Leader of Opposition; (iv) a retired Judge of the High Court nominated by the Chief Justice of the High Court of Kerala; (v)   the Chief Secretary-ex-officio; (vi) the Secretary to Government, Home Department- ex-officio; (vii) the State Police Chief- ex-officio; (viii) three non-official members, who shall be persons of eminence in public life with wide knowledge and experience in maintenance of law and order, administration, human rights, law, social service, management of public administration, nominated by the Governor of whom one shall be a woman.

The Commission shall have the functions, such as (a) to frame general policy guidelines for the functioning of the Police in the State; (b) to issue directions for the implementation of crime prevention tasks and service oriented activities of the Police; (c) to evaluate, from time to time, the performance of the Police in the State in general; (d) to prepare an annual report of the activities of the Commission and submit it to the Government; (e) to prepare the guidelines for the changes to be carried out, from time to time, in the state police; and (f) to discharge such other functions as may be assigned to it by the Government.

139

The Commission is required to submit annual report and the annual report submitted by the Commission shall be placed before the Legislative Assembly. The Act empowers the Commission to evaluate the performance of the police every year. It is submitted that this is a welcome step in as much as police performance is evaluated periodically and, hence, the police will have an apprehension that an extra departmental oversight mechanism is working over their head.

6.7.7. Police Establishment Board

The Kerala Police Act authorizes the Government to constitutea department level Police Establishment Board with the Director General of Police as Chairman and other four senior police officers, not below the rank of Additional Director General of Police of the Department, as members.[80] The Board shall discharge the following functions, namely, (a) to decide on complaints and appeals in respect of service matters like transfer, promotion, etc. of police officers of and below the rank of Inspector after detailed examination of related Acts and rules or submit suitable recommendations in this regard; (b) to study the particular problems in respect of women police officers, decide on grievances in respect of the same and submit recommendations in necessary matters; (c) to review the activities of State Police in general or in respect of special subjects; and (d) such other functions as may be entrusted to the Board by Government from time to time.[81]

The Act provides that the Government shall give due consideration to the recommendations of the Board. However, the Government may, either *suo-motu* or on a complaint by the person concerned, for reasons to be recorded in writing, modify or cancel any decision or order of the Board.[82] The State Police Establishment Board shall nominate an officer of the rank of Deputy Superintendent of Police in each district and such nominated officer shall set apart one day in a week to hear or receive complaints from police officers of and below the rank of Sub Inspector.[83] Such officer shall examine and study the complaints and give recommendations in respect of appropriate redressal measures to the District Police Chief and if the matter is beyond the jurisdiction of the District Police Chief then to the State Police Establishment Board through the District Police Chief.

6.7.8.   *Police Complaints Authorities*

In order to redress the grievances against police effectively, the Kerala police Act now provides for the establishment of Police Complaints Authorities at State and District levels. The establishment of Police Complaints Authority is a significant change that has been brought about by the new Kerala Police Act.

6.7.8.1.   State police Complaints Authority

Section 110 sets out that the Government shall constitute a State Police Complaints Authority for examining and inquiring the,—

(i) complaints on all types of misconduct against police officers of and above the rank of Superintendent of Police;

(ii) grave complaints against officers of other ranks in respect of sexual harassment of women in custody or causing death of any person or inflicting grievous hurt on any person or rape, etc.[84]

The State Police Complaints Authority shall consist of (i)   a retired Judge of a High Court who shall be the Chairperson of the Authority; (ii)   an officer not below the rank of Principal Secretary to Government; (iii)   an officer not below the rank of Additional Director

General of Police; (iv) a person as may be fixed by the Government, in consultation with the Leader of Opposition, from a three member panel of retired suitable officers not below the rank of Inspector General of Police furnished by the Chairman of the State Human Rights Commission; and (v) a person as may be fixed by the Government, in consultation with the Leader of Opposition, from a three member panel of retired District Judges furnished by the State *Lok Ayuktha*.[85]

6.7.8.2.   District Police Complaints Authority

The Act further authorizes the Government to constitute the District Police Complaints Authority at district level for examining and inquiring the complaints against police officers of and up to the rank of Deputy Superintendent of Police. The District Police Complaints Authorities shall consist of i) a retired District Judge, who shall be the Chairperson; ii) the District Collector; and iii) the District Superintendent of Police.[86]

The State Authority and the District Level Authorities shall have all the powers of a Civil Court for conducting inquiries in respect of the following matters, namely, (a) summoning and enforcing the attendance of any person and examining him on oath; (b) requiring the discovery and production of any document; (c) receiving evidence on affidavit; and (d) any other matter as may be prescribed.[87]

All concerned officers shall be bound to carry out the recommendations given by the authority in respect of matters of initiation of department level inquiry, registration of criminal case, *etc.*, against a police officer.[88] Thus, the Kerala Police Act authorizes the State Government to constitute an impartial high power State Police Complaints Authority and district level District Police Complaints Authorities for redressing the grievances against police. It is submitted that the constitution of State and District Police Complaints Authorities is an effective mechanism for the protection of human rights of accused, arrested or detained persons.

The Act also authorizes the people's representatives and others to make complaints against police officers directly to the Police Complaints Authorities. Section 111 provides that the Presidents of Three-tier-Panchayats, Chairpersons of Municipal Councils, Members of Legislative Assemblies, Members of Parliament, Mayors of the Corporations, etc., may give all types of complaints against the police officers that have come to their notice or have been brought to their notice, to the Police Complaints Authority and the Authority shall, after conducting necessary inquiry, inform the result of such inquiry to the representative concerned.

6.7.8.3.   Community policing
The Act also provides for constitution of "community policing". Section 64 empowers the District Police Chief to constitute Community Contact Committees for each Police Station under his jurisdiction. The Community Contact Committee shall comprise the representatives of the local residents of the area give general assistance to the Police in the discharge of their duty. The Committee may also formulate programmes for promoting security awareness, safety awareness, prevention of crimes and legal literacy, *etc.*

Though the Kerala Police Act provides many provisions to uphold human rights and human dignity of persons, transparency, accountability, impartial complaints authorities, State Security Commissions, there are different criticisms about the Act. Regarding the composition of the State Security Commission, proposals were made by different Commissions and Committees such as the National Human Rights Commission, [89] Rebiero Committee, [90] Soli Sorabjee Committee, [91] National Police Commission, [92] *etc.* However, the Kerala Police Act rejected all these models. Dr. P. J. Alexander, former Director General of Police, Kerala State, criticized that the composition of the Security Commission in Section 24 deviates from all the above models both in form and content. [93] Further, while the Supreme Court has stated that the recommendations of the Commission shall be binding on the State Government, proviso to Section 25 (5) states that the State Government may fully or partially reject or modify any recommendation or direction of the Commission.[94] Thus, the Act failed to incorporate the spirit of the Supreme Court for making the State Security Commission devoid of unnecessary interference by the Government. Another criticism is regarding the Police Establishment Board. The purpose of designing a Police Establishment Board by Supreme Court in each State was to decide impartially without political interference on the transfers, postings and promotions and other service related matters of officers of and below the rank of Deputy Superintendent of Police. It was also the intention of the Supreme Court that the State Government shall not interfere with the decisions of the Board except in exceptional cases only after recording its reasons for doing so. In effect the intention of the Supreme Court was to free personnel management issues and service fortunes of officers at the subordinate levels from external interference and pressures. The Police Establishment Board as is provided under the Kerala Police Act would not serve this purpose and it gives more room for governmental and political interference. Dr. P.J. Alexander is of the opinion that the provisions regarding the constitution and the functioning of the Board have to be recast to cure the defect.[95]

Leaving aside the above criticisms, it is submitted that the Kerala Police Act provides many provisions which are more in agreement with human rights aspect of accused, victims and witnesses. The Act also calls for a change in the attitudinal behavioural pattern of the police towards public. The constitution of State Security Commission, Police Establishment Board and Police Complaints Authorities will have far reaching effects in the police-public relationship and

144

prevention of torture, arbitrary arrest, illegal detention, unwanted search and seizure, false implication, failure to take action, etc. The Criticism are too valuable as what is central is to create confidence and trust in the minds of the common man that police will protect their life, liberty, property and human rights and dignity. Though the steps have been taken to make the police more people friendly by giving them training and orientation periodically, it shall be the responsibility of the State Government to ensure a more efficient, effective, and accountable police service for the entire State.

6.7.8. Departmental Disciplinary Actions

The service and disciplinary rules are State affairs in relation to State police establishments. However, the Indian Police Service is controlled by the Central Civil Service Rules that apply to the employees of the Government of India and the All India Service Rules that apply to All India Services such as Indian Administrative Service (IAS), Indian Police Service (IPS) and Indian Foreign Service (IFS). Members of the Indian Police Service are subject to disciplinary sanctions ranging from censure to dismissal.[96] However, in any case, the departmental mechanisms for dealing with police misconduct do not always inspire public confidence. There are allegations that police departments many a times suppress the incidents of criminality or misconduct by police officers because the revelation of the facts could damage the image of the organization or due to fraternity relationship within the department. There have always been allegations of partisanships and manipulations on the investigation of complaints against police officers.

Police officials as public servant enjoy some protection under Section 197 of Code of Criminal Procedure in the case of prosecution proceedings against them. Section 197 provides that Court shall not take cognizance of an offence except with the previous sanction of

Government when any person who is or was a public servant not removable from his office save by or with the sanction of the Government is accused of any offence alleged to have been committed by him while acting or purporting to act in the discharge of his official duty. However, Supreme Court in *Surjeet Singh* v. *Jit Singh*[97] in 1997 held that the protection of Section 197 will not be available in the case of custodial death. Supreme Court relying on its earlier decision in *S.P. Saha* v. *M.S. Kochar*[98] observed that the investigation of an offence is certainly the duty of the police, but it can never be stated that during the course of investigation, the police are entitled to torture a person who was in their custody and thereby cause his death. In such circumstances, it cannot at all be said that they were acting only in the discharge of their duties while they allegedly tortured and caused the death of a person and hence, prosecution for the commission of such offences can never attract the provisions of Section 197 of the Code of Criminal Procedure.

6.7.8.1   Recommendations of the National Police Commission

In order to enhance the image of the police and to increase the trust of general public on the investigation against police atrocities, the National Police Commission, in their First Report suggested arrangements, whereby inquiries would be conducted by departmental authorities and also by an independent authority outside the police. The National Police Commission felt that a large number of complaints against police should be looked into and disposed of by the supervisory ranks in the police hierarchy, but a judicial inquiry should be made mandatory in the following categories of complaints against the police:

    i.   alleged rape of a woman in police custody;

   ii.   death or grievous hurt caused while in police custody; and

iii. death of two or more persons resulting from police firing in the dispersal of unlawful assemblies.[99]

The response of the Government to these recommendations had been very cold for long. However, the Government has incorporated magisterial enquiry into the rape or death cases in police custody by the new Amendment to the Code of Criminal Procedure in 2005.[100]

6.7.8.2.   Departmental Actions as per the Kerala Police Act 2011

The Kerala Police Act provides elaborate provisions for departmental actions. Section 101 of the Act provides for Departmental Enquiry Proceedings. Sub- section (1) provides that any police officer, who commits any misconduct or offence under this Act or any other Act for the time being in force or rule or order made there under may be subjected to departmental enquiry proceedings under the Kerala Police Departmental Enquiries, (Punishment and Appeal) Rules, 1958 notified by the Government. The State Police Chief may order initiation of action against any police officer before the Court in accordance with the provisions of the Code of Criminal Procedure, in addition to the Departmental Enquiry Proceedings under the said Rules.[101] However, the Sub-section (3) of Section 101 makes clear that the official found guilty of disciplinary proceedings shall not be considered as a criminal nor be sentenced to any punishment under the Criminal law. Sub-section provides that the competent officer or the Government may impose any of the following penalties mentioned in items (a) to (q) below against any police officer found guilty on completion of the department level inquiry,—

(a) fine;

(b) extra duty including drill and physical training;

(c) recovery of loss caused to Government from salary; (d) recovery of loss sustained to the concerned party from salary;

147

(e) giving training to improve work and conduct;

(f) prohibit from performing fixed particular duties or assigning fixed particular rank;

(g) warning;

(h) censure;

(i) barring increment without cumulative effect;

(j) barring increment with cumulative effect;

(k) withholding of promotion;

(l) reducing pay without cumulative effect;

(m) reducing pay with cumulative effect;

(n) reduction in seniority or rank;

(o) compulsory retirement;

(p) removal;

(q) dismissal.

Department level enquiry proceedings may be initiated against any police officer for the same matter even though he was exonerated by a criminal court after trial.[102] A police officer if convicted for an offence involving moral turpitude or serious misconduct, the disciplinary authority concerned or the State Police Chief or the Government may, after considering the nature of the offence, make him compulsorily retire or remove or dismiss that officer from service.[103]

6.7.8.3. The Kerala Police Departmental Inquiries (P&A) Rules.

The rules relating to the award of punishments to the members of the Kerala Police Service are provided under the Kerala Police Departmental Inquiries, (Punishment and Appeal) Rules, 1958 as amended from time to time. Since it is imperative that it maintains a higher level of discipline than any other Government department, the disciplinary proceedings of the police Department are of prime significance. The procedure prior to awarding punishments can be split into three categories.

    a. Minor defaults where formal charge need not be framed

    b. Defaults where no oral inquiry is necessary, but a charge is framed

    c. Defaults where a charge is framed and an oral inquiry or personal hearing is held[104]

Thus, in summary, if either the IPS officers or the State police officers commit misconduct, the same shall attract disciplinary proceedings. However, the disciplinary punishments are not considered as criminal sanctions. Nonetheless, there is no restriction to bring other criminal or civil action against the erring personnel. It is submitted that when a police officer commits excess, most of the time, unless there is a hue and cry from public and media, departmental enquiries are not ordered and are not carried out properly due to political pressure or partisanship. Even where the police officer is found culprit, now the practice is that the State takes the responsibility of making the payment of compensation to the victims. It is submitted that in all cases where the police commit human rights violations against common man, the State should make the erring police officer to be personally liable for paying the compensation. This may considerably reduce human rights violations by the police.

6.8. Human Rights Act, 1993

With a view to provide effective protection and promotion of human rights, the Parliament has enacted the Protection of Human Rights Act, 1993. The Section 2 (1) (d) of the Protection of Human Rights Act provides that "human rights" means the rights relating to life, liberty, equality and dignity of the individual guaranteed by the Constitution or embodied in the International Covenants and enforceable by courts in India. The same Section in Sub-section (1) (f) states what includes the international covenants and it provides that "International Covenants" means the International Covenant on Civil and Political Rights and the International Covenant on Economic, Social and Cultural rights adopted by the General Assembly of the United Nations on the 16thDecember, 1966 and such other Covenant or Convention adopted by the General Assembly of the United Nations as the Central Government may, by notification, specify. Originally, when the Protection of Human Rights Act was adopted in 1993, the Act included only two international covenants, *viz.*,the International Covenant on Civil and Political Rights and International Covenant on Economic, Social and Cultural Rights. After the Amendment in 2006 the words "and such other Covenant or Convention adopted by the General Assembly of the United Nations as the Central Government may, by notification, specify" were added to it. The Protection of Human Rights Act provides for the establishment of National Human Rights Commission, State Human Rights Commissions and the Human Rights Courts. It also elaborates the constitution, composition, powers and functions of National Human Rights Commission and State Human Rights Commissions. Accordingly, on October 12, 1993, National Human Rights Commission was established. Invoking section 21 of the Protection of Human Rights Act, the Kerala State Government established Kerala State Human Rights Commission in December 1998.[105] The powers and functions of the State Human Rights Commission are the same as those of the National Human Rights Commission.[106]

The Protection of Human Rights Act also provides for the establishment of Human Rights Courts. Section 30 states that for the purpose of providing speedy trial of offences arising out of violation of human rights, the State Government may, with the concurrence of the Chief Justice of the High Court, by notification, specify for each district a Court of Session to be a Human Rights Court to try the said offences. Section 31 further provides that for every Human Rights Court, the State Government shall specify a Public Prosecutor or appoint an advocate who has been in practice as an advocate for not less than seven years as a Special Public Prosecutor for the purpose of conducting cases in that Court.

6.9. Conclusion

The Indian legal system provides a number of provisions and procedures to protect persons from arbitrary arrest, unlawful detention, interrogation, false implication, vexatious searches and seizures, torture, etc., from police. The Code of Criminal Procedure provides provisionsthat are to be followed in making arrest, detention, search, seizure etc. These procedures are considered to be inadequate to tackle the police excesses. Hence, Supreme Court made guidelines and directives in *Joginder* and *D.K. Basu* cases as a temporary measure until the new legislation has been made by the Government to this effect.

The Indian Penal Code does not provide an exclusive definition of "torture" nor does it prescribe punishment as such for torture committed by police. However, there are various general provisions such as hurt, grievous hurt, assault, public servant concealing design to commit offence which it is his duty to prevent, public servant disobeying law with intent to cause injury to any person, criminal use of force, unlawful confinement, unlawful restraint, etc., which may be used against police atrocities. Nonetheless, the Indian Penal Code provides very few specific provisions such as Sections 330 and 331 which provide for punishment for causing hurt

151

or grievous hurt to extort confession or to compel restoration of property respectively and Section 376 (2) (a) which provides punishment for committing rape in police custody. Since police commit torture and other atrocities in custody where there are no witnesses other than police personnel, the general provisions of the Indian Penal Code have proved to be inadequate in order to bring the erring police officer to justice.

Indian Police Act which was enacted in 1861 during the period of British rule to coerce and suppress people who stood against the rule is still followed in India. This has been criticized by National police Commission, Law Commission of India, Mallimath Committee etc. Many Commissions and Committees such as Dharma Veera Commission (National Police Commission), Reibero Commission, Soli Sorbjee committee, Justice Mallimath Committee, etc., were constituted by the Central Government for making recommendations to the reform of law relating to police from time to time. However, the recommendation of these commissions and Committees were not implemented by the Government of India. Considering the lethargic attitude of the Government in reforming Police Act even after recommendations of the various Commissions and Committees, the Supreme Court in *Prakash Singh* case gave directions to the Government to reform police Acts both at the Centre and States with specific guidelines.

Consequent to the directives of the Supreme Court, the Kerala Government has passed new Kerala Police Act in 2011. The earlier Kerala Police Act, 1960 which was enacted following the foot steps of Indian Police Act was totally replaced by the recent Kerala Police Act. The New Act contains provisions for taking care of human rights and human dignity of individuals. It also provides provisions intending to change the colonial dreaded attitudinal behaviour of police with polished and civilized nature. The Act also ensures increased autonomous for the police department by providing provisions for establishing a Police Establishment Board for posting, promotion and transfer of employment of police with a view to minimize political and Governmental interference at minimal level. Another significant feature of the Act is complaint redressal mechanisms against police personnel by providing for the establishment of State Police Complaint Authority and the District Police Complaint Authorities. The Authority with Retired High Court Judge as Chairperson at State level and Retired District Judge at District level can ensure more impartial mechanism for redressing the complaints/grievances against police atrocities. It is submitted that the mechanism may be considered as a milestone in the protection human rights in the years to come. However, there are criticisms about the form and content of the Security commission and Complaint authorities. Despite the fact of criticism, it is submitted that the Kerala Police Act is a lead ahead for reformation of police in Kerala. Above all, the success of the Act lies on the fact that the public, the Government, the Police Department, the concerned professional groups, the human rights groups and the media must closely monitor police practices to see that provisions are upheld.

Endnotes

[1] Government of India, Third Report: *National Police Commission* (Ministry of Home Affairs, 1980), pp. 30-31.

[2] *Id.*, p.115.

[3] Law Commission of India, 152nd Report (1994), p. 172.

[4] *Id.*, 154th Report (1996), p.13.

[5] See *supra* Ch. 5 n.43.

[6] See *supra* Ch. 5 n.83.

[7] See *supra* Ch. 5 n. 47.

[8] In the light of recommendations of the National Police Commissions, Law Commission of India, the Mallimath Committee on Criminal Justice reform and in the wake of the guidelines issued by the Supreme Court in *Joginder Kumar's* and *D.K Basu's* cases, the Parliament made Amendments in the Code of Criminal Procedure in 2005, 2008 and in 2010. The Criminal Procedure Code (Amendment) Act, 2005 and 2008 provided comprehensive changes for making the criminal justice system more effective. However, there was stiff opposition from lawyers relating to arrest (Section 5 of Amendment Act, 2008), notice of appearance before a police officer (Section 6 of Amendment Act, 2008) and adjournments (Section 21 (b) of the Amendment Act, 2008), and urged the government not to notify these amended laws and hence, the Government decided not to notify Sections 5, 6 and 21 (b) then(*See* Code of Criminal Procedure (Amendment) Act, 2010, Statement of Objects and Reason, p.3.). The other amended provisions of the Code of Criminal Procedure (Amendment) Act 2008 came into effect from December 31, 2009. The matter related with Sections 5, 6 and 21 (b) was then referred to the Law commission of India to take the initiative to bring about a consensus on the issues. Law Commission recommended certain changes and the changes recommended were incorporated into the Amendment Act of 2010 and the Code of Criminal Procedure (Amendment) Act, 2010 came into effect from 1st November 2011.

[9] Code of Criminal Procedure, S. 57 and 76,

[10] *Id.,* S. 51.

[11] In *Sheela Barse's* case, the Supreme Court has provided guidelines to be followed if arrested person is a woman such as (i) when the circumstances so requires that she shall be kept in police station under detention, she must be kept in a separate lock-up separated from male suspects, (ii) if separate lock-ups are not available in a police station and the circumstances so warrants that she is required to be kept in police lock-up, she may be transferred to the nearest police station where separate women lock-up is available, (iii) the interrogation of a woman suspect shall be carried out only in the presence of a female police officer or constable, (iv) if, at any time during interrogation, she needs or wants to consult a lawyer, she shall be given the opportunity to do so.

[12] Act 56 of 2000.

[13] The Juvenile Justice (Care and Protection of Children) Act, 2000 was amended by the Juvenile Justice (Care and Protection of Children) Amendment Act, 2006 (33 of 2006).

[14] Juvenile Justice (Care and Protection of Children) Act, S. 63(1).

[15] *Id.,*S. 18 (1).

[16] *Id.,*S. 18 (2).

[17] Section 119 of the Indian Penal Codeprovides that " whoever, being a public servant intending to facilitate or knowing it to be likely that he will thereby facilitate the commission of an offence which it is his duty as such public servant to prevent, voluntarily conceals, by any act or illegal omission, the existence of a design to commit such offence, or makes any representation which he knows to be false respecting such design; *and* -shall, if the offence be committed, be punished with imprisonment of any description provided for the offence, for a term which may extend to one-half of the longest term of such imprisonment, or with such fine as is provided for that offence, or with both"; or if the offence be punishable with death or imprisonment for life, with imprisonment of either description for a term which may extend to ten years; or, if the offence be not committed, shall be punished with imprisonment of any description provided for the offence for a term which may extend to one-fourth

part of the longest term of such imprisonment or with such fine as is provided for the offence, or with both.

[18] Section 166 of the Indian Penal Code provides "whoever, being a public servant, knowingly disobeys any direction of the law as to the way in which he is to conduct himself as such public servant, intending to cause, or knowing it to be likely that he will, by such disobedience, cause injury to any person, shall be punished with simple imprisonment for a term which may extend to one year, or with fine, or with both".

[19] Section 192 provides that "Whoever causes any circumstance to exist or makes any false entry in any book or record, or makes any document containing a false statement, intending that such circumstance, false entry or false statement may appear in evidence in a judicial proceeding, or in a proceeding taken by law before a public servant as such, or before an arbitrator, and that such circumstance, false entry or false statement, so appearing in evidence, may cause any person who in such proceeding is to form an opinion upon the evidence, to entertain an erroneous opinion touching any point material to the result of such proceeding is said "to fabricate false evidence

[20] Section 299 of the Indian Penal Code provides "whoever causes death by doing an act with the intention of causing death, or with the intention of causing such bodily injury as is likely to cause death, or with the knowledge that he is likely by such act to cause death, commits the offence of culpable homicide".

[21] Section 300 of the Indian Penal Code provides "except in the cases hereinafter excepted, culpable homicide is murder, if the act by which the death is caused is done with the intention of causing death, or- 2ndly.-If it is done with the intention of causing such bodily injury as the offender knows to be likely to cause the death of the person to whom the harm is caused. or- 3rdly.-If it is done with the intention of causing bodily injury to any person and the bodily injury intended to be inflicted is sufficient in the ordinary course of nature to cause death, or- 4thly.-If the person committing the act knows that it is so imminently dangerous that it must, in all probability, cause death, or such bodily injury as is likely to cause death, and commits such act without any excuse for incurring the risk of causing death or such injury as aforesaid".

[22] Section 304-A of the Indian Penal Code provides "whoever causes the death of any person by doing any rash or negligent act not amounting to culpable homicide shall be punished with imprisonment of either description for a term which may extend to two years, or with fine, or with both".

[23] Section 319 of the Indian Penal Code defines hurt as "whoever causes bodily pain, disease or infirmity to any person is said to cause hurt"

[24] Section 320 of the Indian Penal Code defines "grievous hurt" as Emasculation or Permanent privation of the sight of either eye, or Permanent privation of the hearing of either ear, or Privation of any member or joint, or Destruction or permanent impairing of the powers of any member or joint or Permanent disfiguration of the head or face or Fracture or dislocation of a bone or tooth or Any hurt which endangers life or which causes the sufferer to be during the space of twenty days in severe bodily pain, or unable to follow his ordinary pursuits".

[25]Section 330 of the Indian Penal Code provides "Whosoever voluntarily causes hurt for the purpose of extorting from the sufferer, or from any person interested in the sufferer, any confession or any information which may lead to the detention of any offence or misconduct, or for the purpose of constraining the sufferer or any person interested in the sufferer to restore or to cause the restoration of any property or valuable security or to satisfy any claim or demand, or to give

155

information which may lead to the restoration of any property or valuable security, shall be punished with imprisonment of either description for a term which may extend to seven years, and shall also be liable to fine."

[26]Section 331 of the Indian Penal Code provides "Whoever voluntarily causes grievous hurt for the purpose of extorting from the sufferer or from any person interested in the sufferer any confession or any information which may lead to the detection of an offence or misconduct, or for the purpose of constraining the sufferer or any person interested in the sufferer to restore or to cause the restoration of any property or valuable security, or to satisfy any claim or demand or to give information which may lead to the restoration of any property or valuable security shall be punished with imprisonment of either description for a term which may extend to ten years, and shall also be liable to fine".

[27] Section 340 of the Indian Penal Code provides "Whoever wrongfully restrains any person in such a manner as to prevent that person from proceeding beyond certain circumscribing limits, is said "wrongfully to confine" that person".

[28]Section 348 of the Indian Penal Code provides "Whoever wrongfully confines any person for the purpose of extorting from the person confined, or any person interested in the person confined, any confession or any information which may lead to the detection of an offence or misconduct, or for the purpose of constraining the person confined or any person interested in the person confined or restore or to cause the restoration of any property or valuable security or to satisfy any claim or demand, or to give information which may lead to the restoration of any property or valuable security, shall be punished with imprisonment of either description for a term which may extend to three years, and shall be liable to fine."

[29] Section 350 of the Indian Penal Code provides "Whoever intentionally uses force to any person, without that person's consent, in order to the committing of any offence, or intending by the use of such force to cause, or knowing it to be likely that by the use of such force he will cause injury, fear or annoyance to the person to whom the force is used, is said to use criminal force to that other.

[30] Section 351 provides" whoever makes any gesture, or any preparation intending or knowing it to be likely that such gesture or preparation will cause any person present to apprehend that he who makes that gesture or preparation is about to use criminal force to that person, is said to commit an assault.

[31] Section 357 of the Indian Penal Code provides "whoever assaults or uses criminal force to any person, in attempting wrongfully to confine that person, shall be punished with imprisonment of either description for a term which may extend to one year, or with fine which may extend to one thousand rupees, or with both"

[32] Section 356 of the Indian Penal Code provides "whoever assaults or uses criminal force to any person, intending thereby to dishonour that person, otherwise than on grave and sudden provocation given by that person, shall be punished with imprisonment of either description for a term which may extend to two years, or with fine, or with both"

[33]Section 376(2) (a) of the Indian Penal Code provides "whoever being a police officer commits rape-(i) within the limits of the police station to which he is appointed; or(ii) in the premises of any station house whether or not situated in the police station to which he is appointed; or(iii) on a woman in his custody or in the custody of a police officer subordinate to him".

[34] Section 354 of the Indian Penal Code provides "Whoever assaults or uses criminal force to any woman, intending to outrage or knowing it to be likely that he will there by outrage her modesty, shall be punished with imprisonment of either description for a term which may extend to two years, or with fine, or with both".

[35] *See* Indian Penal Code, S. 119.

[36] *Id.,* S. 166.

[37] *Id.,* S. 330.

[38] *Id.,* S.331.

[39] Section 348 of the Indian Penal Code provides "whoever wrongfully confines any person for the purpose of extorting from the person confined, or any person interested in the person confined, any confession or any information which may lead to the detection of an offence or misconduct, or for the purpose of constraining the person confined or any person interested in the person confined or restore or to cause the restoration of any property or valuable security or to satisfy any claim or demand, or to give information which may lead to the restoration of any property or valuable security, shall be punished with imprisonment of either description for a term which may extend to three years, and shall be liable to fine".

[40] *See* Indian Penal Code, S. 357.

[41] *Id.,* S.299 and 304.

[42] *Id.,* S.300 and 302.

[43] *Id.,* S. 300, exception 3.

[44] *Id.,* S.304.

[45] *See* Indian Penal Code, S. 354.

[46] *Id.,* S.375 and 376 (2).

[47] (1979) 2 SCC 143.

[48] Indian Evidence Act, S. 24.

[49] *Id.,* S. 26.

[50] *Id.,* S. 27.

[51] Michael Hor, *The Confessions Regime in Singapore,* Malayan Law Journal(1991), p. 3.

[52] Section 9 (3), the Railway Property (Unlawful Possession) Act, 1996 provides"..... all persons so summoned shall be bound to state the truth upon any subject respecting which they are examined or make statements and to produce such documents and other things as may be required"

[53] Section 108 (3), The Customs Act, 1962 provides "... all persons so summoned shall be bound to state the truth upon any subject respecting which they are examined or make statements and produce such documents and other things as may be required"

[54] Section 32 (3) (a), Prevention of Terrorism Act, 2002 provides "any person who has been convicted of a conspiracy to commit any of the offences under sections 3, 4, 5, 6, 7, 11, 12, 14, or 15 shall be exempted from penalty as specified in subsection (1) and absolutely discharged if, having revealed

the conspiracy to the police or to the Court, he has made it possible to prevent the commission of the offence and to identify the other persons involved in the conspiracy".

[55] The Terrorist and Disruptive Activities (Prevention) Act was enacted on may 23, 1985 to combat disruptive and terrorist activities posing a serious threat to the integrity of the country initially for a period of two years applicable to Punjab only. However, in the context of continued terrorist violence and disruption in the country, a new legislation, Terrorist and Disruptive Activities (Prevention) Act was enacted in 1987 for the whole of India.

[56](1994) 3 S.C.C. 569.

[57]See *supra*Ch.5 n.35 p.222.

[58] Law Commission of India, 48th Report (1972), p. 4.

[59]*See* Ss. 25 and 26 of the Indian Evidence Act and S. 164 of the Code of Criminal Procedure.

[60]*See* Indian Penal Code S. 319.

[61]*Id.,* S.320.

[62]*Id.,* S.330 and 331.

[63]*Id.,* S.166.

[64]*Id.,* S.357.

[65]*Supra Ch.5 n.47, DK Basu's case,* para.10.

[66] S. 46 (2) of theCode of Criminal Procedure provides: "If such person forcibly resists the endeavour to arrest him, or attempts to evade the arrest, such police officer or other person may use all means necessary to effect the arrest"; and 46 (3) provides: "Nothing in this section gives a right to cause the death of a person who is not accused of an offence punishable with death or with imprisonment for life". Section 49of the Code of Criminal Procedure provides: The person arrested shall not be subjected to more restraint than is necessary to prevent his escape.

[67] See *supra* Ch.5 n.35, at p. 120.

[68](2006) 8 S.C.C. 1; (hereinafter referred as *"Prakash Sing'*scase").

[69]*Id.,* para 11.

[70] Kerala Police Act, S. 4 (b).

[71]*Id.,* S. 7.

[72] Kerala Police Act, S. 8 (1).

[73]*Id.,* S. 8 (4).

[74] Kerala Police Act, S. 46 (3).

[75]*Id.,* S. 46 (2).

[76]*Id.,* S. 33 (1).

[77] Kerala Police Act, S. 33 (2).

[78] Kerala Police Act, S. 96 (2).

[79]*Id.,* S. 96 (3).

[80] Kerala Police Act, S.105 (1).

[81] *Id.*, S. 106(1).

[82] *Id.*, S. 106(3).

[83] *Id.*, S. 107(1).

[84] Kerala Police Act, S. 110 (1).

[85] *Id.*, S. 110 (2).

[86] Kerala Police Act, S. 110 (3) and (4).

[87] *Id.*, S. 110 (7).

[88] *Id.*, S. 110 (9).

[89] The National Human Rights Commission proposed the composition of State Security Commission consisting of i) Chief Minister/Home Minister as Chairman, ii) *Lok Ayukta* or in his absence, a retired Judge of High Court to be nominated by Chief Justice or a Member of State Human Rights Commission, iii) A sitting or retired Judge nominated by the Chief Justice of the High Court, iv) Chief Secretary, v) Leader of Opposition in Lower House, vi) DGP as ex-officio Secretary.

[90] Rebiero Committee's proposal was Commission consisting of i)Minister i/c Police as Chairman, ii) Leader of Opposition, iii) Judge, sitting or retired, nominated by Chief Judge of High Court, iv) Chief Secretary, v) Three non-political citizens of proven integrity, vi) DGP as Secretary.

[91] Soli Sorabjee Committee proposed commission consisting of i) Home Minister (Ex-officio Chairperson), ii) Leader of Opposition, iii) Chief Secretary, iv) DGP (Ex-officio Secretary), v) Five Independent Members.

[92] Section 29 of Chapter III, of the 8th and Last Report of the National Police Commission; NPC recommended the composition to consist of i) Minister in-charge of police, Chairman, ex-officio, ii) One member each from State Legislature representing the ruling party and the opposition nominated on the advice of the Speaker, iii) Four members to be nominated by the Chief Minister of the State after approval by the State Legislature, one each from retired Judges of the High Court, Government Servants retired from senior positions, social scientists or academicians of public standing and eminence, iv) Director General, Secretary, ex-officio.

[93] P.J Alexander, *Kerala Police Bill, 2010 requires drastic changes to meet the standards of a legislation fitting for a modern democracy* ,Asian Human Rights Commission, (2010) available at: http://www.humanrights.asia/news/forwarded-news/AHRC-FST-053-2010/?searchterm= (Visited on June 25, 2011).

[94] *Ibid.*

[95] *Ibid.*

[96] Section 311 of the Constitution and The All India Services (Discipline and Appeal) Rules, 1955, as well as the Central Service Rules of India and the individual States, the Police Act, 1861 and the provisions of the Police Acts of the individual Union States.

[97] 1998 Cri.L.J. 3562.

[98]1979 Cri.L.J. 1367; In this case the customs officials dishonestly misappropriated the goods which they had seized and as such were holding in trust to be dealt with in accordance with law. The SC held that section 197 of the Code of Criminal Procedure cannot be construed too narrowly, in the sense that since the commission of offence is never a part of the official duty of a public servant, an act constituting an offence can never be said to have been done or purportedly done in the discharge of official duty, as such a narrow construction, will render the section entirely otiose.

[99]See *supra* Ch.3 n. 27.

[100]Code of Criminal Procedure, S.176.

[101]Kerala Police Act, S. 101 (2).

[102]*Id.*, S.(8) (1).

[103]*Id.*, S.(8) (2).

[104]N.R. Madhava Menon, *Criminal Justice India Series: Kerala*, Vol.6 (2002), p.42.

[105] The Kerala State Human Rights Commission was set up by the Government of Kerala in December 1998 under Section 29 of Protection of Human Rights Act, 1993 vide G.O. (P) No. 523/98/Law dated 11th December 1998 and published as S.R.O. No. 1065/98 in the Kerala Gazette Extraordinary No. 2036 on 11th December 1998; *See* Ch. 7 for details.

[106] Protection of Human Rights Act 1993, S.29; *See* Ch. 7 for details.

III

Chapter 7

NATIONAL HUMAN RIGHTS COMMISSION

The Constitution and the Statutes in India provided various provisions related with human rights protection. However, the only available impartial method of redressal of grievance against violation of human rights was through the tiresome, expensive and lengthy process of Court proceedings. So the effective monitoring of the human rights protection was a major concern for India for long. Enactment of Human Rights Act in 1993 was a milestone in the history of protection of human rights in India. The Act provides for the establishment of human rights Commissions at National and State levels and for the constitution of human rights Courts at Sessions level in the State for the effective protection and promotion of human rights. The preamble of the Protection of Human Rights Act mirrors the purpose as:

> An Act to provide for the constitution of a National Human Rights Commission , State Human Rights Commission in States and Human Rights Courts for better protection of Human Rights and for matters connected therewith or incidental thereto.

Thus, the Human Rights Act provides for the institutionalized monitoring and protection through the establishment of National and State level Human Rights Commissions and Human Right Courts.

7.1. National Level Human Rights Commission

India is the first country to establish the National Human Rights Commission among the South Asian countries, and also few among the National Human Rights Institutions in the World which were established as early as 1990s.[1] In accordance with the Protection of Human Rights Act, the Government of India established National Human Rights Commission on October 12, 1993.[2]

7.1.1. Composition of National Human Rights Commission

The National Human Rights Commission consists of a Chairperson and four Members.[3] The Chairpersons of the National Commission for Minorities, the National Commission for the Scheduled Castes,[4] the National Commission Scheduled Tribes[5] and of the National Commission for Women are ex-officio Members of the National Human Rights Commission. Only a person who has been a Chief Justice of the Supreme Court can be appointed as the Chairperson of the National Human Rights Commission. Two other Members must also be persons who held positions in Higher Judiciary.[6] Other two Members are persons having knowledge of, or practical experience in, matters relating to human rights.[7] Thus, out of five members National Human Rights Commission, three are from the higher judiciary.

There are criticisms on the scheme of the selection as it is mainly limited to persons belong to judiciary who may not have proficiency in or commitment for human rights. In this way, the National Human Rights Commission is "restricted from getting the plurality of perspectives, vocations and diverse experiences from the civil society."[8] It is submitted that since the three Members are from higher judiciary who have proven track record of impartiality and judicious decision making can ensure high fortitude of objectivity and deep sense of responsibility in settling the disputes and recommending the Governments to take appropriate measures to protect the human rights as the matter concerned is human rights, its violation and protection.

7.1.2. Appointment of Chairperson and Members

The appointment of the Chairperson and others Members are made by the President of India upon the recommendation of a high level Committee under the Chairmanship of Prime Minister. The Selection Committee consists of Speaker of the Lok Sabha, Minister in-charge of the Ministry of Home Affairs in the Government of India, Leaders of the opposition in the Lok Sabha, and Rajya Sabha, and Deputy Chairman of the Rajya Sabha as Members.[9] Thus, in the matters of appointment of the Chairperson and Members of the National Human Rights Commission, the leaders of the opposition in the Lok Sabha and Rajya Sabha have a role to be played. Here again, there are criticisms on the selection process, and also about the Selection Committee itself. The first criticism is that the committee recommending selection of the Chairperson and the Members consists solely of politicians. It does not consist of high profile experts in the areas of human rights. Secondly, the process of selection is not transparent because the composition of the National Human Rights Commission is generally decided through "noting in secret files or during closed door meetings between the politicians and their favourite bureaucrats."[10] However, it is submitted that the inclusion of opposition leaders in the appointment process of the National Human Rights Commission may be seen as making the selection on an impartial method rather than as a partisan process of Government.

7.1.3. Autonomy of Chairperson and the Members

The Protection of Human Rights Act makes the office of the Chairperson and the Members impartial and autonomous. The Chairperson and the Members are made ineligible to hold any office under the Central or State Government after retirement from the Commission.[11] This way, to a considerable extent, the Act ensures autonomy and independence of the National Human Rights Commission in as much as they can act impartially without being ambitious to get into any governmental position after retirement. Another significant aspect that makes the office of the Chairperson or Members of the National Human Rights Commission independent and autonomous is that it explicitly prohibits the varying of the salary or allowances or other terms and conditions of service of a Member to his disadvantage after his appointment and during the tenure of office.[12] So the Chairperson and Members can function with out the apprehension of reducing the salary, allowances or term of service by the Government if the decisions of the Commission are adverse to the interest of the Government. Thus, it is submitted that the Protection of Human Rights Act takes possible measures in order to make the office of the Chairperson and its Members to be impartial and autonomous, free, and independent of Governmental interference.

7.1.4. Powers and Functions of the Commission

The National Human Rights Commission enjoys a large number of powers for the promotion and protection of human rights. The powers and functions of the National Human Rights Commission are elaborately provided under Chapter III of the Protection of Human Rights Act.

7.1.4.1. Power to Inquire into the Violations of Human Rights

The most important power that has been entrusted with the Commission is the power to inquire *suo motu* or on a petition presented to it by a victim or any person on his behalf, into the complaint registered against a public servant on charges of violation of human rights.[13]This power can equally be exercised by the Commission even in the case of abetment, or for negligence in the prevention of such violation by a public servant. The Commission has been extensively using *suo motu* power to inquire into the violation of human rights committed by the police. Invoking such powers the National Human Rights Commission has taken action in many cases right from its establishment in 1993. Some of the significant cases where the Commission took cognizance *suo motu* are death of two persons in police firing in Meghalaya,[14] custodial death of Shri.MadanLal in Delhi,[15] amputation of male organ of Shri. Jugtaram in police custody in Barmer, Rajasthan,[16] beating up of Mr. Suseel Kumar and his wife by the Police of Gautam Budh Nagar,[17]firing by security forces in Bijbehara, Jammu & Kashmir killing 60 persons,[18] firing by Armed Forces killing at least 5 persons including a minor in Manipur,[19] killing of innocent citizens in the wake of post Godhra violence in Gujarat,[20] shooting and injuring 21 scheduled castes by the police in a land dispute in Allahabad, UP.[21] There numerous other instances where the Commission has *suo motu* taken action. The National Human Rights Commission has been expansively using the power to inquire and take cognizance of cases of the violation of human rights by the State functionaries.

7.1.4.2.   Power to Intervene in Court Proceedings

Another significant power enjoined by the National Human Rights Commission is the power to intervene under Section 12 (b) in any proceeding involving any allegation of violation

165

of human rights pending before a court with the approval of such court. Invoking the power of intervention the Commission has intervened in many cases in the legal proceedings. The Commission had intervened in a case pending proceedings in the Punjab & Haryana Court relating to the disappearance of Harjit Singh.[22] The infamous *Best bakery case*[23] is another best illustration of it. This case is a vivid illustration of human rights violations committed in the State of Gujarat during the 2002 riots.[24] Fourteen persons were brutally killed by a mob in the presence of police and the police men were reluctant to take any action to prevent the killings. Investigation was not properly conducted by the Gujarat State Administration. The National Human Rights Commission had recommended the State Government and State officials to provide securities for the victims and witnesses for attending the trial, but the recommendations were not seriously taken by the authorities, and as a result, the witnesses turned hostile and accused were acquitted.[25] The Commission, on receiving reports form its own investigation team and deeply concerned with the truth being buried at the hands of human rights violators, took a remarkable step in filing a Special Leave Petition for a separate investigation by an independent agency and for retrial of the case to be conducted out side of Gujarat State as there were serious human rights violations involved in the case. The Supreme Court accepted the plea of the Commission and issued orders in connection with re-investigation and retrial.[26] Thus, the Commission enjoys power to intervene in legal proceedings before a court or to approach a court for appropriate orders.

7.1.4.3.   Power to Make Surprise Visits

The Protection of Human Rights Act empowers the National Human Rights Commission to make surprise visits to police stations, jails or other institutions under the control of the State Government where persons are detained or lodged.[27] In pursuant, the National

166

Human Rights Commission or its officials have visited a number of jails and lock-ups in Andhra Pradesh and Bihar the same year and made a series of observations which are being attended to in consultation with the competent State authorities.[28] The Commission continues the period visits in many jails and lockups in other States and Union Territories.[29] It is submitted that the periodic and surprise visits by National Human Rights Commission works as an oversight mechanism for the police and other detention authorities.

7.1.4.4.   Power of Review of the Laws and Policies

It is one of the functions of the National Human Rights Commission to conduct a systematic review of the human rights policies of the government in order to identify shortcomings in the human rights observance and to suggest ways of improvements.[30]Invoking this authority, the Commission has vehemently criticized the Terrorist & Disruptive Activities (Prevention) Act[31] and also questioned the need for the Prevention of Terrorism Ordinance, 2001.[32] A number of laws and policies have been received the attention of the Commission, in accordance with sub-sections (d) and (f) of Section 12 of Protection of Human Rights Act. On the basis of requests from Governments, the Commission made comments on the draft legislation of Freedom of Information Bill 2000, the Protection from Domestic Violence Bill 2002; the Prevention of Terrorism Act, 2002; draft of Model Prison Manual, Food Safety and Standard Bill, 2005, the draft bill for ratification of Convention against Torture, Copy Right (Amendment Bill), 2010.[33]Thus, the Commission plays a vital role in the reviews of the laws, policies, regulations and draft legislations from the point of human rights perspective and provide comments/ recommendations to the Governments.

7.1.4.5.   Power of a Civil Court

While inquiring into the complaints, the National Human Rights Commission enjoys all the powers of a civil court trying a suit in respect of the following matters, *namely*:

(a) summoning and enforcing the attendance of witnesses and examine them on oath;

(b) discovery and production of any document;

(c) receiving evidence on affidavits;

(d) requisitioning any public record or copy thereof from any court or office;

(e) issuing commissions for the examination of witnesses or documents;

(f) any other matter which may be prescribed.[34]

Besides, the National Human Rights Commission shall have power to require any person to furnish information on matters that may be useful for / relevant to the subject matter under inquiry and any person so required shall be deemed to be legally bound to furnish such information within the meaning of Section 176[35] and Section 177[36] of the Indian Penal Code.[37] Further, the Commission or any officer authorized by the National Human Rights Commission, may enter any building or place where the National Human Rights Commission has reason to believe that any document relating to the subject matter of the inquiry may be found, and may seize any such document or take extracts or copies there from subject to the provisions of section 100[38] of the Code of Criminal Procedure, 1973, in so far as it may be applicable.[39] Thus, it is submitted that wide powers are given to the National Human Rights Commission in the matters of summoning persons or public servants, searching for finding documents and seizing of such materials.

7.1.4.6.   Power to Initiate Criminal Proceedings in Certain Cases

The National Human Rights Commission is generally deemed to be a civil court. However, when wilful omission are committed by the public servant in the view or presence of the Commission, it can, after recording the facts constituting the offence and the statement of the accused as provided for in the Criminal Procedure Code, forward the case to a Magistrate having jurisdiction to try the same.[40] The Magistrate to whom any such case is forwarded shall proceed to hear the complaint against the accused as if the case has been forwarded to him under Section 346[41] of the Criminal Procedure Code.[42]These provisions reveal that the National Human Rights Commission has no independent prosecuting power.

7.1.4.7.   Power of Investigation

When the National Human Rights Commission gets reports of human rights violations, it can make necessary inquiries with the help of its independent investigative agency. The Protection of Human Rights Act casts an obligation on the Central Government to make available an officer not below the rank of a Director General of Police and other necessary staff for the purpose of the investigation. The Investigating Officer submits a report to the Commission within the specified period after the investigation.[43] The Commission may verify the correctness of the report of such investigation.[44]It is submitted that assistance form the investigating experts is advantageous for the Commission to gather information directly from the spot where violations of human rights took place.

7.1.5. Enforceability of Decisions after inquiry

The following steps may be taken by the Commission after the completion of an inquiry:[45]Implementation

(1) where the inquiry discloses violation of human rights or negligence in the prevention of violation of human rights by a public servant, the Commission may recommend to the concerned Government or authority the initiation of proceedings for prosecution or such other action as the Commission may deem fit against the concerned person or persons;

(2) approach the Supreme Court or the High Court concerned for such directions, orders or writs as the Court may deem necessary;

(3) recommend to the concerned Government or authority for the grant of such immediate interim relief to the victim or the members of his family as the Commission may consider necessary;

(4) provide a copy of the inquiry report to the petitioner or his representative (subject to the provisions of clause (5) of section 17;

(5) the Commission shall send a copy of its inquiry report together with its recommendations to the concerned Government or authority and the concerned Government or authority shall, within a period of one month, or such further time as the Commission may allow, forward its comments on the report, including the action taken or proposed to be taken thereon, to the Commission;

(6) the Commission shall publish its inquiry report together with the comments of the concerned Government or authority, if any, and the action taken or proposed to be taken by the concerned Government or authority on the recommendations of the Commission.

In fact, the National Human Rights Commission is established primarily as a recommendatory body. The Commission submits an annual report to the Central Government and to the State Government concerned.[46] It may, at any time, submit special reports on any matter which, in its opinion, is of such urgency or importance that it should not be deferred till submission of the annual report.[47] The reports of the Commission are required to be placed in the Parliament or to the State Legislature, as the cases may be, with the memorandum of action taken or proposed to be taken by the Government. Article 20 sub-section (2) further provides that if the government considers that the recommendations of the Commission cannot be complied with, it must furnish reasons for non-acceptance of the recommendations.

7.1.6. Complaints Received by the Commission

After the establishment in 1993, the National Human Rights Commission has started functioning actively bringing out many cases that wouldn't have come to lime light but for the efforts of the Commission. In the beginning, the number of complaints received was very less. However, the number of complaints gradually increased over the years. During 1993-94, the very year

Year	2001-02	2002-03	2003-04	2004-05	2005-06	2006-07	2007-08
Complaints received	69,083	67,354	71,427	72,775	74,444	82,233	100,616
Complaints disposed off/concluded	50108	82,231	57,694	64,369	80,923	93,421	102,848

Table 1: Number of Complaints received by the National Human Rights Commission from 1st April 2001 till 31st March 2008 (*Source: NHRC, Annual Reports 2001-02 to 2007-08*)

of inauguration of the National Human Rights Commission, and immediately thereafter, the

Commission received 496 complaints of violation of human rights.[48] Over the years, the number of complaints has increased progressively and during the period from 1st April2007 to 31st April 2008, it received 100,616complaints.[49]

Whereas the number of complaints received during 2001-02 were 69,083.[50] There is an increase of 45.64 per cent during 2001-02 and 2007-08. The Table.1 below shows a gradual increase from the year 2001-02 to 2007-08 except for the year 2002-03 where there was slight decrease in the number of complaints/ intimations received by the Commission than the previous

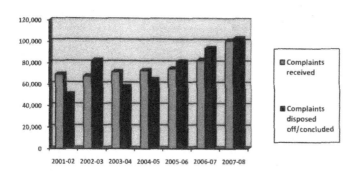

Chart 1: Graphic Chart Based on the Table 1

year 2001-02. The Commission claims that "the phenomenal increase in the number of complaints is indicative of growing awareness amongst the people in the country as well as increased trust in the Commission".[51]

7.1.6.2.   Complaints Disposal off by the Commission

During 2007- 08 the Commission disposed off/concluded 1,02,848Complaints. This includes the pending cases from the previous year as well. The number of complaints received during the year 2007-08 was 100,616. The Table 1above shows the year wise number of complaints received and complaints disposed off or concluded cases from 2001-02 to 2007-08. Form the table 1, on an average the disposal rate is higher than the complaints received. Further, Table 1 shows that there is a gradual increase in the number of cases disposed off by the Commission from 2001-02 to 2007-08 except for the year 2003-04.Comparing complaints received and complaints disposed off it is submitted that the more the number of complaints received the more the number of disposal of cases. Thus, the Commission is very quick and active in disposing off the complaints/ intimations received by it.

7.1.6.3.   Interim Relief/Remedy

During the year 2009-10, the National Human Rights Commission recommended for the payment of interim relief by the Government agencies in 400 cases amounting to Rs. 63,483,000/-.[52] In 2007-08, the amount recommended by the Commission was only Rs. 32,000,000/- to be paid in 199 cases.[53] There was an increase almost exactly twice the amount of interim relief and twice the number of complaints within a span of two years. While in the year 2002-2003 the Commission recommended for compensation amounting to Rs.3,140,000/- be paid in 39 cases.[54] These figures show the dramatic increase in the amount of interim relief recommended by the Commission in appropriate cases. In addition to recommending interim relief, Commission also recommends for disciplinary action. In 2007-08 it recommended for the disciplinary action in 11 cases and prosecution in 2 cases.[55] From the above it is submitted that the work of the National Human Rights Commission is on the right direction settling a large number of complaints annually.

7.1.6.4.   Complaints against Police

It is pathetic to state that the majority of the complaints received by the Commission are against police personnel.[56] The Commission is subdued about police excesses and atrocities and it recommends takes stern action against erring police personnel. For this study purpose the complaints against police are broadly classified into two heads depending on the seriousness of offence committed, namely, (i) custodial death/rape cases and (ii) torture/illegal arrest/unlawful detention and other cases.

i. Custodial Death/Rape cases

The National Human Rights Commission has been taking serious measures against custodial violence in the cases of deaths or rapes by police ever since its commencement of functioning. Immediately after the establishment, one of the significant stepsthat were taken by the Commission was directing all the States and the Union Territories require District Magistrates and Superintendents of Police to report directly to the Commission any instance of death or rape in police custody within twenty four hours of its occurrence.[57] It was also made clear by the Commission that failure to send such reports would lead to a presumption that an effort was being made to suppress the facts.[58] The communication stated: "in view of the rising number of incidents (custodial deaths/rapes)[59] and reported attempts to suppress or present a different picture of these incidents with the lapse of time, the Commission has taken a view that a direction should be issued forthwith to the District Magistrates and Superintendents of Police of every district that they should report to the Secretary General of the Commission about such incidents within 24 hours of occurrence or of those officers having come to know about such incidents. Failure to report promptly would give rise to presumption that there was an attempt to suppress the incident. "[60]

Another significant step that has been taken by *Commission* is in relation to post mortem. Since there is no credible and reliable witnesses or evidences in custodial death cases, the only important evidence is post mortem report. As the officials involved in the custodial death crime are police/jailors, there are all possibilities of manipulation in such post mortem reports either by influence or by coercion of surgeons conducting the post mortem. Understanding such manipulations, the *Commission* had recommended to the State Governments to video-film all post-mortem examinations and to send the cassettes to the *Commission*.[61] Thus, the *Commission* made solemn designs to make the higher officials of the Government responsible for the acts of death in custody.

There were 2222 complaints of deaths in police custody received by the National Human Rights Commission from 1-9-1993 to 31-3-2008 and all these deaths were reported within 24 hours to the Commission.[62] Out of the above 2222 deaths reported, 1485 deaths in police custody were turned out to be deaths due to natural causes but 158 deaths were due to police brutality. The Commission recommended for interim relief, prosecution and departmental

Custodial Death/ Rape	2001-02	2002-03	2003-04	2004-05	2005-06	2006-07	2007-08
Complaints received on All India	165	183	162	136	139	119	188
Complaints received from Kerala	4	4	4	6	5	3	6

Table 2: Number of Complaints of deaths in Police Custody from 1st April 2001 till 31st March 2008.
(Source: NHRC, Annual Reports 2001-02 to 2007-08.)

action against defaulting personnel in these 158 cases.[63] From 1st April 2007 to 31st March 2008 the *Commission* received 188 cases of death in police custody.[64] The Table2 below shows the number of complaints of deaths in police custody received by the National Human Rights Commissionfrom all over India and from Kerala during the period from 2001-02 to 2007-08.

From the Table 2 above, it can be understood that there were decrease in the complaints of deaths in police custody received by the Commission for the period 2001-02 to 2006-07, though there were slight increase in the year 2003-04 and 2005-06 than its previous years. It is, however, unfortunate that again in 2007-08, number of complaints of deaths in police custody rose up to 188 than the number of 119 in the previous year 2006-07s. This shows there was a steep increase of 63 per cent. This is astonishing that irrespective of the stringent measures that are being taken by the Commission, there takes place a number of incidents of custodial deaths.

Chart2: Graphic Chart based on the Table 2

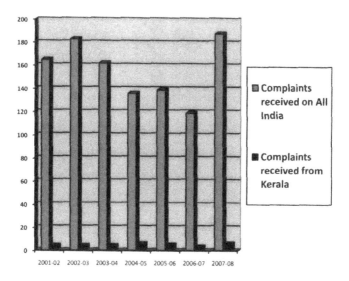

The national average[65] of number of complaints of deaths in police custody is thirty one during the period from 2001-02 to 2007-08. However, the number of complaints received from Kerala State by the National Human Rights Commission during the same period is thirty two only (Table 2). This indicates that the number of complaints from Kerala State is above the national average. Surely, it is pain staking to note that Kerala, the most literate state in India, is also perpetrating the deaths in police custody.

ii.   Torture/unlawful arrest/detention and other cases

Besides causing death or rape in custody, the police generally indulge in torture, unlawful arrest, illegal detention, false implication etc. In relation to prevention of torture in custody, the National Human Rights Commission took major efforts to eradicate such practices in India. The major initiation by the National Human Rights Commission was to make India sign the UN Convention against Torture. The Commission wrote a number of letters to this effect to the Prime Minister of India and, as a result, on October 14, 1997 the Government of India signed the Convention against Torture.[66]But, unfortunately, India has not ratified the convention yet. However, there is a move for the ratification of the Convention by the Government of India in this regard. As part of it, the Prevention of Torture Bill, 2010 has been passed by the*Lok Sabha* and is now pending before the *Rajya Sabha* for approval. The bill provides up to 10 years imprisonment for public servants responsible for torturing any person.[67] It is submitted that the Bill will act as a deterrent for the police and other public servants indulging in custodial violence. The National Human Rights Commission played a vital role in bringing the bill into the Parliament.

The Commission categorizes complaints against police into eight categories, *namely,* Custodial Violence, Illegal Arrest, Unlawful detention, False implication, Failure in taking action, Fake encounter, Disappearances and Other Police Excesses. The Table 3 below provides the number of complaints registered against police before the National Human rights Commission during the period from 2002-03 to 2007-08:

Sl. No.	Category of complaints	2001-02	2002-03	2003-04	2004-05	2005-06	2006-07	2007-08
1	Custodial Violence	160	706	1	16	7	4	2
2	Illegal Arrest	476	612	188	210	183	155	318
3	Unlawful detention	1496	2983	472	876	741	605	675
4	False implication	1768	2783	420	1213	606	489	254
5	Failure in taking action	6143	9978	1766	6833	3397	2682	1589
6	Alleged Fake encounters	0	118	34	84	45	89	57
7	Alleged disappearances	80	263	5	24	19	15	32
8	Other Alleged Police Excesses	9638	9622	2344	6488	4248	3740	4248
	TOTAL	19764	27065	5230	15744	9246	7779	9246

Table 3: Number of complaints against police registered before the National Human Rights Commission from April 1, 2002 to March 31, 2008.[68]
(Source: NHRC, Annual Reports 2001-02 to 2007-08)

The Table 3 above shows that there is gradual decrease in the number of complaints before the National Human Rights Commission against police excesses during the period 2001-02 to 2007-08, except during 2002-03 where there was the highest number of complaints and during 2003-04 here there was the lowest. In 2001-02, the number of complaints admitted was

19,764 and in 2007-08 the number was 5,550. There is a steep decrease in the number of cases registered against police in the case of torture, unlawful arrest, illegal detention, *etc*. It is significant to note that in the case of death in police custody, there was considerable decreaseduring the period from 2001-02 to 2006-07, where as in the case of torture, unlawful arrest,

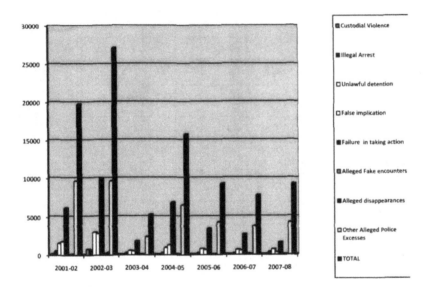

Chart 3: Graphic Chart based on the Table 3

illegal detention, *etc*., there is steep decrease during the same period. It is submitted that decrease in the number of cases of torture, unlawful arrest, illegal detention, *etc*., may be due to the reason that police personnel are becoming cautious about the consequences of the matter if it reaches to the National Human Rights Commission. Earlier, complaints against the police could

National Human Rights Commission is entirely a different body, devoid of political pressure. The policy of the National Human Rights Commission is very vivid and it calls for "stringent action against those who are responsible for perpetrating inhuman treatment and torture" to persons while in custody.[69]

7.1.6.5.   Remedy and Relief against Police Excesses

Since the National Human Rights Commission is a recommendatory body, it cannot enforce its decisions. It can only recommend to the State or Central Governments to implement its decision.[70] The Government may implement its decision. However, the Commission, in a large number of cases, has recommended interim relief where there occurred police torture, false implication, and illegal arrest.

There are numerous cases where the commission recommended for interim reliefs. In many appropriate cases the Commission recommended for disciplinary action and prosecutions. The space may not enough to mention the cases in which the Commission had recommended for interim relief. Very few instances are given to make known the diversified areas where the Commission awarded interim relief. In the case of illegal detention and torture by the police of three persons by Rajasthan police, the Commission recommended the State of Rajasthan to pay interim compensation for all the three victims.[71] A young girl was tortured first and then gang rapedby three police officers in Tripura on 26/5/2003. The Commission directed the Government of Tripura to pay an amount of Rs.50,000/- as immediate interim relief to the victim.[72] In a daring incident of beating of Mr.Suseel Kumar and his wife by Police of Gautam Budh Nagar, UP, the Commission recommended to pay Rs.25,000/- to Suseel and Rs.50,000/- to his wife.[73] A *dalit* woman made a complaint to the police against a person in her locality. The Police colluding with the opposite party raided the house of the complainant during night, abused the family members, outraged the modesty of the complainant who was stripped naked and kept in lock up by the police officer. The Commission found that the police helped the opposite partyand in a show cause notice issued by the Commission, the Home Secretary of the State of Bihar sanctioned Rs.50,000/- to the victim.[74] The instances are many where due to the intervention of the Commission the interim reliefs were paid to the victims of police atrocities.[75]

The Commission has been actively interfering for protecting human rights and recommending for remedial action in the event of human rights violations, particularly in the matters of police atrocities and inaction against common man. Interference by the Commission in the infamous Gujarat Communal violence cases is a best illustration for its credit. It was but for the active involvement of the Commission that many police officials and culprits involved in the Gujarat communal riots in 2002 was brought before justice. The Commission issued as many as 11 orders in relation to the human rights situations after the Gujarat riots in 2002 and in "Best Bakery case".[76]Thus, it is submitted that the Commission takes serious steps towards unearthing the police excesses either *suo motu* or on the basis of complaints made to it. The Commission is only a recommendatory body and within its jurisdiction, it recommends the Governments to provide remedies and reliefs to people. It is appreciable that the Commission disposes off the cases quickly affording speedy remedy to the people.

7.2. Conclusion

When the National Human Rights Commission was established, though there were some hopes for the protection of human rights, it was doubtful in many quarters regarding the effective enforceability of its decisions, because the Commission is created primarily as recommendatory body. Now, it will not be wrong to submit that the National Human Rights Commission is working actively solving many human rights violations. The National Human Rights Commission has dealt with many death and torture cases in police custody which would not have come to lime light but for the involvement of the Commission. It is submitted that the National Human Rights Commission, due to its impartial and commendable activities in the protection of human rights, and as a defender of violation of human rights gained credibility among the people. Hence, the recommendations submitted of the Commission to the Governments are also generally complied with. This is evident from the fact that the number of cases pending for compliance of the Commission's recommendations by State Governments was only 89for the payment of monitory relief/disciplinary action/prosecution during the year 2007-08. [77] Mr. Sharma, a Member of the National Human Rights Commission, in an interview stated that 99% of the recommendations of the Commission are complied with by the Governments.[78] It is, thus, submitted that the recommendations of the Commission operate as forceful as an order of it. The follow-up mechanisms of the Commission on the implementation of its recommendation by the Governments are also praise worthy. When the Commission recommends for monetary relief to be paid by the Government to the person affected by the violation of human rights, it demands the compliance report from the Government along with a payment receipt. In this way the Commission ensures that its recommendations are complied with in a time bound manner.

Endnotes

[1] The Human Rights Commission of Sri Lanka was established under the *Human Rights Commission of Sri Lanka Act, No. 21 (1996)* and became operational in September 1997. The National Human Rights Commission of Nepal is an independent and autonomous statutory body established in the year 2000

under the Human Rights Commission Act 1997. *See Also* Manoj Kumar Sinha, *Role of the National Human Rights Commission of India in Protection of Human Rights,* Internet publication<http://www.rwi.lu.se/pdf/seminar/manoj05.pdf> *accessed* on 12-12-2010

[2] S. 3 of the Protection of Human Rights Act empowers the central government to constitute the National Human Rights Commission and also sets out the composition of office bearers and members of the Commission.

[3] Protection of Human Rights Act, S. 3(2).

[4] Substituted by Amendment Act 43 of 2006 for "The National Commission for the Scheduled Castes and Scheduled Tribes".

[5] Substituted by Amendment Act 43 of 2006 for "The National Commission for the Scheduled Castes and Scheduled Tribes".

[6] S. 3 (2) of the Protection of Human Rights Act states that one Member shall be a person who is a sitting or a retired judge of the Supreme Court and another Member, a sitting or a retired Chief Justice of a High Court.

[7] Protection of Human Rights Act, S. 3(2).

[8] Joshi JP, *National Human Rights Commission - Need for Review,* Commonwealth Human Rights Initiative Publications, New Delhi, *available at:*

http://www.humanrightsinitiative.org/programs/aj/police/papers/gpj/national_human_rights_commission.pdf (Visited on July 12,2010).

[9] Protection of Human Rights Act, S. 4(1).

[10] *Supra* n. 8.

[11] Protection of Human Rights Act, S. 6 (3).; The Chairperson shall hold office for a period of five years or until he attains seventy years of age, whichever is earlier and the Members also hold office for a period of five years or until he attains seventy years of age, whichever is earlier.[11] However, Members can be reappointed for one more term of five years.

[12] *Id.,* S.8.

[13] Protection of Human Rights Act 1993, S.12 (a).

[14] National Human Rights Commission, Annual Report 1993-94 (1994), para 5.6; the inquiry was made by the National Human Rights Commission on the basis of a broadcast over All India Radio on 5 November 1993.

[15] *Ibid.* The inquiry was made by the National Human Rights Commission on a report published in a newspaper dated 30 November 1993 captioned "Two Cops Suspended for Custody Death".

[16] *Ibid.* The inquiry was made by the National Human Rights Commission on a News paper report dated 10 February 1994 and captioned "Cops Cut off Man's Penis".

[17] National Human Rights Commission, Annual report 2007-08 (2008), p. 44; The inquiry was made by the National Human Rights Commission on a news report published in the "Times of India" on the 16th September 2006 under the headline: "Brutal Cops Batter Noida Couple".

[18] National Human Rights Commission, Annual Report 1993-94 (1994), p.13; The inquiry was made by the National Human Rights Commission on the press report.

[19] National Human Rights Commission, 2001-02 Annual Report (2002), p. 175; the inquiry was made by the National Human Rights Commission on Press report.

[20] National Human Rights Commission, 2007-08 Annual Report (2008), p.52; cognizance was taken by the National Human Rights Commission on the basis of a programme, "Operation Kalank" telecast on TV channel 'Aajtak' on 25th October 2007, accusing the State functionaries of Gujarat, including the Chief Minister, Minister of State for Home Affairs and Police Officers, for abetment of killing of innocent citizens in the wake of post Godhra violence.

[21] National Human Rights Commission, 2007-08 Annual Report (2008), p.58; the inquiry was made by the National Human Rights Commission on a distressing report captioned "21 SCs Shot due to Land Dispute", which appeared in a publication by the 'Indian People's Tribunal on Untouchablity".

[22] National Human Rights Commission, *Human Rights Newsletter*, vol.2, n.7 (1995), p.1.

[23] *National Human Rights Commission v. State of Gujarat*,Crl.M.P. No.10719/2003 in WP (Crl.) No. 109/ 2003, available at: www.indiankanoon.org/doc/168922/?type=print

[24]*ZahiraHabibulla v State of Gujrat*, A.I.R. 2004 S.C. 3114; Notoriously known as "Best Bakery Case".

[25] Case No. 1150/6/2001/2002, National Human Rights Commission, Annual Report, 2002-03 (2003), p.188.

[26] The other notable incidence where the National Human Rights Commission involved in bringing protection of human rights are *Starvation death case* in Orissa Case No.37/3/97-LD, National Human Rights Commission, 2002-03 Annual report (2003), p.197; and the *Mass Cremation case* in Punjab and protection of Mentally disabled persons (Case No. 1/97/NHRC; Two writ petitions, Writ Petition (Crl.) No. 497\95, *ParamjitKaur v. State of Punjab,* and Writ Petition (Crl.) No. 447\95, *Committee for Information and Initiative on Punjab v. State of Punjab* were filed before the Supreme Court containing serious allegations about large-scale cremations resorted to by the Punjab Police of persons allegedly killed in what were termed as "encounters".

[27] Protection of Human Rights Act, S.12 (c); Inserted by Protection of Human Rights (Amendment) Act 43 of 2006.

[28]National Human Rights Commission, Annual Report 1998-99, para.3.26; *See* also Annual Reports of 1999-2000, 2000-01, 2001-02, 2002-03, 2003-04, 2004-05, 2005-06, 2006-07, 2007-08.

[29]Visited Thihar jail on 14th June, 2007, (*See*, National Human Rights Commission, Annual Report 2007-08 (2008) p.26); Visited District jail at Shillong and Jowai from 6-8 June, 2006, (*See* National Human Rights Commission, Annual Report 2006-07(2006), p.15); Visited Central jail, Raipur, Chattisghar on 14th February, 2006 (*See* National Human Rights Commission, Annual Report 2005-06(2006), p.18); Visited jails in Tripura, Kerala, Andhra Pradesh, Goa and Chandigarh during the year 2004-05 (*See* National Human Rights Commission, Annual Report 2004-05 (2005), p.17-18).

[30]Kaur Jaskaran, *A Judicial Blackout: Judicial Impunity for Disappearances in Punjab, India*, Harvard Human Rights Journal, Vol.15 (2002) p. 269; *See also* Reenupaul, *National Human Rights Commission of India: A Human Rights Evaluation(*, 2003), (Unpublished MA thesis, London School of Economics, London).

[31]National Human Rights Commission, Annual Report 1993-94 (1994), Para 7.3.

[32]*Id.*, Annual Report 2001-02(2002), p.48.

[33] National Human Rights Commission, Annual Reports 2007-08, p.143, 2005-06,p.205, National Human Rights Commission, Human *Rights Newsletter* (May 2003); National Human Rights Commission: India, Office of the High Commission for Human Rights publication, 2010; the other functions, *inter alia*, include to review the factors, including acts of terrorism that inhibit the enjoyment of human rights and recommend appropriate remedial measures; study treaties and other international instruments on human rights and make recommendations for their effective implementation; undertake and promote research in the field of human rights; spread human rights literacy among various sections of society and promote awareness of the safeguards available for the protection of these rights through publications, the media, seminars and other available means; encourage the efforts of non-governmental organizations and institutions working in the field of human rights; and any other functions as it may consider necessary for the protection of human rights.

[34] Protection of Human Rights Act, S.13(1).

[35] Section 176 of the Indian Penal Code, provides "Whoever, being legally bound to give any notice or to furnish information on any subject to any public servant, as such, intentionally omits to give such notice or to furnish such information in the manner and at the time required by law, shall be punished with simple imprisonment for a term which may extend to one month, or with fine which may extend to five hundred rupees, or with both; or, if the notice or information required to be given respects the commission of an offence, or is required for the purpose of preventing the commission of an offence, or in order to the apprehension of an offender, with simple imprisonment for a term which may extend to six months, or with fine which may extend to one thousand rupees, or with both; 2*[or, if the notice or information required to be given is required by an order passed under sub-section (1) of section 565 of the Code of Criminal Procedure, 1898 (5 of 1898), with imprisonment of either description for a term which may extend to six months, or with fine which may extend to one thousand rupees, or with both.]".

[36] Section 177 of the Indian Penal Code, provides Furnishing false information: Whoever, being legally bound to furnish information on any subject to any public servant, as such, furnishes, as true, information on the subject which he knows or has reason to believe to be false shall be punished with simple imprisonment for a term which may extend to six months, or with fine which may extend to one thousand rupees, or with both; or, if the information which he is legally bound to give respects the commission of an offence, or is required for the purpose of preventing the commission of an offence, or in order to the apprehension of an offender, with imprisonment of either description for a term which may extend to two years, or with fine, or with both.

[37] Protection of Human Rights Act, S.13(2).

[38] Section 100 (1) of the Criminal procedure Code 1973 provides "Persons in charge of closed place to allow search: Whenever any place liable to search or inspection under this Chapter is closed, any person residing in, or being in charge of, such place, shall, on demand of the officer or other person executing the warrant, and on production of the warrant, allow him free ingress thereto, and afford all reasonable facilities for a search therein."

[39] Protection of Human Rights Act, S.13(3).

[40] Protection of Human Rights Act, S.13 (4); Such offences are described in the S. 175, 178-180 and S.228 of the Indian Penal Code.S. 175 of the Indian Penal Code deals with Omission to produce document to public servant by person legally bound to produce it;S. 178 of the Indian Penal Code deals with Refusing oath or affirmation when duly required by public servant to make it;S. 179 of the Indian

Penal Code deals with Refusing to answer public servant authorized to question;S. 180 of the Indian Penal Code deals with Refusing to sign statement;S. 228 of the Indian Penal Code deals with Intentional insult or interruption to public servant sitting in judicial proceeding.

[41] S. 346 of the Criminal Procedure Code provides that "if the court in any case considers that a person accused of any of the offences referred to in section 345 (Section 345 of the Criminal Procedure deals with certain offences of contempt as described in section 175, section 178, section 179, section 180 or section 228 of the Indian Penal Code, 1860) and committed in its view or presence should be imprisoned otherwise than in default of payment of fine, or that a fine exceeding two hundred rupees should be imposed upon him, or such Court is for any other reason of opinion that the case should not be disposed of under section 345, such Court, after recording the facts constituting the offence and the statement of the accused as hereinbefore provided, may forward the case to a Magistrate having jurisdiction to try the same, and may require security to be given for the appearance of such person before such Magistrate, or if sufficient security is not given shall forward such person in custody to such Magistrate. The Magistrate to whom any case is forwarded under this section shall proceed to deal with, as far as may be, as if it were instituted on a police report".

[42] Protection of Human Rights Act, S.13(4).

[43] *Id.*, S.14 (4).

[44] *Ibid.*

[45] Section 18 has been substituted after the amendment in the Protection of Human Rights Act in 2006 for providing the course of action that is required to be taken by the Commission after the completion of the inquiry.

[46] Protection of Human Rights Act, S.20.

[47] *Id.*, S.20 (1).

[48] 13th Asia Pacific Forum Meeting at Kuala Lumpur, *Report of National Human Rights Commission of India* (2008), p.3.

[49] Asia Pacific Forum, *Activities of the National Human Rights Commission-India 2009-10*, Report to 15th Annual Meeting (2010), p.8.

[50] National Human Rights Commission, Annual Report 2001-02 (2002), p. 138.

[51] *Supra* n. 49 p.3.

[52] *Supra* n. 50.

[53] National Human Rights Commission, Annual Report for 2007-08 (2008), p.184.

[54] National Human Rights Commission, Annual Report for 2002-03 (2003), p.170.

[55] National Human Rights Commission, Annual Report for 2007-08 (2008), p.184.

[56] Joshi, GP, Police Accountability in India, Commonwealth Human Rights Initiative, New Delhi, available at: www.humanrightsinitiative.org/.../police/.../police_accountability_in_india.pdf(*Visited on May 14, 2010*)

[57] Letter No. 66/SG/NHRC/93, dated 14th December 1993, National Human Rights Commission, Annual Report 1993-94 (1994), Annexure IV.

[58] *Ibid.*

[59] *Emphasis added.*

[60] *Supra* n. 59.

[61] National Human Rights Commission, Annual Report 1997-98 (1998), p. 53.

[62] Supra n. 49 at p.9.

[63] National Human Rights Commission, Annual Reports from 1993-94 to 2007-08 (2008).

[64] National Human Rights Commission, Annual Report 2007-08 (2008), p.175.

[65] Total number of complaints of deaths during 2001-02 to 2007-08 i.e.,1092 divided by thirty five (twenty eight States and seven union territories)

[66] National Human Rights Commission, Annual Report, 1994-95 (1994), para 4.27; However, India has not ratified the Convention; *See also* The UN General Assembly Res. A/53/150, 17 August 1998.

[67] PTI, "Bill for Prevention of Torture in Introduced in LS", The Hindu, April 26, 2010; The Bill was passed by the LokSabha on May 6th 2010.

[68] Source of data: National Human Rights Commission, Annual Reports 2001-02 to 2007-08.

[69] NareshMahipal, The Protection of Human Rights Act 1993(No. X of 1994), Expert Column (2009), *available at*: http://expertscolumn.com/content/protection-human-rights-act-1993-no-x-1994 (Visited on January 14, 2011).

[70] Protection of Human Rights Act, S.18 (a).

[71] National Human Rights Commission, Annual Report, 1997-98 (1998), p. 47.

[72] Case No. 5/23/2003-2004-WC, National Human Rights Commission, Annual Report, 2003-04 (2004), P.36.

[73] Case No.28117/24.2006, National Human Rights Commission, Annual Report 2007-08 (2008), Para 6.74.

[74] Case No.1375/13/2006, National Human Rights Commission, 2007-08 Annual Report (2008), p.82.

[75] Illegal detention/abduction of Rama Rao by Andhra Police, Case No.5828/95-96/NHRC; Illegal detention and torture of Anil Kumar: Maharashtra, Case No.517/13/98-99; Illegal detention and torture of D.M. Rege: Maharashtra, Case No.1427/13/98-99; Illegal detention by Police: Uttar Pradesh, Case No.13161/24/98-99; Unlawful Detention of Manoharan: Tamil Nadu, Case No.213/22/2001-2002; Illegal Detention and Torture in Police Station, Shikarpur: Uttar Pradesh, Case No.17171/24/1999-2000; Illegal detention and torture of ShriZamir Ahmed by the police at Sayana, Bulandshahr, UttarPradesh, Case No: 14071/24/2001-2002; False implication and torture of Rajiv Rattan by the Police, Case No. 9302/95-96; False Implication of the Complainant and Others and Torture by police, Delhi, Case No. 3069/30/1999-2000; False implication of MadhukarJetley: Uttar Pradesh, Case No.2385/24/2000-2001; False implication of Rajinder Singh: Haryana, Case No.810/7/98-99; False implication of Manoj Kumar Tak and NarenderTak, Madhya Pradesh, Case No.667/12/98-99-FC; False implication of NaviUllah under NDPS Act, Uttar Pradesh, Case No. 13501/24/2000-2001.

[76] *Suomotu* case taken by National Human Rights Commission in Case No: 1150/6/2001-2002 orders dated 1st March, 2002; 1st April, 2002; 1st May, 2002; 31st March, 2002, 10th June,2002; 1st July,2002; 25th September 2002; in "Best Bakey case" 30th June 2002; 3rd July 2002 and 11th July 2002; "In re.

Custodial death of Samirkhan Sarfarazkhan Pathan", Case Number: 452/6/2002-2003 dated 28th October, 2002.

[77]National Human Rights Commission, Annual Report 2007-08 (2008), p.185.

[78] Rahman, Azera, *UP police: The biggest violator of human rights,* Human Rights published, iGovernment, 2010,*available at*: http://www.igovernment.in/site/police-biggest-violator-human-rights%E2%80%99-37465 (Visited on June 7, 2011).

Chapter 8

STATE HUMAN RIGHTS COMMISSIONS

The Protection of Human Rights Act, besides establishing National Human Rights Commission, provides for the establishment of State level Human Rights Commissions also.[1] Chapter V of the Act provides for the composition, appointment, removal and the term of office of Chairperson and Members, and powers and functions of the State Human Rights Commissions. The State level Human Rights Commission shave the power, functions, procedure for investigation, inquiry and reporting after inquiry same as that of National Human Rights Commission.[2] However, the Act provides for transfer of cases from National Human Rights Commission to State Human Rights Commissions. Section 13 subsection (6) of the Act provides that National Human Rights Commission may transfer a complaint filed or pending before it to the State Human Rights Commissions where the former considers it necessary or expedient to do so for disposal.[3] However, the National Human Rights Commission shall not transfer such complaint unless the State Human Rights Commissions has authority to entertain the same.[4] In respect of the jurisdiction, section 21 subsection (5) provides that a State Human Rights Commissions may inquire into the violation of human rights only in respect of matters relatable to any of the entries enumerated in List II[5] and List III[6] in the Seventh Schedule to the Constitution of India. However, the State Human Rights Commissions should not inquire into a complaint which is already inquired into by the National Human Rights Commission or any other Commission constituted by law.[7]

8.1. Composition of State Human Rights Commissions

The State Human Rights Commissions shall consist of one Chairperson and two Members.[8]The Chairperson or a Member of one State Human Rights Commissions may be appointed as Chairperson or Member of the State Human Rights Commissions of another State with the consent of such Chairperson or Member, and with the prior approval of the Selection Committee as per section 22.[9]Only a person who has been a Chief Justice of the High Court can be appointed as Chairperson.[10] One Member of State Human Rights Commissions shall be a person who held position as High Court Judge or as District Judge with seven years experience in that position.[11] Another Member is to be appointed from amongst persons having knowledge of, or practical experience in, matters relating to human rights.[12] Thus, out of 3 Member Commission, two persons are from Judiciary who do not require any back ground in human rights for their appointment as Chairperson or Member of the State Human Rights Commissions. It is submitted that the same criticism that usually forwarded against National Human Rights Commissions may again be significant here as the selection is limited to a narrow band of persons who, just by belonging to judiciary, need not reflect any particular expertise in or commitment to human rights.[13]

8.2. Appointment of Chairperson and Members

The appointment of the Chairperson and Members are made by the Governor of the State, upon the recommendation of a high level Selection Committee under the Chairmanship of the Chief Minister of the State. The Selection Committee shall consist of Speaker of the

Legislative Assembly, Minister in-charge of the Ministry of Home in the State, Leader of the opposition in the Legislative Assembly.[14] Thus, in the matters of appointment of the Chairperson and Members of the State Human Rights Commissions, the leader of the opposition in the Legislative Assembly has a role to play. Here again, there are criticisms, same as in the case of National Human Rights Commission, on the process of selection such as the Selection Committee consist only of politicians which may yield to political bias, the selection is not transparent as public has "no say" in the selection process, *etc.*[15] However, it is submitted that the inclusion of opposition leader in the selection process of the State Human Rights Commissions ensures some degree of impartiality in the selection process.

The Protection of Human Rights Act makes the office of the Chairperson and the Members as impartial and independent as possible. The Chairperson and the Members of the State Human Rights Commissions are made ineligible to hold any office under the Central or State Government after the retirement from the State Human Rights Commissions.[16] This way, to a considerable extent, it ensures the independence of the State Human Rights Commissions in as much as they can act impartially without being ambitious to get into any governmental position after their retirement. Another significant aspect in order to make the office of the Chairperson or Members of the State Human Rights Commissions independent and autonomous is that Protection of Human Rights Act specifically prohibits the varying of the salary or allowances or other terms and conditions of service of the Chairperson or of a Member to his disadvantage after his appointment and during the tenure of office.[17]Thus, it is submitted that in the case of State Human Rights Commissions also the Act takes possible measures in order to make the office of the Chairperson and Members to be impartial and independent of Governmental interference.

8.3. Powers and Functions of the SHRC

Regarding the powers and functions of State Human Rights Commissions, Section 29 provides that the provisions of sections 12 (Functions), 13 (Powers relating to inquiries), 14 (Investigation), 15 (Statement made by persons to the Commission), 16 (Persons likely to be prejudicially affected to be heard), 17 (Inquiry into complaints), and 18 (Steps during and after inquiry) applicable to National Human Rights Commission, shall apply to a State Human Rights Commissions as well. Thus, the powers, functions, inquiry, investigation and procedure of the State Human Rights Commissions are the same as that of the National Human Rights Commission. Hence, the State Human Rights Commissions has also the power to inquire *suomotu* on a complaint registered against a public servant on charges of violation of human rights, its abetment or the negligence in preventing such violation.

8.4. Enforceability of the Decisions

Like in the case of National Human Rights Commission, State Human Rights Commissions also functions as a recommendatory body and submits its annual report or special reports, in case of urgency, to the State Government concerned.[18] The State government is required to place such reports before the State Legislative Assembly along with action taken/ proposed to be taken memorandum. [19] However, if the Government considers that the recommendations of the State Human Rights Commission cannot be complied with, it must furnish reasons for non-acceptance of the recommendations. [20] Thus, the concerned State Government is required to give a memorandum on the action taken/or proposed to be taken on the recommendations of concerned State Human Rights Commission. In this way, the Protection of Human Rights Act ensures that the recommendations of the State Human Rights Commissions are complied with to the possible extend.

8.5. Jurisdictional Issue between National and State Commissions

Section 36 of the Protection of Human Rights Act provides that the National Human Rights "Commission shall not inquire into any matter which is pending before a State Commission or any other Commission duly constituted under any law for the time being in force". However, this provision has created a confusion regarding the jurisdiction of National and State Human Rights Commissions. The question was whether the National Commission has authority to enquire into a matter (i) which has not been initiated by the State Commission, and (ii) which has not been properly inquired into by the State Commission. It was because of this confusion that the National Human Rights Commission has been demanding for the amendment of section 36 of the Protection of Human Rights Act with a view to establisha clear functional relationship between National and State Commissions.

It would be of significance to consider a case that relates to a conflict about jurisdiction between National Human Rights Commission and West Bengal State Human Rights Commission.[21] In the Case No.624/25/2000-200, the National Human Rights Commission took cognizance of a complaint received from an advocate, TamaliSengupta of west Bengal, alleging that atrocities had been committed by the police in the villages in Midnapore district on 29thDecember 2000. The National Human Rights Commission called for an investigation report from the State Government, and directed on 3rd January 2001 that a team of officers of the National Commission proceed to the area for an on-the-spot investigation and collection of facts in respect of the allegations made in the complaint.

193

The National Human Rights Commission received a resolution from the West Bengal Human Rights Commission on 22ndJanuary 2001 stating that since the matter was pending before the West Bengal State Human Rights Commissions, the National Human Rights Commission is prevented from inquiring into the matter by virtue of section 36(1) of the Protection of Human Rights Act. The resolution of the West Bengal Human Rights Commission was considered by the National Human Rights Commission in its proceedings on 24thJanuary 2001 and it did not agree with the view of the West Bengal Human Rights Commission. National Human Rights Commission observed that:

(i)   the opinion required to be formed for the purpose of Section 36(1) is of the National Human Rights Commission itself which is not obliged to act on the view taken by the State Commission and the National Human Rights Commission is not to be governed merely by the view of the State Commission in formation of its opinion; and

(ii) the Protection of Human Rights Act does not exclude any part of India from the jurisdiction of the National Human Rights Commission nor does it prohibit any person from approaching the National Human Rights Commission in respect of violation of human rights anywhere in the country, simply because a State Commission exists for that area. Prior clearance of the State Commission is also not needed by the National Human Rights Commission to exercise its functions in any part of India."[22]

The National Commission further observed that the overall purpose of Section 36(1) of the Act is to empower the National Human Rights Commission to avoid multiplicity of proceedings where another Commission is fully seized of the matter.[23]

Though the West Bengal Human Rights Commission did not respond to the above observation of the National Human Rights Commission, it didn't mean the matter is settled thereas the wording of Section 36 (1) is not clearly demarcating the jurisdictions of the Commissions. Thus, it is submitted that though the Protection of Human Rights Act provides for the establishment of National Human Rights Commission and State Human Rights Commissions, but their jurisdictions are not clearly defined. It is also not clear from the Act that where a complainant who is not satisfied with the inquiry conducted by the State Human Rights Commissions, if approached National Human Rights Commission what course of action would be taken by the National Human Rights Commission. Thus, there needs further review with regard to working relationship, power and functional sharing between National Human Rights Commission and State Human Rights Commissions for the smooth and effective functioning.

8.6.   Kerala State Human Rights Commission

Invoking Section 21 of the Protection of Human Rights Act, 18 States in India have established the State Human Rights Commissions in their respective States.[24]The Government of Kerala established the Kerala State Human Rights Commission in December 1998.[25] The Kerala State Human Rights Commission enjoys the same powers and functions of the National Human Rights Commission within the State of Kerala.[26] Since the State Human Rights Commission enjoys the same powers and functions like that of the National Human Rights Commission, it could also take up *suo motu* matters connected with human rights violations.

8.6.1. Work of the Kerala State Human Rights Commission

The Kerala State Human Rights Commission made recommendations to the Government in 34 cases during the year 2005-06. During the same period, it recommended the Government to pay compensation amounting to Rs.4, 85,000/- be paid in 8 cases. In addition, the Commission directed the government to take disciplinary action in 3 cases. In all these cases, by follow up action, the Commission requires the Government to submit compliance letter to the Commission. Hence, the Commission ensures the compliance of its recommendations by the State Government.

8.6.2. Visits made by the Kerala State Human Rights Commission

In fulfillment of the statutory responsibility entrusted to the State Human Rights Commissions under section 12(c) of the Protection of Human Rights Act, Kerala State Human Rights Commission made visits to police lock ups.[27] The visits are made to verify that the police stations are maintained in accordance with the directions of the Supreme Court in *D.K. Basu* v. *State of West Bengal.*[28] There is an obligation on State Human Rights Commissions to monitor whether the 11 requirements laid down by the Supreme Court in *DK Basu's* case were being carried out by the police stations and also to take all further steps to ensure that those requirements were met.[29] Thus, Commission periodically, or as a surprise, visits the police stations for oversight and monitoring the conditions and activities in the police stations in the State.

8.7. Human Rights Violations by Police in Kerala

A number of violations of human rights by the police have been reported from Kerala to both National and State Human Rights Commissions. The following study throws light to the extent of violations in Kerala.

8.7.1 Complaints to National Human Rights Commission

Complaints from Kerala to the National Human Rights Commission can broadly be divided into two depending on the serious nature of the violations committed by the police, *namely,* complaints of death in police custody and other complaints such as torture, unlawful arrest, illegal detention, etc.

8.7.1.1   Complaints of Death in Custody

The National Human Rights Commission while assessing the number of death in police custody in 1999 stated that the number of deaths in police custody during 1998-99 had shown a decline in States, with the exception of Kerala, Gujarat, Meghalaya, Rajasthan, West Bengal and Delhi.[30]This shows the situation of custodial death in Kerala during the period 1998-99 than its previous years. The Table.2 above also depicts a picture not different from the above observation of the Commission regarding the death in police custody in Kerala during the period from 2001-02 to 2007-08. From the Table 2 above, it can be under stood that during the period from 2001-02 to 2007-08 also there was increase in the number of complaints of deaths in police custody received by the National Human Rights Commission from Kerala, except for the year 2006-07 and 2005-06 where there were slight decrease than the previous years respectively. In one instance the National Human Rights Commission has taken cognizance in the case of death of a person immediately after the release from the police custody. In this case, the Police in *Wynadu* district of Kerala had taken Mr. Hussain on suspicion that he was a gambler, and had beaten him so brutally that his spinal cord broke. Later he was released, but died when he was under treatment in a hospital.[31] On the complaint of a resident of the locality, the National Human Rights Commission recommended the State Government to pay a sum of Rupees Two lakhs to the next of kin of Hussain as immediate interim compensation. The Commissionalso directed the State Government to institute criminal action against the concerned police officials for the murder of Hussain, and also to expedite the departmental proceedings against them. The National Human Rights Commission stated that the Government was at liberty to deduct the amount of Rupees Two lakhs from the salary of the guilty police officials. The Kerala Government complied with National Human Rights Commission's recommendation below.

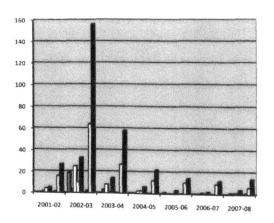
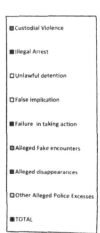

Chart 4: Chart based of the Table 4

The National Human Rights Commission took *suo motu* cognizance of an instance of police brutality where a college lecturer was beaten mercilessly by the police as he had dared to question the fare demanded by the driver of an "Auto Rickshaw".[32] When the lecturer became unconscious, his legs and hands were tied and he was shifted to a mental hospital, and a case was made out that he was a violent mental patient. The Commission issued notices to the Chief Secretary and Director of General of Police, Government of Kerala. The Government had suspended two Sub-Inspectors of Police, one Assistant Sub-Inspectors, one Head Constable, three Police Constables and an enquiry was ordered against them.

Again, the National Human Rights Commission took *suo motu* cognizance of a case where some tribal youths, mostly students, were picked up by the police when they were agitating against the opening of liquor shops in *Appappara* and were treated in a very harsh manner, and made them to strip off.[33]Upon the recommendation of the National Human Rights Commission, the Kerala Government had sanctioned payment of compensation of Rs 10,000 to each of seven boys who were stripped off and forced to spend two nights in the police lock-up at *Tirunelli* in *Wayanad* District in Kerala. Necessary action has also been initiated by the State Government for recovering, through departmental proceedings, the total compensation amount of Rs. 70,000 from the delinquent police officers.

The Christian Cultural Forum, Kollam made a complaint to National Human Rights Commission alleging that police officials of *Agali* in *Attappaddi* in Palakkad district in Kerala arrested three *Adivasis*, Manikandan, Parameswaran and Kuppamma on 25.5.1997 and kept them in illegal custody for 23 days.[34] During detention, one of the detenue Kuppamma, an *Adivasi* woman was beaten black and blue by the police and chilly powder was stuffed into her vagina.

199

According to the complainant, the Circle Inspector of Police had falsely implicated around 100 *Adivasis* in a fabricated case and as a result *Adivasis* had left their houses. In response to the notice issued by the Commission, the Superintendent of Police, Palakkad reported that an enquiry into the matter was conducted by the Superintendent of Police, Crime Branch/CID and it was found that police at *Agali* Police Station detained two boys, namely, Manikandan and Parameshwaran illegally on 27-5-97 till 17 June 1997, without any complaint having been registered against them; that the Circle Inspector, Assistant Sub- Inspector and two Police Constables who were involved in the incident had been suspended and criminal cases were instituted against them; and that Kupamma, the mother of Parmeshwaran did not make any allegations of torture, when she was produced before the Court in a criminal case. In response to the show cause as to the payment of interim relief issued by the Commission, the State Government informed the Commission that the State was not in a position to make any payment till disposal of criminal cases pending before the Court, since the alleged delinquent officers are liable to pay compensation, if any, awarded by the Court. But the Commission informed that the proceedings u/s 18(3) of HR Act is independent and the pendency of criminal case is no impediment to the award of immediate interim relief and recommended that a sum of Rs. 10,000/- to each of the victims as immediate interim relief. Pursuant to the directions of the Commission, the Government of Kerala paid the interim relief to the victims.

It is submitted that the Commission by not accepting the contention of the Government of Kerala that the interim relief cannot be paid due to the pendency of the case before the court by the Government, laid a stern footing that interim reliefs as per Protection of Human Rights Act is independent of Court proceedings or the out come of the Court Proceedings. This way, the

Commission has widened the scope of application of its authority to recommend the interim relief irrespective of the court proceedings or prosecution or other disciplinary action.

8.8. Conclusion

The greater advantage of approaching the Human Rights Commissions than on Courts in relation to human rights violation committed by the police is that there is speedy remedy. Earlier, the police could have violated the human rights and the only effective and impartial remedy available was from the Courts. The problem with the court system is that there is no independent investigative team for courts and, hence, in majority of the cases, the police and other violators used to hush up or manipulate the case and escaped from the justice system. So the people who suffer at the hands of police normally keep silent as there can be further revenge from police due to the complaint made to the court. Even it took longer times to determine such cases by Courts. Due to the prolonged struggle in getting "unsure" justice, people, often, do not approach the Courts unless there is a compelling and grave circumstance.

Where as the State Human Rights Commissions have its own investigative teams and send its own investigative team to probe the case, as when required finding the truth and, hence, the investigation cannot be sabotaged or manipulated by State or other State agencies. In this way the Human Rights Commissions get first hand information about the happenings and conclude its findings quickly even in complex cases and recommends the matters to the Governments for appropriate action and interim relief. There are also no procedural hurdlesof formal court procedure and lawyerings in the case of Human Rights Commissions.

Nevertheless, the works of National Human Rights Commission and State Human Rights Commissions have suffered due to certain infirmities and deficiencies in the law

201

governing its functioning.[35] The power of the National Human Rights Commission and State Human Rights Commissions to inquire in to the complaints against violation of human rights committed by Armed forces is restricted by Section 19 of Protection of Human Rights Act. What is more aggravating is that the definition of "armed forces" not only includes the naval, military and air force but "any other armed forces of the Union", such as Border Security Force, Central Reserve Protection Force, *etc.*[36] This may be seen as a major lacuna of the Protection of Human Rights Act.

Further, under the Act, the National Human Rights Commission and State Human Rights Commissions has no power to enforce its decisions.[37] According to the Act, where the enquiry conducted by the National Human Rights Commission and State Human Rights Commissions discloses a violation of human rights, it can only advise or recommend the Government concerned to take action against the guilty persons or grant relief to the victim.[38] If any State government refuses to accept the advice, there is no provision in the law which empowers the National Human Rights Commission and State Human Rights Commissions to force the government to implement its advice.[39] Nevertheless, it is a fact that the State Governments, generally, comply with the recommendations of National Human Rights Commission and State Human Rights Commissions.[40] If any State Government does not comply with its recommendations, the only mechanism available to National Human Rights Commission and State Human Rights Commissions is to approach the Supreme Court or the concerned State High Court seeking directions to enforce it. Hence, the National Human Rights Commission and State Human Rights Commissions are, sometimes, described as "toothless" or a "paper tiger" or a "pen pusher."[41] However, it is submitted that the reliability and esteem that has been achieved by the National Human Rights Commission over the years has produced cautiousness on the government and officials that non-compliance to the recommendations of the National Human Rights Commission creates a disturbing image on the political face of the Government.

Considering the stand of the Kerala State Human Rights Commission against police excesses, it is submitted that it provides remedy against police action. In many cases the Commission awarded compensation where there were violations of human right by the police and in some cases it recommended to the Government to take disciplinary action against erring police personnel. However, there are many criticisms about the working of the Commission. The Asian Center of Human Rights criticizes the works of the Commission as unsatisfactory and blames that except for awareness raising the Commission remained ineffective.[42] It further asserts that a five-member jury of "a People's Tribunal on Police Torture" comprising former judge of the Mumbai High Court H. Suresh, former Acting Chairpersons of Kerala State Human Rights Commission, S. Balaraman, former Pro-Vice Chancellor of Kerala University, N A Karim, *inter alia*, stated that the Kerala State Human Rights Commission had failed to initiate action in most cases of police torture brought to its attention.[43] The Kerala State Human Rights Commission also reportedly attempted to block access to right to information when Jomon Puthenpurackal, a social activist, who had sought certain information under the Right to Information Act, 2005. The information was provided only after the Chief Information Commissioner of Kerala ruled in favour of the applicant on appeal.[44] Though there are criticisms about the actions of Kerala State Human Rights Commission, it is submitted that at least, there is an autonomous authority, not consisted of politicians and police, who can be approached in the event of police atrocities and other human rights violations.

Comparing the works of the National Human Rights Commission and Kerala State Human Rights Commission, it is submitted that that the National Human Rights Commission is far ahead both in terms of functionalism and remedial measures. One reason may be that Kerala State Human Rights Commission was established much later in 1998 than the establishment of National Human Rights Commission. Even when Kerala State Human Rights Commission was established, from time to time, the State Governments were skeptical and non-accommodative. At some points it became necessary even for the High Court to knock the State Government in the matters of appointment of Chairperson of Kerala State Human Rights Commission. On 28 July 2006, the High Court stayed the working of the Kerala State Human Rights Commission until appointment of a full-time Chairperson according to the Protection of Human Rights Act.[45]Following the interventions of the High Court, on 16 August 2006 the State Government appointed a full time Chairperson of the Kerala State Human Rights Commission. It is submitted that the National Human Rights Commission could penetrate and come out from the clutches of political/Governmental interference due to the prominent leaderships of Justice Ranganatha Mishra, Justice A.S. Anand, Justice M.N. Venkatachellaya, Justice J.S. Varma, and Justice S. Rajendra Babu. The working of the National Human Rights Commission, from its inception, was attractive. National Human Rights Commission, over the period of its splendid activities, established a trust and goodwill among the people as a protector and defender of human rights by affording quick remedy.

Endnotes

[1]Protection of Human Rights Act, S.21.

[2] *Id.*, S.29.

[3]*Id.*, S.13 (6).

[4]*Id.*, S.13, *proviso* to Sub-section (6); inserted by the Protection of Human Rights (Amendment) Act 43 of 2006.

[5]List II sets out the subject matter of State jurisdiction.

[6] List III sets out subject maters where Union and States have Concurrent jurisdiction.

[7] Protection of Human Rights Act, S.21, *proviso* to Sub- section (5).

[8] *Id.*, S.21 (2); inserted by the Protection of Human Rights (Amendment) Act 43 of 2006.

[9] *Id.*, S.21 (6); inserted by the Protection of Human Rights (Amendment) Act 43 of 2006.

[10] *Id.*, S.21 (2) (a); inserted by the Protection of Human Rights (Amendment) Act 43 of 2006.

[11] *Id.*, S.21 (2) (b); inserted by the Protection of Human Rights (Amendment) Act 43 of 2006.

[12] *Id.*, S.21 (2) (c); inserted by the Protection of Human Rights (Amendment) Act 43 of 2006.

[13] See supra Ch.6 n.56, Joshi GP.

[14] Protection of Human Rights Act, S.23 (1); Where there is a Legislative Council in a State, the Chairman of that Council and the Leader of the Opposition in that Council shall also be members of the Committee, and also that no sitting Judge of a High Court or a sitting District Judge shall be appointed except after consultation with the Chief Justice of the High Court of the concerned State.

[15] See *Supra*Ch6n. 8.

[16] Protection of Human Rights Act, S.24 (3); The Chairperson shall hold office for a period of five years or until he attains seventy years of age, whichever is earlier and the Members also hold office for a period of five years or until he attains seventy years of age, whichever is earlier. However, Members can be reappointed for one more term of five years.

[17] *Id.*, S.26.

[18] Protection of Human Rights Act, S.28 (1).

[19] *Id.*, S.28 (2); The report shall be laid to each Houses of the State legislature where the House consists of two Houses.

[20] Protection of Human Rights Act, S.28 (2).

[21] Case No.624/25/2000-2001;National Human Rights Commission, Annual Report 2001-02 (2002), p.183.

[22] Case No.624/25/2000-200, National Human Rights Commission, Annual Report 2000-01 (2001).

[23] *Ibid.* (Case No.624/25/2000-200).

[24] The States that established State Human Rights Commissions are Andhra Pradesh, Assam, Himachal Pradesh, Jammu & Kashmir, Kerala, Karnataka, Madhya Pradesh, Maharashtra, Manipur, Orissa, Punjab, Rajasthan, Tamil Nadu, Uttar Pradesh, West Bengal, Chhattisgarh, Gujarat, and Bihar.

[25] G.O.(P)No.523/98/Law dated 11th December 1998.

[26] Protection of Human Rights Act, S.29.

[27] The Kerala State Human Rights Commission also visited many jails such as Central Prison, Kannur, Special Sub jail Alappuzha, Sub Jail Ernakulam, Sub Jail Mavelikkara, Sub Jail, Pathanamthitta, Mental Health Centre Trissur, Taluk Hospital Harippad, Taluk Hospital Neyyattinkara, Taluk Hospital Kottarakkara, Govt. Hospital Varkala, Social Welfare Complex at Thavanur in Malappuram, Shelters provided for the Tsunami victims, Sub jail Kozhikode, Open jail, Nettukaltheri, Taluk hospital Cherthala etc.

[28]1997(1) SCC 416.

[29] Kerala State Human Rights Commission, Annual Report, 2006-07 (2007); *available at; http://www.kshrc.kerala.gov.in/archives.htm*(Visited on July 21, 2011).

[30]National Human Rights Commission, Annual Report, 1998-99 (1999), para.3. 18; However, there was reported a marginal increase in Andhra Pradesh, Arunachal Pradesh, Assam, Karnataka, Madhya Pradesh, Maharashtra, Punjab, Tamil Nadu and Pondicherry.

[31]Case No. 64/11/1999-2000, National Human Rights Commission, Annual Report, 1999-2000 (2000), para.7 (B).

[32]Case No.166/11/98-99, National Human Rights Commission, Annual Report 1998-99 (1999), para 7; The action was taken by the National Human Rights Commission on the basis of a report published in the Hindustan Times on 3 September 1998, under the heading "Police Brutality Again in Kerala".

[33]National Human Rights Commission, Annual Report 1995-96 (1996), para 9.20; the action was taken by the National Human Rights Commission on the basis of a press reports which stated that the case of stripping of teenagers by police.

[34]Case No. 208/11/97-98, National Human Rights Commission, Annual Report 2004-05 (2005), p.37.

[35]See *Supra* Ch.6 n.56.

[36]S.2(1) (a) of the Protection of Human Rights Act defines "armed forces" as "armed forces" means the naval, military and air forces and includes any other armed forces of the Union.

[37]See *Supra* Ch.6 n.56.

[38]Protection of Human Rights Act, S. 18, 1993.

[39]See *Supra* Ch.6 n.56.

[40]*Supra* Ch.6 n. 78, Azera Rahman.

[41]*Ibid.*

[42] The Asian Center of Human Rights, Indian Human rights Report (2009), p 106.

[43]Special Correspondent, Tribunal looks into police torture, *The Hindu*, 4 April, 2008.

[44]"State Human Rights Commission provides information on *suomotu* cases" *The Hindu*, 25 April, 2008.

[45]GirishMenon, "Freeze on SHRC hits filing of rights cases, *The Hindu*, August7 (2006).

Chapter 9

INCIDENTS OF HUMAN RIGHTS VIOLATIONS BY POLICE IN KERALA- EMPIRICAL STUDY

The police in India have not relived from the clutches of the colonial British brutality even after sixty four years of freedom from British rule, and they continue to use the same old methods of investigation and interrogation procedures for the detection and prevention of crimes. Consequently, the Indian police are known for their human rights violations than for their protection. The researcher conducted an empirical study in the Kerala State to find out the extent of violation of human rights by the police in respect of custodial death, torture, unlawful arrest, illegal detention, false implication, failure in taking action, *etc.*

9.1. Methods of data collection

The Police commit numerous human rights violations in India and the problems of human rights violation by police are common for all States. The researcher has selected the State of Kerala for the empirical study. Several police excesses are reported in Kerala within the past three to four decades and some of which are horrendous and gruesome. There have been instances of custodial death, torture, unlawful arrest, illegal detention, harassment, ill treatment and failure or negligence in taking action. The information was gathered through empirical study from the victims of police excesses, investigating police officials, human rights activists, Members of the Kerala State Human Rights Commission, top ranking police officers, professionals, human rights experts and witnesses.

9.1.1. Mode of Interview

Interview method was adopted for the purpose of collecting data. Interviewees were divided into two categories. The first category consisting of victims of police arrests, investigating police officials (they generally include Circle Inspectors, Sub-inspectors and Assistant Sub-Inspectors) who generally make arrest and human rights activists. The second category consisted of the members of the Kerala State Human Rights Commission, top level police officers, human rights experts, professionals and witnesses. For interviewing the first category, different sets of questionnaires were prepared for each sub category, *viz.*,the victims, investigating police officers, and human rights activists as these sub categories stood in different segments. Data were gathered from persons thorough one- to- one personal visit to each person. Information is gathered from victims of police arrests who are either arrestees in lock up or now under trial prisoners, or convicts or persons set free by the Courts. For interviewing the investigating police officers, selected police stations both urban and rural were visited and questionnaire got answered from Circle Inspectors, Sub- Inspectors and Assistant Sub-Inspectors. For interviewing human rights activists, activists relevant to the study were identified and personally visited each of them. Each question in the questionnaire contained a statement which bases a three point scale, namely, "Yes", "No", and "No Opinion". Besides questionnaire, personal interviews were also conducted for gathering information from those who are victims, investigating police officers, and human rights activists.

For the second category, personal interviews were conducted to gather information from the Members of the Kerala State Human Rights Commission, top level police officers, human rights experts, professionals and witnesses. The personal interviews were one-to-one, and generally lasted one hour. For both categories of interviewees, first it was made known that the interview is conducted for the purpose of academic research and then, an assurance was given to each person to maintain the confidentiality of the information passed on as part of the interview.

Overall six hundred and ninety seven people were interviewed. Two hundred and seventy two victims, one hundred and thirty seven Circle Inspectors, Sub-Inspectors and Assistant Sub-Inspectors, and one hundred and fourteen human rights activists participated in the questionnaire. Besides, sixty nine victims of crime and complainants were also interviewed. Informal interviews were conducted on sixty eight experts including members of the Human Rights Commission, top level Police officials, human rights Lawyers and Professionals. Thirty seven relatives and/or witnesses were also informally interviewed.

9.2. Analysis of data

The data gathered by the above methods are analysed to obtain a finding. The incidents of human rights violation by the police in specific cases, extent of violation of human rights by the police, the adequacies of the law to safeguard the human rights and human dignity of people, the problem in the implementation of the law related with human rights from being violated by the police, and the suggestions of the experts to improve the law and the system in this aspect are analysed to test the feasibility of the hypothesis. The findings of the empirical study are discussed below.

9.3. Findings

The results of the empirical study reveal that the Police commit violation of human rights very frequently. The common method of violation of human rights that are perpetrated by the police in Kerala are torture, unlawful arrest, illegal detention, false implication, ill treatment, failure in taking action, *etc*. The finding of the empirical study is detailed below.

9.3.1.   *Violation of Human Rights by Torture*

Among the violations of human rights by police, torture is the most barbarous and heinous act. Torture is a very common method for Kerala Police, and it has different magnitude from simple beating to causing death by torture. Torture also leads to disappearances and deaths in 'fake encounters'. Besides, it also causes fatal injuries, permanent disabilities, mental derailment, loss of faculties and psychological trauma.

9.3.1.1. Methods of Torture

Police employ different methods of torture on persons in custody. During the course of informal interview, some of the police officials and the victims of police torture informed the researcher about the different methods of torture that are perpetrated by the police in Kerala. The methods of torture that are followed by the police are as follows.

i.   *Uruttal* Method (Rolling Method)

In the case of *Uruttal* method (Rolling method) as shown in picture 1 below, the victim is made to lie on the floor or on a bench and then a heavy wooden log or iron rod in the shape of a roller is placed over both the thighs of the victim. One or two police men sit/stand on the log/rod and they roll it up and down which gives severe pain for the victim as the thigh muscles are crushed and separated from the bone due to the rolling. This is a brutal and barbarous kind of torture, but is still practiced in Kerala. This has come to the lime light after the infamous Regional Engineering College student *Rajan*'s case[1] of custodial death during emergency and the last known of its series is the *Udayakumar*'s case[2] of custodial death in the Fort police station, Thiruvananthapuram.

Picture 9.1: Showing the rolling method of torture*(Source: frontlinepunjabiyouth)*[3]

Mr.Rajan was subjected to *uruttal*method and was brutally tortured and killed in the camp. He was first beaten up severely by eight police men in the camp, and then tied to a wooden bench with his hands and legs down. A heavy wooden roller was rolled over his thighs with a police man standing on the roller. He was not able to withstand the pain due to the crushing of thigh muscles and hence, he cried aloud. In order to prevent crying out, the police pushed a piece of cloth into his mouths. Later, he was brought into another room where the then Deputy Inspector General of Police was sitting with sharpened pencil. As part of questioning, Deputy Inspector General of Police pierced the pencil edge into the already crushed thigh muscles which gave unbearable pain to Rajan and he cried aloud. At that time, a Sub Inspector of Police standing nearby started kicking him on his stomach with his heavy police boots. Then Rajan fell down, became unconscious and died.

211

In *VarkalaVijayan*'s case,[4] one Vijayan from *Varkala* disappeared during internal emergency in 1975 after the police arrest. There were witnesses that Vijayandied in the police custody due to the *Uruttal* method employed on him. He was first beaten up severely by six policemen and then, they made him to lie on his back on the floor. Two policemen caught hold of his legs and two policemen his hands. Then a wooden rod was placed on his thigh and one policeman sat on the rod and made it to role up and down causing sever pain. In order to avoid loud cry, policemen pushed cloths into his mouth. Due to the unbearable pain, he fell unconscious and died.

Udayakumar, who died in police custody on the night of 27-9-2005, was taken into custody along with his companion Mani from Thiruvananthapuram and brutally manhandled, tortured and killed while in police custody at Fort Police Station, Thiruvananthapuram. The torture method employed on Udayakumar was also *uruttal* method. After beating him heavily by three policemen, Udayakumar was asked to lie on his back on a bench and repeatedly beaten on the soles of his feet with a cane. Thereafter, a heavy G.I. pipe was forcefully rolled down and up over his thighs resulting in the crushing and separation of his thigh muscles and flesh from the bone. When he was crying aloud, a piece of cloth was pushed into his mouth. At 10.20 p.m. when he was removed to the Medical College Hospital from the Fort Police Station he was pronounced dead.

Thus, the Police in Kerala resort to *uruttal* method of torture as a method to inflict severe pain to the accused person in custody.

ii. Rocket Method

In this method, the police make the victim hang on a piece of wire or a rope with his head downwards and legs upwards position, i.e., in reverse direction. He will be placed hours together in this position and, from time to time, made to swing like a pendulum. Then he may be tortured with bats, rods or whips. It gives severe pain and suffocation due to prolonged keeping, and it seriously affect the internal organs and stress. In *Sampath's* case[5] this method was employed to torture Sampath[6] who died in the police custody on the night of 29-3-2009. Sampath was hung with his head down on a rope and tortured by using rubber rod, *lathi*, building block enclosed in cloth. He was kicked by boots and beaten with baton.[7] Many bones in his body were fractured due to the torture and he had 63 *ante mortem* injuries.[8] The other two suspects in the same case, Kanakaraj and Manikandan, were also tortured by hanging upside down and then, torturing by using rubber rod, *lathi*, building block enclosed in cloth.

iii. Burning with Hot Iron Box

This is a method whereby the police make the iron box (used for pressing clothes) very hot and then, place it on the body parts of the victim. It may, sometimes, be placed on the abdomen or at the buttocks or on the back of the body or even on the private parts. This gives severe pain due to the heat and burn. The below given picture 3 shows the burnt iron box marks on the abdomen of a victim of torture. In *Sampath*'s case, Sampath was tortured by burning his buttocks using hot iron box, besides torturing by rocket method.

213

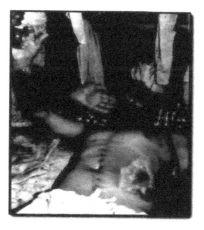

Picture 9. 2: Showing burnt iron box marks on the abdomen(*Source: frontlinepunjabiyouth*)[9]

iv. Aeroplane Method

In this kind of torture victims are forced to bend over while holding their legs straight. The person's head is bent down until it cannot go down any further, while the hands are pulled up and held up to the highest point. The hips have to point up. The body in this position looks like the shape of an airplane, which is how this torture derived its name. When it is prolonged it gives severe pain to the victim. This is generally employed for theft suspects and the like, and is used quite often in many police stations in Kerala.

v. Heavy Electric Shocks

Electric shock is another severe painful method of torture. There are different techniques in the electric shock method. One technique is that a person may be asked to urinate into the live electric wire. Due to the urination, the victim gets continuous electric shock through his private part. Second technique is that a person may be asked to sit on a chair with his hands tied up and, then, electric current is passed to him through live wires. Third one is the technique of giving electric shock to the genitals or nipples directly. Electric shock method is a highly painful technique of torture. This method was widely practiced in Kerala during 1970s by the police for the Naxalite hunt.

vi. Leg Roller Method

The victim may be made to lie facing the floor. His legs are then bent up and a wooden log/iron rod is kept in between his bent legs and thighs. Then the

Picture 9. 3: Showing how the torture is employed *(Source: frontlinepunjabiyouth)*[10]

bent legs are pushed towardshis buttocks very forcefully by one or two police men while one police man may sit on his shoulder and two others stand on each of the spread hands crushing his fore hands. Due to thecrushing of leg muscles and thigh muscles, it may be very painful for the victim. This method is less severe than *uruttal* method as there is no complete crushing of thigh muscles. This method is sparingly used in Kerala.

vii. Making Victims Lie on Ice Blocks

In this method, the victim will be forced to lie on the ice blocks continuously for longer period and three or four police men will be forcing him to lie over the ice blocks. Some times,

215

his body will be tied up with the ice blocks. It will create severe pain and irritation on the body because of the stoppage of blood flow due to freezing. As this does not leave any marks on the body of the victim, police frequently use this kind of method to gather information from the accused or witnesses.

viii. Dipping in Water Continuously

In this method of torture, the victim is tied upside down with the help of a rope i.e., with his head down wards and feet upwards, and then dipped his head continuously for a number of times into the below kept big container of water. Due to the continuous and speedy dip in the water with the head down, water may get in to the nose and lungs. It can create severe breathing problems and damage lungs tissues. This method of torture also does not leave any marks on the body of the victim as in the case of ice block torture. This method is sparingly used by the Kerala police. When the case becomes sensational news and media is at the back of the case, torturing may not possible to extract the information. At that juncture this method is used by the Kerala Police so that injuries are not inflicted on the body of the accused.

ix. Cutting off Eyelashes

This method is employed with a view to prevent the sleep of the victim. When the eyelashes are cut off, the victim's sleep is deprived off due the growth of new eyelashes which gives pain for eyelids that makes him unable to sleep. Sleep deprivation may be seen as a less painful method, but when the victim is unable to sleep for days together, it would be torturous and may lead to breakdown of the nervous system and other serious physical and psychological damages. This is used to extract the secrets from hardened and habitual offenders of robbery, theft, *etc*.

216

x. Pulling Mustache or Beard Hair

Pulling mustache or beard forcefully, or plucking it off is another method of torture employed by the police. Pulling or plucking off the hair from mustache or beard is intended to inflict pain to the victim. If it is plucked off in group, it can cause bleeding also. Since the mustache or beard is found in soft portions of the body, it gives sever pain for the victim. This is used to extract the secrets from hardened and habitual offenders of robbery, theft, *etc*.

xi. Garudan Thookkam

In this method of torture, as shown in the Picture 4, the victim's arms are tied behind their back, a rope is then tied to the wrists and then, suspended in the air. Placing the victim in this position for prolonged period gives tremendous pain and sufferings. In addition to hanging in this position, some times tortured with rods and batons, and in some cases, electric shocks may also beadded for extra pain. Suspending aperson in this way and giving shocks can

Picture 9. 4: showing Garudan thookam(*Source: gypsypalace*)[11]

217

dislocate the shoulders of the victim. This is a method commonly employed by the police in many cases for proving cases of robbery, theft, assault, etc.

xii. **Finger Nail Torturing**

Another painful method of torturing is finger nail pulling. There are different techniques in finger nail pulling. First, the finger nail may be plucked off by using forcing pliers or by a device meant for the purpose (as shown in the picture 4 below). This can cause severe pain and severe bleeding to the victim. The second technique is inserting pins underneath the nail along

Picture 9.5: With the help of a devise the finger nails are removed(Source: gypsypalace)[12]

the flesh. This also causes severe pain to the victim. To make it more painful, the police may make the instrument vey hot before inserting. This is used to extract the secrets from hardened and habitual offenders of robbery, theft, etc.

xiii. Agony Light

In this method, the victim is kept under the heavy powered light so that he may not be able to open his eyes. This is considered to be a low level torturing method. When excessive or high power lightings are made, it can affect a person's mental condition. This is considered to be a bloodless torture method. This is practiced in modern times by police who does not want to physically torture the suspect or the suspect is a dignitary.

xiv. Stuffing Chilly Power

In some cases where the detained person is a woman, the police stuff chilly powder into the private part of the woman causing unbearable burning sensation, severe pain and irritation. In a case before the Kerala State Human Rights Commission an *adivasi* woman, Kuppamma, was arrested and illegally detained in custody at *Agali* Police Station, beaten up severely and then chilly powder was stuffed into her private part.[13]

xv. False Encounter

In this method, the suspect is caught and, then, shot dead by the police. Later, they make the record of encounter death. There are police who are specialist in false encounters. In some cases the police demand money from the suspect not to be shot dead in encounter. In *Naxalite Varghese's* case,[14] Varghese was caught by police first and then he was taken to *Thirunelli* forests in North *Wayanadu* and brutally shot dead on February 18, 1970. This was kept a secret for about three decades until the police constable who shot Varghese confessed about the reality of Varghese murder.

xvi.   Other Methods of Torture

Besides the above methods, there are other methods of torture that are employed by the police. In some cases the police may insert iron wires into the male genital holes causing severe pain and bleeding. This method is employed by the police when the arrestee is a suspect in rape case or in a case of molestation of a woman. Another method is inserting pepper into the private part of females. In some cases the police may insert *lathi* into the private part of the female victims. During Communist and Naxalite movement in Kerala, police inserted *lathi* or rod into the private part of many female suspects. At times, male police may insert their private part into the mouth of the female suspect or witnesses. Simple torture by beating or injuring the body is employed frequently by the police. When female prostitutes were caught, the police used to cause burns on their private parts causing severe and unbearable pain to the victims. Custodial rape, gang rape, and molestation of woman victim are common form of torture employed by the police on women.

The above explained the methods are known for employing torture on the victims by the police. It reveals how cruel and barbarous methods are used by the police on the victims violating their human rights and human dignity. Irrespective of the prohibition by Supreme Court,[15] police still continue to employ brutal torture on suspects and witnesses.

9.3.1.2. Victims of Police Torture

Even though the Supreme Court prohibited any form of torture, the police continue to practice it. Torture and 'third degree methods' employed by the police are controversial everywhere in India. Kerala is also not an exception. There are a number of instances in Kerala where arrested persons are brutally tortured by the police and caused death in police custody. *Sampath*'s case,[16] *Udayakumar*'s case,[17] *Rajan*'s case,[18] *Vijayan*'s case[19] and *Varghese*'s case[20] are the best illustrations for the police torture resulting into the death in police custody in Kerala. The National Human Rights Commission has even taken cognizance in a case in Kerala where the death caused after his release from the police custody. In this case, the Police in *Wynadu* district of Kerala had taken Mr. Hussain on suspicion that he was a gambler, and had beaten him so brutally that his spinal cord broke. Later he was released, but died when he was under treatment in a hospital.[21] On the complaint of a resident of the locality, the National Human Rights Commission recommended the State Government to pay a sum of Rupees Two lakhs to the next of kin of Hussain as immediate interim compensation. The Commission also directed the State Government to institute criminal action against the concerned police officials for the murder of Hussain, and also to expedite the departmental proceedings against them. The National Human Rights Commission stated that the Government was at liberty to deduct the amount of Rupees Two lakhs from the salary of the guilty police officials. The Kerala Government complied with National Human Rights Commission's recommendation.

There are instances where victims are admitted to the hospital in Kerala after torture and the Kerala State Human Rights Commission has entertained petitions in this regard. In a case before the Kerala State Human Rights Commission, Mr. V.V. Prabhakaran, Sub Inspector of Police and other Police Constables, went to the petitioner's house on 30-3-2001 at about 11.30 am, shouted with filthy words and was taken into a jeep.[22] Since then, he was assaulted by the Sub Inspector and constables brutally on his back of chest and other parts of the body. Police used abusive language against the other members of the family also. Petitioner was, then, taken to the police station and released on bail on 31-3-2001. On release, he made complaints to Superintendent of Police and Deputy Inspector General of Police. He was, then, admitted to the Medical College, *Thrissur* and treated in the casualty.

No action was taken on his complaints to the Superintendent of Police and Deputy Inspector General of Police. Commission required the Superintendent of Police, *Thrissur* to file a report on the incident, and the report was found not satisfactory by the Commission. Then, the Chief Investigating Officer was asked by the Commission to investigate and Chief Investigating Officer filed report after enquiry stating that the allegations in the petition are true and correct. Hence, the Commission recommended that the Government shall: (i) give necessary direction to Director of General of Police to take disciplinary action against the Sub Inspector, Mr. V.V. Prabhakaran, and Police Constable Yohannan; and (ii) pay an amount of Rs.5000/- as interim relief to the petitioner and recover the same from the erring police personnel. Thus, the Kerala State Human Rights Commission is a support for the parties whose human rights are violated by the police.

It is because of the never ending controversies and the significance of violations of human rights attached with the torture by the police, the researcher endeavoured to conduct a survey to know the extent of torture by police in Kerala and how it affects victim's health and employment capacity. Table 9.1 below shows the response of the victim of human rights violation by torture.

Table 9.1: *Showing the response on human rights violation by torture*

| Sl. No | Nature of arrest | Response from victim | | | Law which is violated |
		Yes (%)	No (%)	No Opinion (%)	
1	The Police tortured me for extracting information	17.24	75.37	7.39	violative of Article 21of the Constitution of India[23]
2	The police tortured me for admitting the guilt	5.88	82.36	11.76	*Ditto*
3	The police tortured me in retaliation as I stood against abuse of power by police	5.51	87.86	6.63	*Ditto*
4	The police tortured me due to political influence by the opposite party	8.81	84.2	6.99	*Ditto*
5.	The police tortured me due to bribery by the opposite party	8.09	80.15	11.76	*Ditto*

The data in Table 9.1 above shows that police continue torture irrespective of its prohibition by the Supreme Court in *Kishore Singh* v. *State of Rajastahn*[24]in which case the Supreme Court held that torture in any form is violative of Article 21.[25] The study reveals that 17.24 percent torture was employed for extracting information. The torture employed by the police due to the political influence of opposite party constituted 8.81 percent, and this occupies only half of the responses of the torture employed for extracting information. In 8.09 cases the torture was employed by reason of the bribes paid by the opposite party to the police and it is more orless equal with response for political influence for torturing i.e. 8.81 percent. In 5.88percent cases the police tortured for admitting guiltandin 5.51 cases the police tortured

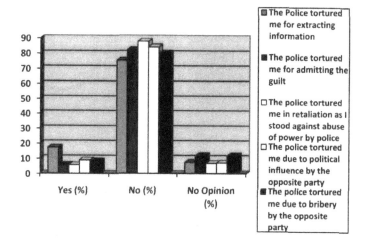

Chart 9.1: *Showing the response onhuman rights violation by torture*

in retaliationfor standing against abuse of power by police. Thus, the study reveals that torture by the police takes place very frequently for different reasons in Kerala and it comes around 45.53 percent. This demonstrates that the police torture people in custody quite often irrespective of its prohibition by the Supreme Court as it violates Article 21 of the Indian Constitution.

9.3.1.3. Impact of Torture on Victim

From time to time, the torture by the police affects the health of the victim. There can be physical and mental injuries due to severe police torture. The impacts generally are fractures, burn injuries, impairment of hearing, loss or reduction of eye sight, psychic trauma, *etc*. The torture may also affect adversely the earning capacity. Due to the significance of the impact of torture on victims, the researcher conducted a survey on it and the details are as shown in Table 9.2.below.

Table 9.2: *Showing the response on the impact of torture from torture victims*

Sl. No	Nature of unlawful arrest	Response from torture victim			Injury caused by torture
		Yes (%)	No (%)	No Opinion (%)	
1	The torture by police has/had bad impact on health	43.12	50.73	6.15	Back pain, impairment of eye sight and hearing, difficulties in walking, etc.
2	The torture affected negatively on earning capacity	12.83	82.76	4.41	Easily exhausted while on work, incapacity, partially incapacitated, *etc.*

Table 9.2.shows that out of the total number of tortured people (45.53 %: Table9.1), 43.12 percent has/had bad impact on the health due to torture. This

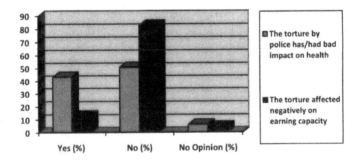

225

include back pain, impairment of eye sight and hearing, fracture of born, difficulties in walking, *etc.* Out of this 43.12 percent, 12.83 percent had serious health problem affecting the earning capacity such as easily exhausted while on work, incapacitated or partially incapacitated due to fracture, *etc.* This depicts that the police brutally torture to the extent of affecting badly on the heath of the arrestee and also, in some cases, incapacitating them from their daily earnings.

9.3.1.4. Police Officer's Opinion on Torture

Though the responses of the victims are as above, the researcher conducted a survey to gather the information on the opinion of the investigating police officers for the research study. The opinions of the police officials are as shown in Table 9.3 below.

Table 9.3: *Showing the response on the opinion of police officers about torture*

	Response from police officers				Reasons for supporting torture
Sl. No	Opinion about torture	Yes (%)	No (%)	No Opinion (%)	
1	Third degree method is necessary to deal with hardened criminals	68.18	20.06	11.76	It is difficult to prove complex cases within 24 hours without employing third degree method
2	Torture is necessary where a person commits a cruel and heinous crime	48.13	36.06	15.81	The criminals may escape from the court by taking advantages of benefit of doubt and torture by the police is the minimum punishment in such cases.

The police officers expressed the view that third degree methods is necessary to deal with hardened and habitual criminals. This view has been affirmed by 68.18 percent of the respondents. They expressdifferentreasons foremploying tortureoncriminals. Firstly, it isbecause of the reason that within 24 hours the accused is required to be produced before the

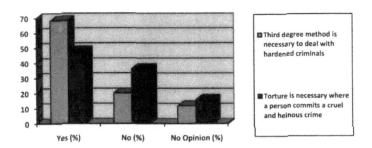

Chart 9.3: *Showing the response on the opinion of police officers about torture*

Magistrate. This 24 hours custody time[26] is too short for eliciting facts and information from habitual and hardened criminals, particularly in complex crimes or crimes which have links in more than one districts or States. Within the short span of 24 hours, police have to investigate the crime, collect evidences from different places, interrogate different witnesses, make recovery of the weapons used to commit crime, prepare statements and records, *etc*. Like this, many crimes may occur in a day. Hence, it would be difficult for completing all the procedures within 24 hours. So the third degree methods are employed or accused may be kept in illegal custody with out recording arrest. Further, employing scientific method requires more time. So, illegal custody or torture is an alternative. Many police officials argue that the custodial time of 24 hours to produce the arrestee before the Magistrate should be increased to avoid these problems.

Response of 48.13 percent of the police officers affirmed that torture is necessary where a person commits a cruel and heinous crime. They consider that where a person commits a cruel and heinous crime, if torture is not inflicted on him, there is no meaning in using the police uniform. These categories of the police officers consider themselves that they are the one who give real punishment to cruel and inhuman criminals. They believe that in Court, the criminals may engage good criminal lawyers and may be set free due to the loopholes in law and benefit of doubt. Even if Court punishes, criminals do not suffer any pain and pain is inflicted only by torture. So they admit that torture is necessary in some cases to inflict on cruel and inhuman criminals. This shows that they are more of emotional than of legal.

9.3.1.5.   Expert's Opinion on Torture

Former and current Members of the Kerala State Human Rights Commission opine that the attitude and behavior of the police generally is harsh and are still in the hang over of colonial brutality. They confirm that the basic defect lies with the training that is given to the police. Some Judicial officers also expressed the same view, but added that the work load and working conditions of police further aggravates the situation. Some human rights experts expressed that police brutality is a political trick because politician in either side need a police who is loyal to them and brutal to the public, so that people will feel that politician have power. So the government is not interested in controlling the police. Some human rights activist expressed that even the good people after getting the police training become cruel and inhuman. They added that the training programme is given in such a way that how they become cruel and torturous towards common man.

According to some top level Police officers, it is a false notion that police can detect crimes by using third degree methods only. They added that any corporal punishment is not going to correct a person. They believe that crime is a disease and it has to be cured. Torture is not going to help any person or the society, and police do not have any authority to inflict torture. According to them what is important is that police should follow what is right in accordance the law. Emotions do not help the police. The police must not act in accordance with moral wrong or right but they should act in accordance with what is right or wrong according to the law.

Senior Police Officers of Police Training College, Thiruvananthapuram asserted that in order to change the attitude and behaviour of the police, the Training College has made several human rights courses as part of the basic training programmes. Apart from this, several refresher courses on human rights have also been introduced to educate the lower ranking police officials with a view to reduce the human rights violation by the police. In addition to these, legal consequences of violation of the rights of the accused, the complainants, the victim, etc., are taught to the police to create awareness about these rights. He added that now, due to all these efforts there is change in the attitude of the police.

However, the study reveals that disregard to the prohibition, there takes place torture to a great extent. Majority of the investigating police officers support torture in certain cases such as in the case of hardened criminals and to punish a criminal who commit cruel and inhuman crimes. Nonetheless, top level police officials are of the opinion that the police investigating officers should act in accordance with the law and not with emotions. They categorically declare that police have no authority to punish a person and to be emotional with a particular circumstance. This shows that there exist a gap between the investigating police officials and top level officers. Unless this gap is filled positively, investigating police officials will continue torturing arrestees.

9.3.2.   *Violation of Human Rights by Unlawful Arrest*

The Third Report of the National Police Commission states that around 60 percent arrests made by the police are unnecessary and without justification.[27] The unlawful arrest is made by the police for different reasons. First, it is made with a view to falsely implicate a person in a crime; secondly, it is made in retaliation for complaints of police abuse; thirdly, due to bribery offered by the opposite party; fourthly, due to political influence; fifthly due to the influence of powerful local figures. The Police quite often fail to comply with the protective provisions of the Article 22 of the Constitution of India, requirements of the Criminal Procedure Code in matters of arrest and the directives of the Supreme Court in *D.K Basu* v.*State of West Bengal*[28]. Unlawful arrest also derogates a person's dignity, social status and reputation. Considering its impact on the people, the researcher conducted an empirical study by questionnaire to know the extent of unlawful arrests by the police. Table 9.4 below shows the picture of unlawful arrest by the police. In more than 80 percent of the cases the human rights of the victims were violated by the police since they were subjected to unlawful arrest due to the non-compliance of procedure prescribed for arrest by the law. In more than 80 percent of the cases the police failed to inform the grounds of the arrest to the victims or to give 'notice of appearance' to appear before the police officer or to inform the relatives or friends about the arrest. In 97.79 percent cases the police did not ask whether the matter of arrest should be informed to friends or relatives. In 79.77 percent cases when the arrestee asked for the reason for the arrest, the police abused using filthy language.

In more than 50 percent of the cases police did not show the arrest memo to the arrestee or to his family members or friends, or did not inform that the arrestee can obtain bail since the offence was bailable one, or the police arrested due to bribery by the opposite party. In around 50 percent cases the police made arrest due to political influence of the opposite party. This shows that in majority cases the police do not comply with the arresting procedures properly. In 11.03 percent cases the arrestee was hand cuffed even when the arrestee was obeying the police officer. As per the Supreme Court direction in *Premshankar* v. *Delhi Administration*[29] there is a prohibition for hand cuffing unless there exist an exceptional circumstance of suspecting that the arrestee may escape from the custody. The study reveals that the police still use hand cuffing in unnecessary situations even when the arrestee is following the police officer. This is done with intent to harass the arrestee by hand cuffing. The responses also show that in more than 40 percent cases, the arresting police official did not wear the name tag. This reveals that in all these cases the police officials violated the Section 41-B (a) of the Criminal Procedure Code which is inserted by the Code of Criminal Procedure (Amendment) Act, 2008 and the Supreme Court direction in *D.K. Basu's* Case. The details of the study are tabulated in Table 9.4.

9.3.2.1.   Arrest of woman

The arrest of woman was made by male police officer in 25 percent of the cases and in 18.1 percent cases, the arrest was made in the absence of a female police officer. The police officer arrested women accused after sunset and before sunrise in 20.95 percent cases and in 8.09 percent cases the male police officer touched the body of the women arrestee to make the arrest. Thus, the study reveals that there takes place violations rights of women in matters of arrest also. However, the violations of special provisions for women are comparatively less. But the significant of these violations lies in the fact that these violations are committed against the

231

prohibition of the newly added proviso to Section 46 (I) of Criminal Procedure Code[30] and the Supreme Court directions in *Sheela Barse v. State of Maharashtra.*.[31]The detail of the study is tabulated and given in Table.9.4 below.

Table 9.4: *Showing the response on human rights violation due to unlawful arrest*

Sl. No	Nature of Unlawful Arrest	Response from the Victim			Law which is violated in the response "yes"
		Yes (%)	No (%)	No Opinion (%)	
1	I was not informed of the grounds of arrest at the time of arrest	83.46	13.97	2.57	Article 22 of the Indian Constitution, and Section 50 of the Criminal Procedure Code
2	Police did not give me notice to appear before the police officer before making an arrest	88.60	2.57	8.83	Section 41-A of the Criminal Procedure Code.
3	The Police did not inform my relatives / friends about my arrest	80.88	10.29	8.83	Section 41-B of the Criminal Procedure Code, and Supreme Court direction in *D.K. Basu's* case.
4	The arrest memo was not shown to me or to my family members or friends	67.65	24.98	7.35	Section 41-B (a) of the Criminal Procedure Code, and Supreme Court direction in *D.K. Basu's* case
5	When I asked the reason for my arrest police abused me using filthy language	79.77	11.40	8.83	Article 22 of the Indian Constitution, and Section 50 of the Criminal Procedure Code.
6.	Even though the offence was bailable, the police officer did not inform me that I can obtain bail	56.61	23.90	19.49	Section 50 of the Criminal Procedure Code.
7	The police officer who arrested me did not wear the name tag with designation	34.92	47.43	17.65	Section 41-B (a) of the Criminal Procedure Code, and Supreme Court Direction in *D.K. Basu's* Case
8	The police did not ask me whether my arrest be informed to friends or relatives	97.79	2.21	0	Section 41-B (c) of the Criminal Procedure Code, and Supreme Court Direction in *D.K. Basu's* Case
9	I did not do any wrong, but the police arrested me	43.01	18.02	38.97	Sections 192 and 340 of Indian Penal Code

232

	on false grounds				
10	Police hand cuffed me even when I was obeying the police officer	11.03	88.97	0	Supreme Court direction in *Prem Shankar's* case.[32]
11	Police arrested me due to political influence of the opposite party	49.26	40.81	9.93	Sections 192 and 340 of the Indian Penal Code
12	Police arrested me due to bribery by the opposite party	57.73	33.45	8.82	Sections 192 and 340 of the Indian Penal Code
13	Even though I am a woman, I was arrested by a male police officer	25.00	70.96	4.04	Section 46(1) of the Criminal Procedure Code, and Supreme Court direction in *Sheela Barse's* case[33]
14	When I was arrested, woman police was absent on the scene	18.01	79.78	2.21	Section 46(1) of the Criminal Procedure Code, and Supreme Court direction in *Sheela Barse's* case
15	Even though I am a woman, police arrested me after sunset and before sunrise	20.95	75.75	3.30	Section 46 (4) of the Criminal Procedure Code
16	Even though I am a woman, male police officer who arrested me touched my body to make the arrest	8.09	87.50	4.41	Section 46 (1) of the Criminal Procedure Code

Thus, in summary, the study reveals that the police continue to make unlawful arrest in a large number of cases either one way or the other. These violations are made by the police in clear disregard to the the safeguards of Article 22 of the Constitution of India, requirement of Criminal Procedure Code in matters of arrest, and the directions of the Supreme Court in *D.K. Basu's* Case,[34] *Sheela Barse's* Case[35] and *Prem Shankar's* Case[36]. The finding of the study underpins the Third Report of the National Police Commission which stated that more than 60 percent of the arrests are unnecessary and unjustified.

There are many instances where complaints on the unlawful arrest have been filed before the Kerala Human Rights Commission. A best illustration is found in the *K Surendra's* case.[37] In this case, the petitioner, K.Surendran, a sub-contractor, while supervising the cable work done by the labourers, G. Venu, the Sub Inspector of Police and other policemen alighted there in a private jeep, and without disclosing anything started beating him They kicked the petitioner indiscriminately and on sustaining the same he fell down. The Sub Inspector and the other policemen, then, took him into custody and put him on the platform of the jeep. On the way also he was brutally assaulted. After half-an- hour the policemen brought him back. He was admitted in the District hospital and treated for several days. The Kerala State Human Rights Commission obtained the report of Superintendent of Police, *Kottayam* and the report stated that the Sub Inspector only warned the petitioner and not taken him in the custody. On the side of the petitioner three witnesses were examined by the Commission. All of them categorically sworn before the Commission that the petitioner was assaulted by the Sub Inspector and his party without any provocation and took the petitioner in to the jeep and assaulted him. Documentary evidences also were produced by the petitioner. The Commission recommended the State Government to grant an interim relief of Rs.25, 000/- to the petitioner.

9.3.3.   Violation of Human Rights by Illegal Detention

Illegal detentions are another controversial area whereby the police commit violations of human rights. As in the case of arrest, in illegal detentions also the police quite often fail to comply with the protective provisions of the Article 22 of the Constitution of India, provisions of Criminal Procedure Code in matters of detention and the directives of the Supreme Court in *D.K. Basu*'s Case.[38]Illegal detention affects the personal liberty and the dignity of individuals. Considering its impact on the detainees, the researcher conducted a survey by questionnaire to know the extent of illegal detentions made by the police. Table 9.5 below shows the responses in relation to illegal detention.

Table 9.5 demonstrates the responses in relation to illegal detention. More than 60 percent of the respondents affirmed that they were not produced before the Magistrate within 24 hours. What is more astonishing is that in 97.06 percent cases, the policedid not inform the arrestees about their right to consult a lawyer. As per the newly substituted Section 54 of the Criminal Procedure Code, the accused person shall be medically examined immediately after the arrest. However, in 56.61 percent cases the police did not make medical examination 'immediately' after the arrest.[39] Around 80 percent respondents (78.67 %) stated that the venue of the detention was not notified to the relatives or friends. Clear stipulations are provided under newly inserted Section 41-C (2) of the Criminal Procedure Code, and also in the direction of the Supreme Court in *D.K. Basu's* case to inform the venue of the detention to the relatives or friends, but police frequently violates it.The details of the study are tabulated in Table 9.5.

Table 9.5: *Showing the response on human rights violation by Illegal Detention*

	Response from the Victim				Law which is violated in the response "Yes"
Sl. No	Nature of Illegal Detention	Yes (%)	No (%)	No Opinion (%)	
1	I was not produced before the Magistrate within 24 hours	60.67	36.76	2.57	Article 22 of the Indian Constitution and Section 56 of the Criminal Procedure Code
2	I was not asked whether I wish to consult a lawyer	97.06	0	2.94	Article 22 of the Indian Constitution, Section 41-D of the Criminal Procedure Code [40], and Supreme Court direction in *D.K. Basu's* Case

235

| 3 | I was not examined by a doctor immediately (within six hours) of my arrest | 56.61 | 23.90 | 19.49 | Section 54 of the Criminal Procedure Code, [41] and Supreme Court direction in *D.K. Basu's* Case |
| 4 | Venue of my custody was not notified to my relatives or friends. | 78.67 | 11.76 | 9.56 | Section 41-C (2) of the Criminal Procedure Code, [42] and Supreme Court direction in *D.K. Basu's* Case |

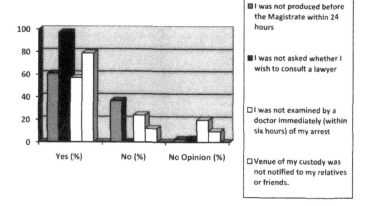

Chart 9.4: *Showing the response on human rights violation by Illegal Detention*

Thus, the study reveals that there take place illegal detentions very frequently in Kerala. They take place in clear violation of the Article 22 of the Indian Constitution, Section 41- D of the Criminal Procedure Code[43]andSupreme Court direction in *D.K. Basu's* Case.

9.3.4.   False Implication

In some cases, the police may falsely implicate an innocent person. This happens when police have retaliation against a person in some other crime. When a person accused in a crime takes anticipatory bail, the police may fabricate another case to arrest and detain that person. It may also happen due to political influence against rival groups. Due to the strength of bribes paid to the police, the police may falsely implicate a person. In order to hush up the abuse of power by the police, the police may falsely implicate the victim or the relatives of the victim or witnesses to persuade them to be on their side. In this way police violate the human rights of people.

Mani who was arrested along with Udayakumar who was tortured and caused death in police custody in Fort Police station,[44] narrated that they were sitting in *Sreekanteswaram* park in Thiruvananthapuram when two police constables appeared and asked whether they were drunk and then the police put their hand into Udaykumar's and his pocket. Udayakumar had around three thousand rupees in his pocket for buying cloths for his mother for the then forthcoming *onam* festival. Immediately, they were taken to the Fort police station and after taking money they were set free. But Udayakumar demanded the money back. The police got enraged and hence, tortured and killed Udayakumar there. After causing death of Udayaumar, the police registered a false case of theft against Mani and Udayakumar in order to reduce the aggravation of causing death of Udayakumar. This is only a single instance but there takes place a number of cases where the police falsely implicate innocent persons. Considering its significance, the researcher included the statement related with false implication in the questionnaire. The Table 9.3 above shows the data related with false implication. In 40.01 percent of the cases, the respondents affirmed that they were falsely implicated. False implication affects the rights and liberties of a person and also is a crime under Sections 192 and 340 of the Indian Penal Code. However, police continue to practice it.

237

The *Savithri*'s case before the Kerala State Human Rights Commission depicts a case of this kind.[45]In this case the petitioner, Savithri, alleged that her son, Biju, was falsely implicated as accused in a case of *Thrikkunnapuzha* Police Station by the Circle Inspector, *Haripaad*. In connection with the said crime he was taken in to custody at 10.10 am on 25-6-95 along with four others. While under police custody, Biju was tortured by the police both mentally and physically. He was then produced before the Judicial First Class Magistrate Court, *Harippad*, and thereupon he was kept under judicial custody for 60 days. Thereafter, he was released on bail. Upon complaint, the case against Biju and others were reinvestigated by the Crime Branch of the State Police and found that Biju had not involved in the incident and he was innocent and removed from the list of accused on 25-7-1997. The petitioner specifically alleged that even after he was removed from the array of the accused by the Crime Branch, the Police personnel were threatening him that they will implicate Biju in false cases. They used to go to his residence and place of work and used to torture him. On account of the torture and erroneous action of police Biju had suffered mental anguish and physical deprivation and he committed suicide on 19-6-2000. The Commission observed that even though the loss of her son cannot be compensated in terms of money, yet it recommended Government: (1) to pay an amount of Rs.100, 000/- as an interim relief to the petitioner; and (2) to provide Government job to any of the dependants of deceased Biju.

In *Mohanan*'s case before the Kerala State Human Rights Commission, a petition was filed against fabrication of false crimes, harassment and torture committed by the Sub Inspector of Police.[46] In this case Mr. Vyasan Pillai, Sub Inspector of Police, accompanied by a group of police constables went to the house of the petitioner, Mr. Mohanan and searched his house, took away his vehicle R/C book, pass book, documents, *etc*. He proceeded to the police station along with his Advocate and got back the valuables taken from his house, but he was not permitted to go out from the police station. He was detained in the station till 3.30p.m.on the same day and implicated in Crime No.328/2001. As he was a patient of peptic ulcer and as he was remaining in the police station without any food or drink, he started vomiting. He was then hospitalized. On 31.8.2001 the Circle Inspector of Police, Mr. Shahul Hameed came to his house and taken him to *Harippad* Police station and detained there and falsely implicated as accused in an *Abkari* case along with two others. Another case, Crime No.329/2001 under *Abkari Act* also was registered against him, after planting a few litres of spirit in a plastic container at his residence in the same night. He was then produced before the Magistrate and remanded to judicial custody.

The Kerala State Human Rights Commission required the Chief Investigating Officer to inquire and file report on the matter. The Chief Investigating Officer filed report which set out that the petitioner was falsely implicated in Crime No.328/2001 of *Harippad*Police station, the seizure of illicit liquor from the house of the petitioner in the night of 31.8.2001 also is a false story and the FIR in Crime No.329/2001 also is a fabricated one. The Commission expressed its concern over the matter that the police Officers who are duty bound to protect the life, liberty and property of every citizen, but are fabricating false case against any citizen to wreak vengeance. The Commission recommended the Government that (i) disciplinary action may be taken against the Circle Inspector of Police, Mr. Shahul Hameed and Sub Inspector of Police Mr. Vyasan Pillai; (ii) a vigilance enquiry may be made regarding the allegation of demand of bribe; and (iii) an amount of Rs.25, 000/- each be recovered from the counter petitioners, Circle Inspector and Sub Inspector, and pay to the petitioner for the mental agony suffered by him.

The police falsely implicate even witnesses simply in a crime. Due to this reason, witnesses, in many cases, do not come forward to inform the police about the occurrence of crime. Thus, the police commit violation of human rights by falsely implicating persons in some crime which they have not committed.

9.3.5. *Failure to take Action*

The Police, in many cases, do not register cases nor conduct proper investigations on the complaints of the victim. Sometimes, the action taken may not be sufficient in the circumstances of the case. The Police inaction generally affects the victim of crime. *Satheesh Kumar*'s case[47] decided by the Kerala State Human Rights Commission is a glaring illustration for depicting the extent of failure in taking action by the police. In this case, some culprits who were the illicit liquor sellers caused the death of one Satheesh kumar on 1-11-1999 at *Harippad* in the presence of the police, but the police did nothing for its prevention. Edavattom G.Vasavan, an Advocate, complained to the Kerala State Human Rights Commission on watching the news items about the police inaction. The Commission called for the report of the Superintendent of Police, *Alappuzha*. Since the Commission felt that the report of the Superintendent of Police is unsatisfactory, the Chief Investigation Officer of the Kerala State Human Rights Commissionwas asked to investigate the matter and file report. The report of the Chief Investigation Officer had shown that on sustaining injuries Mr. Satheesh Kumar fell unconscious and the accused obstructed in taking the injured to the hospital for about 20 minutes and that the incident occurred only 150 meters away from the police picketing. The Commission observed that there was gross negligence and inaction on the part of the police and, consequently there is vicarious liability on the State. Hence, the Commission recommended that the State is requested to grant an interim relief of Rs.200, 000/- to the father and mother of the deceased. The Government complied with the recommendation of the Commission and paid an amount of Rs.2, 00,000/- to the father and mother of the deceased Satheesh Kumar towards interim relief.

On many occasions, the police do not conduct the investigation properly either because they are negligent or because they make themselves negligent due to bribery by the opposite party. One Mr. Eachen Antony alleged that the police did not properly and fairly investigate the death of his son, Tintu, and the police simply referred the case as drowning and his *bona fide* belief was that somebody murdered his son.[48] As per the direction of the Commission, the Chief Investigating officer investigated the matter and reported that the death cannot be presumed as accidental and proper investigation has not been conducted by the police officer. Hence, the Commission recommended the State Government to reinvestigate the death of Tintu either by the Crime Branch or Central Bureau of Investigation.

The inaction on the part of police violates the human rights of people as it may adversely affect their right to life, liberty and property of individuals. Due to its significance, the researcher conducted a survey on the victims/complainants to know the extent of police inaction. 42.86 percent responded that there was police inaction or the action taken was not satisfactory for the victims/complainants. There are various reasons for police inaction or failure to take action. First, the police officials are under pressure of workload. In order to reduce the work load the police may not register new cases. Second, there may be political influence not to register cases against some particular persons. Third, some crime victims who are poor cannot afford to pay bribes that the police ordinarily demand for registration of First Information Report. This way police violate the human rights of the victim of crime.

9.3.6. Reports of the National Human Rights Commission on Torture in Kerala

The total number of complaints admitted for disposal by the National Human Rights Commission from Kerala during 2001-02 was 27 but it reached up to a total of 156 during2002-03 i.e., around six times greater in just one year. But

Category of Cases	2001-02	2002-03	2003-04	2004-05	2005-06	2006-07	2007-08
Custodial Violence	0	19	0	0	1	0	0
Illegal Arrest	0	3	3	0	0	0	1
Unlawful detention	1	25	8	2	0	1	1
False implication	4	10	1	2	0	0	1
Failure in taking action	5	33	14	6	3	2	4
Alleged Fake encounters	0	0	0	0	0	0	0
Alleged disappearances	1	2	0	0	0	0	1
Other Alleged Police Excesses	16	64	27	12	10	9	6
TOTAL	27	156	58	22	14	12	14

Table 9.6: Number of Complaints against police admitted by the National Human Rights Commission from Kerala from 1st April 2001 till 31st March 2008. (Source: NHRC, Annual Reports 2001-02 to 2007-08.)

There was a gradual decrease until 2006-2007 where it was 12; but again slightly increased to 14 during 2007-08. It is submitted that although there is no marked decrease in the number of complaints of deaths in police custody to the National Human Rights Commission from Kerala,

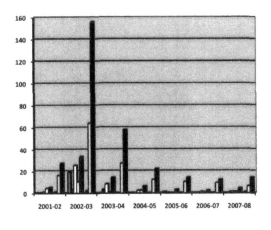
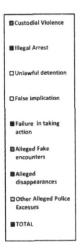

Chart 9.5: Chart based of the Table 9.6

yet there is marked decrease in other complaints such as custodial torture, illegal arrest, unlawful detention, false Implication, etc.[49]This may be due to two factors: first, the National Human Rights Commission has given directionsto all State Governments and Authorities to intimate custodial deaths -natural or unnatural- within 24 hours of the occurrence to the Commission. Thus, all custodial deaths are reported directly to the National Human Rights Commission. Secondly, the Kerala State has constituted the Kerala State Human Rights Commission in 1998, and thereafter, Kerala State Human Rights Commission started functioning on complaints related with human rights violations including police atrocities such as custodial torture, illegal arrest, unlawful detention, false Implication, failure in taking action, etc. Thirdly, the number of incidents may also have reduced from the part of police due to the awareness among the police that that the National and Kerala State Human Rights Commissions are established which sternly recommend the Government for action against erring police personnel.

243

Even though there is a decrease in the human rights violations by the police, what is more significant to be noted from the report of the National Human Rights Commission is that there takes place a number of human rights violations by the police in Kerala. This is in agreement with the result of the empirical study conducted by the researcher which also depicts the same fact. Hence, the report of the National Human Rights Commission also strengthens the finding of the empirical study.

9.4. Conclusion

The Supreme Court has prohibited torture as violative of Article 21. However, the study reveals that torture by police is a common phenomenon in Kerala. The police employ a range of methods of torture such as *uruttal*, rocket, aeroplane, ice block method to simple beating. The study reveals that 17.24 percent tortures are employed for extracting information, 8.81percent are employed due to the political influence of the opposite party, 8.09 percent by reason of the bribes paid by the opposite party, 5.88 percent for admitting guilt and 5.51 percent as retaliation for standing against abuse of power by the police. Torture also affects health and earning capacity. 43.12 percent of tortured victims had bad impact on health, and for 12.83 percent of them, the torture affected negatively on the earning capacity.

However, the opinion of the majority investigating police officers favours torture. 68.18 percent responded that torture is necessary to elicit facts from hardened and habitual offenders. It is submitted that they consider that the accused is the best source of information and by using third degree methods information about the crime can be elicited from the accused. This shows that they totally ignore the 'right to silence' guaranteed to the accused by the Constitution of India. They also consider torture as a short cut method. Majority police officers responded that the custody time of 24 hours for producing before the Magistrate is too short and within the short span of 24 hours, it is difficult for the police to complete the investigation, interrogation, collection of evidences, preparation of statements and records. For all these, more time is required and hence, the police employ short cut methods of torture rather than going for a detailed investigation.Further, 48.13 percent of the police officers affirmed that torture is necessary where a person commits a cruel and heinous crime. It is submitted that this category of police officers consider that they are the one who give real punishment to cruel and inhuman criminals. They consider that in the court, the criminals may engage good lawyers and be able to set free themselves due to the loop holes in law and the benefit of doubt. They believe that even if the court punishes, criminals do not suffer any pain, and the pain is really inflicted only by torture. So they admit that torture is necessary in some cases on hardened, cruel and inhuman criminals.

However, the top level police officials do not support this view. They opine that police have no authority to torture any person. They suggest that the police should act in accordance with law, not by emotions. They assert that the police are supposed to do what is legally right and not what is morally right. However, the investigating police officers resort to torture. It is submitted that there lies a wide gap between the top level police officers and investigating police officers and this gap is to be removed by educating the investigative police officers.

Some judicial officers opined that in some cases simple torture may be necessary and can be admitted if it is in a human way. This view is formed due to the growing crimes in the society and the prevalent socio-political situations in the State. It is submitted that in order to curb the growing crimes, some times, simple beatings by the police can be justified; however, the fear is

245

that if such permission is given to the police, the police may misuse it on innocent persons. Hence, the purpose would be defeated.

There are legal and procedural requirements for arrest. However, the study reveals that in majority cases police continue unlawful arrest. Around 80 percent cases the police commit violation of human rights such as not informing the grounds of arrest, not issuing the notice of appearance before making an arrest, not informing the relatives or friends about the arrest and not asking whether the arrest be informed to any friends or relatives. Besides, in around 50 percent cases the police commit violations of human rights such as not showing the arrest memo to the arrestee or his family members, not informing the arrestee that he can obtain bail even though the offence was bailable one or the police arrested due to bribery or political influence by the opposite party.

There is a prohibition for handcuffing unless there exists an exceptional circumstance of suspecting that the arrestee may escape,[50] but study reveals that police continue to hand cuff persons (11.03 percent of the arrestees) unnecessarily. The study also reveals that around 25 percent violation of special rights of women also takes place in Kerala. Considering all the above facts it is submitted that the extent of unlawful arrest in Kerala is very high and the situation is grave.

Illegal detention by the police is also very common in Kerala. The study reveals that in more than 60 percent cases arrestee were not produced before the Magistrate within 24 hours. What is more astonishing is that in 97.06 percent cases, the police did not inform the arrestees about their right to consult a lawyer. In majority cases, the police did not inform the venue of detention (78.67 percent) to the relatives or friends. These are clear violation of the Article 22 of the Indian Constitution, Section 41- D of the Criminal Procedure Code [51] and the Supreme Court directions in *D.K. Basu's* Case; but the police continue to practice it.

False implication of innocent persons in a crime by the police and Failure in taking action on complaints are also crucial in relation to human rights violations by the police. The study reveals that in a considerable number of cases the police falsely implicate(41.01 percent) people in the crimes or they either failed to take action on the complaint or the action taken by the police was insufficient (42.86 percent).

Thus, in summary, the study reveals that there takes place violations of human rights by the police in Kerala State in different ways such as unlawful arrest, illegal detention, torture, false implication, failure in taking action on complaints, *etc.* The extent of violation is very high in unlawful arrest and illegal detention. The police recurrently employ third degree methods, even though torture is prohibited. False implication and failure to take action on complaints are also not uncommon. These violations take place irrespective of Constitutional guarantees, criminal procedural requirements, and the direction of Supreme Court in different cases. Hence, it is submitted that the major problem lies not with the laws but with the implementation of laws.

Endnotes

[1] *T.V. EacharaVarier* v. *Secretary to the Ministry of Home Affairs, Government of Kerala*, 1977 K. L. T. 335; *K. Karunakaran* v. *T V EacharaWarrier*, 1978 AIR 290; 1978 SCR (2) 209; 1978 SCC (1) 18; *See also* T.V. EacharaVarier, *Memories of a Father* (2004), p.47.

[2] WP(C) No. 24258 of 2007(K), High Court of Kerala; See*also*CaseNo.S.C. 1542/06, Addl. Sessions Court (Fast Track - III), Thiruvananthapuram

[3] *Available at:*http://frontlinepunjabiyouth.blogspot.com (Visited on March 7, 2011).

[4] J. Reghu, *Custodial Death of the Author of Play Called "Liberation* (2006) available at:http://www.zcommunications.org/the-custodial-death-of-the-author-of-the-play-called-liberation-by-j-reghu(Visited on July 23,2011).

[5] *Central Bureau of Investigation* v. *Murukeshan*, Special Leave to Appeal (Crl) No(s).774/2011(From the judgment and order dated 22/12/2010 in I.A. No.16944of 2010 in WP No.13426/2010, High Court of Kerala).

[6]The prime suspect in a murder case notoriously known as *"Puthur*Sheela murder case".

[7]A kind of rod used by I.P.S. officers.

[8] Injuries a body has received before his death.

[9]*Available at:*http://frontlinepunjabiyouth.blogspot.com(Visited on March7, 2011).

[10]*Available at:*_http://frontlinepunjabiyouth.blogspot.com_(Visited on March7, 2011).

[11] Available at http://*www.gypsypalace.com*(Visited on March8, 2011).

[12] Available at http://*www.gypsypalace.com*(Visited on March8, 2011).
[13] See *supra* Ch. 8 n. for details.

[14]*Niyamaved*i*v.Central Bureau of Investigation,* 1999(1) KLT 56; *Seealso*S.Muralidhar, *Public Interest Litigation,* International Environmental Law research Center(1999), p. 487.

[15]*Kishore Singh v State of Rajastahn,* A.I.R. 1981 S.C. 625 (hereinafter referred as *"Kishore Singh*'s Case"); *FancisCoralieMullin* v *Union Territory of Delhi,* 1981 S.C.R. (2) 516; A.I.R. 1981 S.C. 746 (hereinafter referred as *"FancisCarolie Mullin's* case").
[16]*Supra* n.5.
[17]*Supra* n.2.
[18]*Supra* n.1.
[19]*Supra* n.4.
[20]*Supra* n.14.

[21]Case No. 64/11/1999-2000, National Human Rights Commission, Annual Report, 1999-2000 (2000), para.7 (B).
[22]Case No. H.R.M.P.1100/2001, Kerala State Human Rights Commission.

[23]*Ibid.*

[24]1981 SCR (2) 516.

[25]*Id.,* p. 518.

[26] The Constitution and criminal procedure code provides that the arrestee shall be produced before the court within 24 hours.

[27] Third Report, the National Police Commission, (1980) Para 22, 23, pp. 30-31.

[28]A.I.R. 1997 S.C. 610; (*D.K. Basu*'s Case).

[29] A.I.R. 1980 S.C. 1535.(*PremShanker*'s case)

[30]Inserted by the Code of Criminal Procedure (Amendment) Act, 2008.

[31] (1983) 2 SCC 96.(*SheelaBarse*'s case).

[32]*Supra*n.29.

[33]*Supra* n.31.

[34]*Supra* n.28.

[35]*Supra* n.31.

[36]*Supra* n.*32.*
[37]Case H.R.M.P. No.401/2002, Kerala State Human Rights Commission.

[38]*Supra* n.28.

[39]In order to make it more specific what does 'immediately' means, six hours time was specified in the questionnaire in parenthesis.

[40]Inserted by the Code of Criminal Procedure (Amendment) Act, 2008.

[41]*Ibid.*

[42]Inserted by the Code of Criminal Procedure (Amendment) Act, 2010.

[43]*Ibid.*

[44] WP(C) No. 24258 of 2007(K), High Court of Kerala.
[45]Case No. H.R.M.P. 2259/2000, Kerala State Human Rights Commission.
[46]Case No. H.R.M.P. 255/2002, Kerala State Human Rights Commission.
[47]Case H.R.M.P.No 1192/1999, Kerala State Human Rights Commission.
[48]Case H.R.M.P. No.2280/2000, Kerala State Human Rights Commission.

[49]Table 7,Number of Complaints against police disposed off by the National Human Rights Commission from Kerala from 1st April 2001 till 31st March 2008.

[50]*Supra n.32.*

[51]Inserted by the Code of Criminal Procedure (Amendment) Act, 2010.

Chapter 10

EFFECTIVENESS OF INSTITUTIONAL PROTECTION- EMPIRICAL STUDY IN KERALA

There are mainly two administrative institutions which play vital roles in redressing the grievances against police in Kerala, *namely*, the Kerala State Human Rights Commission and the Public Grievance Cell against police actions in Kerala. The role played by these institutions in protecting human rights is appreciable in many cases. However, it is pertinent to examine the effectiveness of these institutions in terms of satisfaction of those who are in contact with these institutions.

10.1.   Effectiveness of the Kerala State Human Rights Commission

In order to asses the effectiveness regarding the working of the Kerala State Human Rights Commission, a survey has been conducted by the researcher on the "victims" and the "human rights activists" who had contacts with the Commission.

10.1.1.   Opinion of the Victims

It is surprising to note that more than 80 percent respondents expressed their dissatisfaction with the working of the Kerala State Human Rights Commission. 82.72 percent expressed that they are not happy with the remedy given by the Kerala State Human Rights Commission. Regarding delay in settling the dispute, 77.94 percent expressed dissatisfaction. 67.65 percent affirmed that the Commission is not impartial in its decision making process.86.76 percent expressed dissatisfaction withthe implementation of the decisions of the

Table 10.1: *Showing the response on the opinion of victims on the working of the Kerala State Human Rights Commission*

Sl. No	Response from victim				Reasons for the opinion "Yes"
	Nature of Opinion	Yes (%)	No (%)	No Opinion (%)	
1	I am not happy with the remedy given by the Kerala State Human Rights Commission	82.72	11.39	5.89	Decision of the Commission had no impact on the offender
2	I am not happy with the delay in settling the dispute	77.94	13.97	8.09	Delay dilutes the effectiveness of the remedy
3	The Kerala State Human Rights Commission is not impartial	67.65	15.81	16.54	Biased due to influence of politics
4	I am not happy with the implementation of the Commission's decisions	86.76	9.19	3.05	Decisions are recommendations to the Government and the Government may delay or may not implement it.
5	Totally the Kerala State Human Rights Commission is an ineffective body and should be dismissed	87.87	9.92	2.21	Decisions are not enforceable and the Commission is biased, and hence, it is an unnecessary wastage of State fund for the establishment of the Commission

Commission. 87.87 percent expressed that the Kerala State Human Rights Commission is anineffective body and should be dismissed. The details are tabulated in Table. 10.1. Thus, from the above survey it is clear that the victims are dissatisfied with the working of the Commission.

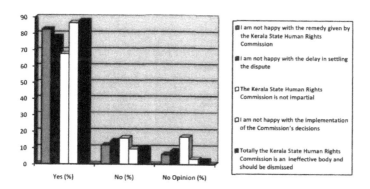

Chart 10.1: *Showing the response on the opinion of victims on the working of the Kerala State Human Rights Commission*

10.1.2.   Opinion of the Human Rights Activists

Human rights activists dealing with victims of human rights violation by the police had to approach the Kerala State Human Rights Commission for the redressal of victim's grievances. Table 10.2 below shows the opinion of the human rights activists on the working of the Kerala State Human Rights Commission. More than 80 percent of the human rights activists expressed their dissatisfaction with the working of the Kerala State Human Rights Commission. Regarding remedy given to the victims by the Commission, 83.82 percent of the activists expressed theirdissatisfaction. 87.88 percent expressed dissatisfaction on the delay in settling the dispute and 81.99 percent expressed that the Commission is not impartial in its decision making. 92.65 percent expressed dissatisfaction regarding the implementation of the decisionsof the Commission90.87 percent respondentsanswered affirmatively that the Commission is an

Table 10.2: *Showing the response on the opinion of human rights activists on the working of the Kerala State Human Rights Commission*

Sl. No	Response from Human Rights Activists				Reasons for the opinion "Yes"
	Nature of opinion	Yes (%)	No (%)	No Opinion (%)	
1	I am not happy with the remedy given to the victims by the Kerala State Human Rights Commission	83.82	11.76	4.42	Decision of the Commission had no impact on the offender
2	I am not happy with the delay in settling the dispute by the Commission	87.88	8.82	3.30	Delay dilutes the effectiveness of the remedy
3	The Kerala State Human Rights Commission is not impartial	81.99	12.87	5.15	Biased view due to influence of politics
4	I am not happy with the enforceability of the Commission's decisions	92.65	7.35	0	Decisions are recommendations to the Government and the Government may delay or may not implement it.
5	Totally Kerala State Human Rights Commission is an ineffective body and should be dismissed	90.81	6.99	2.20	Decisions are not enforceable and the Commission is biased, and hence, it is an unnecessary wastage of State fund for the establishment of the Commission

ineffective body and should be dismissed. Thus, from the above survey it is clear that the activists also, like the victims, dissatisfied with the working of the Commission.

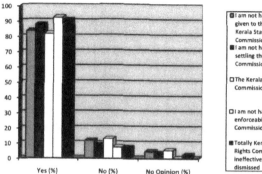

▣	I am not happy with the remedy given to the victims by the Kerala State Human Rights Commission		
▦	I am not happy with the delay in settling the dispute by the Commission		
☐	The Kerala State Human Rights Commission is not impartial		
☐	I am not happy with the enforceability of the Commission's decisions		
■	Totally Kerala State Human Rights Commission is an ineffective body and should be dismissed		

Chart 10.2: *Showing the response on the opinion of human rights activists on the working of the Kerala State Human Rights Commission*

It is significant to note that in all the five points in the questionnaire, the reasons for the opinion expressed by the victims and activists are more or less the same. It supports strongly the argument that Kerala State Human Rights Commission is a failure in providing remedy effectively to the victims. One of the major reasons for ineffective remedy is that the Commission cannot implement its decisions. Since the Commission is not giving remedy, but only recommends to the Government, the victims and activists are not happy the way the Commission is working.

10.1.3. Opinion of Experts

During the interview all Members of the Kerala State Human Rights Commission agreed that a large number of cases had been dealt with by the Commission relating to the human rights violation by the police. However, some Members expressed that the violations of human rights by the police do not come frequently to the Commission the way it should have come because of the apprehension of the people that if they complain against police, police can still take revenge by falsely implicating in another case or torturing the complainant in some other way. All the Members further stated that the Commission is only a recommendatory body. It decides cases, recommends to the Government, and then waits for the Government to execute it. The problem with this system is, firstly, that the decisions of the Commission may or may not be implemented by the Government. Secondly, even if the Government implements it, it suffers from bureaucratic formalities which further delays the process and people do not get speedy remedy especially in the cases violation of human rights by the police. So it is suggested that Protection of Human Rights Act should be amended to provide powers to the Commission to execute its decisions. This can increase the efficiency of the Commission to a greater extent.

Majority members said that Commission lacks a full fledged Investigation team. Now the investigating team is appointed form the regular State police service and they cannot provide impartial report in many cases since they conduct investigation against police brethren from where they came for the service of the Commission. They are on deputation and are not appointed permanently for the service of the Commission. Hence, Commission cannot get an impartial report against police in many cases involving violation of human rights by police. This problem can be solved by appointing separate and independent permanent police staff for the Commission. Such staff can work with integrity and cooperation with the Commission to find out the truth of violation of human rights by the police.

Some human right activist and professionals stated that Kerala State Human Rights Commission is suffering a lot because:

255

i.   It has no power to implement its own decisions. This is nothing but a political trick. If power to implement its decision is given, then political interference with police will be reduced and the Commission can easily punish erring police personnel. The politicians and police do not want this.

ii. Now, the Chairperson is a retired Chief Justice of the High Court which reduces the power of the Commission.

iii. Commission has no prosecuting power to prosecute police who commit violations of human rights.

They suggested that instead of a retired Judge, the Chairperson should always be a sitting judge of the High Court, so that the Commission will be more authoritative. Secondly, the prosecuting power should be given to the Commission in the case of violation of human rights by the police. If that is not possible, the Commission should be given authority to frame charges against erring personnel and pass it to appropriate court of Magistrate or Sessions. In this way the Commission can be made more powerful and authoritative. Now the Commission acts as a recommendatory body.

However, the Commission Members acknowledge that more than 85 percent of the recommendations are implemented by the Government. Nonetheless, some former Members specifically pointed that in some gross violation of human rights by the police, as in the case of the then Circle Inspector of Police, Kollam, who hit a person with wireless set, the Kerala State Human Rights Commission found him fault and recommended the government to take disciplinary action against him. But the recommendation was not implemented by the Government even after repeated demand from the Commission.

10. 2.   Effectiveness of the Public Grievances Cell

In order to redress the grievances of the public against police, a public grievance cell was opened under the supervision of an Assistant Inspector General of Police at the Police Head Quarters in Thiruvananthapuram. Assistant Inspector General (Public Grievances) (AIG (PG)) receives complaints against police from public from all over Kerala State. AIG (PG) informed in the interview that the majority of the complaints received by the Public Grievances Cell were related with lower level police officials from the rank of Sub Inspector up to the rank of Deputy Superintendent of Police. Complaints mainly related with police inaction or the police action was insufficient, police unnecessarily make arrest or detention, torture by police, false implication, police favour the opposite party by taking bribe or by political influence, etc. He stated that the action taken by the Cell was to call for report from the Superintendent of Police of the concerned district. In urgent and serious cases General Diary will be called for inspection and verification. He further added that ninety percent of the complaints are not genuine and, in many cases, complainants "expect more from police than the authority of the police". If a police official is found to have committed any thing as complained of, Public Grievance Cell will recommend to the State Police Chief for taking appropriate action against the erring police officer. However, the victims of crimes and human rights activists are not happy with the working of the Public Grievance Cell.

10.2.1.   Opinion of Victims about Public Grievance Cell

The victims approach the Public Grievance Cell generally to redress the grievances against police officer. The complaints, normally, are that the police officer failed to take action on the complaint made to the police, or the police made false implication, or police tortured, or

257

unlawfully arrested or illegally detained, *etc*. The responses of the victims on the working of the Public Grievance Cell are tabulated in Table 10.3 below.

Table 10.3: *Showing the response on the opinion of victims on the working of Public Grievance Cell (against police)*

| SI. No | Nature of Opinion | Response from Victims | | | Reasons for the opinion "Yes" |
		Yes (%)	No (%)	No Opinion (%)	
1	I have approached Public Grievance cell, but the response was not satisfactory	82.91	12.82	4.27	There was no enthusiasm to inquire into the complaint
2	The police officer hearing the complaint was rude to me	77.78	16.24	5.98	The attitude of the officer was not friendly
3	I did not get any remedy from there or the remedy received was insufficient	84.62	12.82	2.52	The Decision had no impact on the offender
4	The Grievance Cell was favouring the police officer against whom I made the complaint	74.35	13.68	11.97	There was no proper action on my complaint

More than 70 percent respondents expressed their dissatisfaction towards the public grievance cell. 82.91 percent expressed that working of the Cell is not satisfactory. 77.78 responded that the officers were rude with the victims who went to complain against the police. Further, 84.62

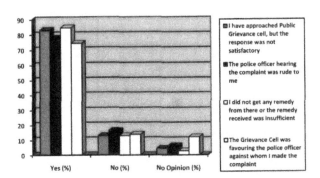

Legend:
- ◼ I have approached Public Grievance cell, but the response was not satisfactory
- ◼ The police officer hearing the complaint was rude to me
- ◻ I did not get any remedy from there or the remedy received was insufficient
- ◻ The Grievance Cell was favouring the police officer against whom I made the complaint

X-axis: Yes (%), No (%), No Opinion (%)

Chart 7: *Showing the response of victims on the working of Public Grievance Cell.*

responded that they did not receiveany remedy or the remedy received was not satisfactory. 74.

35 percent responded that the Cell favours the police officials against whom complaint was made

by the victim. Thus, the study reveals that the work of the Public Grievance Cell is not

satisfactory in redressing the grievances of the victims against police officers.

10.2.2.   Opinion of Activists about Public Grievance Cell

Human rights activists also approach the public grievance cell to provide justice

to victims of police excesses. Since the activists are acquainted with the working of the Cell, the

researcher conducted a survey on their opinion also. The responses of the human rights activists

are tabulated in Table 10.4 below which shows that more than 80 percent respondents are

dissatisfied with the working of the Public Grievance Cell. 88.89 percent responded that when

approached the Cell with the complaint, the response was not satisfactory. 82.91 percent

expressed that

Table 10.4: *Showing the responses on the opinion of human rights activists on the working of Public Grievance Cell (against police)*

		Response from human rights activists			Reasons for the opinion "Yes"
Sl. No	Nature of opinion	Yes (%)	No (%)	No Opinion (%)	
1	The response of the public grievance cell is not satisfactory towards victims	88.89	7.69	3.42	The Cell was not active to inquire into the complaints
2	The police officer hearing the complaint is generally rude towards victims	82.91	10.26	6.83	The attitude of the officer was not friendly
3	I am not happy with the remedy given by the Cell to the victims of police action	86.32	11.11	2.57	The Decision had no impact on the offender
4	The Grievance Cell generally favours police officers against whom victim make the complaint	89.74	5.98	4.28	There was no proper action on victims complaint

the police officer receiving complaint was rude. Further, 86.32 responded that the remedy given is not satisfactory and 89.74 percent responded that the cell favours the police officials against whom complaint was made by the victim.

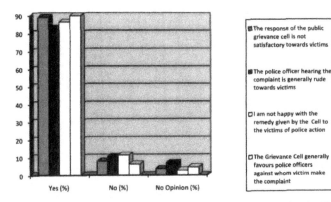

Showing the responses of human rights activists on the working of Public Grievance Cell

Thus, the study reveals that the work of the Public Grievance Cell is very much unsatisfactory from the view point of victims and human rights activist. The study also shows that more than 70 percent victims and more than 80 percent human rights activists are totally dissatisfied with the working of the Public Grievance Cell. It is submitted that the Public Grievance Cell is working for nothing but as an 'eye wash' against police excesses.

10.3.   Conclusion

Majority of the victims and human right activist interviewed expressed their dissatisfaction with the working of the Kerala State Human Rights Commission. More than 80 percent of the victims and activists expressed their dissatisfaction on the remedy given by the Commission and enforceability of the decisions of the Commission. 87.87 percent victims and 90.81 percent activists did not have any hesitation to express that Commission is an ineffective body and should be dismissed. 67.65 percent of the victims and 81.99 percent of the activists expressed that the Commission is not impartial. Thus, the general trend is that Kerala State Human Rights Commission is a defunct body and does not provide effective and impartial remedy. However, the Commission members opined that they provide remedy in appropriate cases within the legal frame work. Nonetheless, they admit that since it is a recommendatory body, it cannot execute its decisions, it can only recommend to the Government, and hence, implementation of the decision of the Commission may not be effective. In order to make the Commission more effective, members of the Commission and some human rights experts suggest that (i) power to implement its decision is to be conferred on the Commission, (ii) Commission should always be chaired by a sitting High Court Judge, and (iii) prosecuting power shall be given to the Commission, at least, in the case of violation of human rights committed by the police.

Victims of police excesses and human rights activists are of the opinion that the Public Grievance Cell under Director General of Police is an ineffective mechanism due to the partisanship of the officials in the Public Grievance Cell with other police officers. More than 80 percent of the human rights activists and 70 percent of victims expressed their dissatisfaction with the working of the Cell.

Thus, the study reveals that the Kerala State Human Rights Commission and the Public Grievance Cell are not functioning properly to the satisfaction of the victims. Hence, it is necessary to take steps to improve the working of these institutions so that victims can get effective remedy.

Chapter 11

PROTECTION OF HUMAN RIGHTS FROM POLICE-POSITION IN REGIONAL SYSTEMS

When domestic institutions fail to protect human rights, or when they themselves are the violators of human rights, it may become necessary to seek redress beyond national boundaries. Regional legal frameworks give victim of violations of human rights in a nation within the region a chance to bring his case before a regional body provided that the country in question is a Member State of the Regional Treaty such as European Union, African Union, *etc.* Regional systems can further help strengthen the protection of human rights. The known regional systems that exist for the protection of human rights now are the European, American, African systems. There are some countries such as former Soviet Russian member countries which are not part of European Union, Arab countries in the Middle East, South Asian Countries, *etc.*, which do not have an effective mechanism to check the violation of human rights on national or international basis. However, these countries are now emerging with new system of regional mechanism for the protection of human rights within their region which in turn intends to protect individuals within their nations in the region. However, the protection of the human rights in European, American, African, Arab and Asian countries are not uniform due to factors such as the difference in economic and ideological diversity that determines the status of nations as developed/ developing, democratic/ communist, and also the diverse religions that is adopted as State religion in many countries within the regions e.g. Saudi Arabia, Qatar, Iran. A detailed analysis is made on how the human rights protection mechanism works in regional systems.

11.1 EUROPEAN SYSTEM

When League of Nations was formed human rights issues were not given much significance due to which there were large numbers of human rights violations by nations which ended up in Second World War. When Second World War was about to end the allies determined to set up a new global regime, the United Nation Organization which would, *inter alia*, protect human rights violations. As both world conflicts originated in Europe, many European States believed that in addition to the United Nation Organization, there had to be a specific European regional response concentrating on human rights. As a result Europe had developed different documents in order to protect human rights. The principal document that relate with human rights protection especially in relation to civil and political rights is the European Convention on Human Rights and Fundamental Freedoms, 1950.

11.1.1 European Convention on Human Rights, 1950

The European Convention on Human Rights and Fundamental Freedoms or shortly, The European Convention on Human Rights, is an international regional treaty under which the Member States of the Council of Europe promise to secure fundamental civil and political rights, not only to their own citizens but also to everyone within their jurisdiction.[1] The Convention that came into existence as a result of the establishment of the Council of Europe for a number of reasons, *inter alia*, as a reaction to Second World War atrocities and determination to avoid future repetition; to encourage cooperation rather than conflict between European states; and to avoid the dangers that arose from the punishment and humiliation inflicted on Germany after the First World War.[2] The Convention, which was signed on 4th November 1950 in Rome, came into force on 3rd September 1953 and the emphasis is on individual and political rights rather than collective economic, social and cultural rights.

Among the existing regional mechanisms for the protection of human rights, it is submitted that the Europe has the most advanced system in terms of the scope, influence and enforceability. The preamble of the European Convention on Human Rights provides that considering the Universal Declaration of Human Rights which aims at securing the universal and effective recognition and observance of the human rights this enactment is made for the effective protection and promotion of the human rights. The provisions of the convention are more or less similar to that of earlier Universal Declaration of Human Rights in relation to protection of civil and political rights.[3] The convention contains 66 Articles in five sections. Any Member of the European Council can be a party to the Convention and Article 65 (2) makes it clear that any Member country which shall cease to be a member of the Council shall also cease to be a party to the convention.

European Convention on Human Rights provide specific protection for the right to life[4], liberty and security of person[5], freedom from unlawful arrest and detention[6] and right against torture and in human treatment.[7] These are categorized as absolute rights and cannot be derogated even in the case of national emergency.[8] Article 5 of the convention specifically guarantees for the liberty and security of persons. It provides:

> Everyone has the right to liberty and security of person. No one shall be deprived of his liberty save in the following cases and in accordance with a procedure prescribed by law:
> (a) the lawful detention of a person after conviction by a competent court;
> (b) the lawful arrest or detention of a person for non-compliance with the lawful order of a court or in order to secure the fulfillment of any obligation prescribed by law;
> (c) the lawful arrest or detention of a person effected for the purpose of bringing him before the competent legal authority on reasonable suspicion

of having committed an offence or when it is reasonably considered necessary to prevent his committing an offence or fleeing after having done so;

(d) the detention of a minor by lawful order for the purpose of educational supervision or his lawful detention for the purpose of bringing him before the competent legal authority;

(e) the lawful detention of persons for the prevention of the spreading of infectious diseases, of persons of un-sound mind, alcoholics or drug addicts or vagrants;

(f) the lawful arrest or detention of a person to prevent his effecting an unauthorized entry into the country or of a person against whom action is being taken with a view to deportation or extradition.

2. Everyone who is arrested shall be informed promptly, in a language which he understands, of the reasons for his arrest and of any charge against him.

3. Everyone arrested or detained in accordance with the provisions of paragraph 1 (c) of this Article shall be brought promptly before a judge or other officer authorized by law to exercise judicial power and shall be entitled to trial within a reasonable time or to release pending trial. Release may be conditioned by guarantees to appear for trial.

4. Everyone who is deprived of his liberty by arrest or detention shall be entitled to take proceedings by which the lawfulness of his detention shall be decided speedily by a court and his release ordered if the detention is not lawful.

5. Everyone who has been the victim of arrest or detention in contravention of the provisions of this Article shall have an enforceable right to compensation.

Thus, Article 5 protects persons from arbitrary arrest and detention by the Member State machineries and also provides a right to claim compensation in the event of unlawful encroachment to liberty. Thus, the European Convention on Human Rights provides effective protection for right to life, liberty and freedom from unlawful arrest, illegal detention and torture.

The significant part of European Convention on Human Rights is the enforceability mechanism that is made available to a person whose human right has been violated and has not been satisfied by the decision of the national tribunal. In such cases the European Convention on Human Rights provides for the establishment of the European Court of Human Rights.[9] The European Court of Human Rights has jurisdiction over Member States of the Council of Europe which has opted to accept the jurisdiction of the European Court of Human Rights.[10] Once a State has accepted the jurisdiction, all the decisions of the Court in connection with the State are binding to it. Judges are elected to the Court by the Parliamentary Assembly of the Council of Europe. The Court accepts applications of instances of human rights violations from individuals as well as States. However, it is rare for a State to submit allegations against another State, unless the violation is severe. For an application to be accepted by the Court, all domestic legal remedies available to the applicant must have been exhausted.[11] Additionally petitioner must bring the case to the Court within six months of the final domestic ruling on it. The petitioner must not be an anonymous person. The issue must be a violation of a guarantee set forth in the European Convention on Human Rights. Article 25 provides that any person, non- governmental organization or group of individuals claiming to the victim of a violation of human rights specified in the convention.

The Court then holds a public hearing to determine if there has been a violation to the Convention.[12] The Court normally sits as a Chamber of nine judges[13], including one from the country in question, but in rare instances can seat a Grand Chamber consisting of 21 judges.[14] If the application is declared *admissible*, the Court pursues for reaching a friendly settlement, which ranges from a change in the law(s) to compensation.[15] If not possible, Court proceeds with hearing. Chamber judgments may be appealed to the Grand Chamber until they become final after three months; Grand Chamber judgments are always final. Once the Court considers a case as a violation, States are obliged to prevent similar violations from occurring in the future. In appropriate cases the decision of the Court can afford "just satisfaction"[16] to the victims, including compensation paid by the State at fault.

The Committee of Ministers[17] of the Council of Europe monitors whether the Court's judgments are being complied with by the Member States.[18] The Committee of Ministers also observe that the requisite changes are made following a judgment, such as changes in legislation, case law, rules, and practices, building prisons or the appointment of new domestic judges.[19] The mechanism for the effective protection of human rights through a supranational European Court of Human Rights and the monitoring by the Committee of Ministers of Council of Europe whether the decision of the European Court of Human Rights are properly implemented in the respective national jurisdictions of Member States makes the European regional system a distinctive mechanism for the protection of the human rights.

11.1.2 European Convention for the Prevention of Torture

Besides the European Convention on Human Rights, there exists another Convention knows as the European Convention for the Prevention of Torture and Inhuman or Degrading Treatment or Punishment, 1987.[20] The main purpose of the convention is to provide effective remedy form police action and state brutality within the Council of Europe. The Convention creates the European Committee for the Prevention of Torture to monitor the implementation of the Convention provisions in the Member States.[21] Any State whether member of Council of Europe or not can become a party to the Convention.[22] Once a State, whether Member of Council of Europe or otherwise, has become party to the Convention, it shall be bound by the monitoring mechanism provided by the Convention.

11.1.2.1   Committee for the Prevention of Torture

The Convention provides for the constitution a Committee for the Prevention of Torture for effective monitoring mechanism to determine that no acts of torture takes place within the domain of any Member State. The Committee shall consist of as many members as the number of the State Parties.[23] According to its mission statement "the Committee shall, by means of visits, examine the treatment of persons deprived of their liberty with a view to strengthening, if necessary, the protection of such persons from torture and from inhuman or degrading treatment or punishment."[24] The Committee visits places of detention, such as police stations, prisons, detention centers, *etc.,* in any Member State.[25] Before the visit, the Committee shall give notice to the Government of the Party concerned of its intention to carry out a visit. After such notification, it may at any time visit any place of detention center.[26] The Member State shall provide the Committee with: (a) the free access to its territory and the right to travel without restriction; (b) full information on the places where persons deprived of their liberty are being held; (c) unlimited access to any place where persons are deprived of their liberty, including the right to move inside such places without restriction;(d) other information available to the Party which is necessary for the Committee to carry out its task.[27] The Committee may interview in private persons deprived of their liberty and may communicate freely with any person whom it believes can supply relevant information.[28] If necessary, the Committee may immediately communicate observations to the competent authorities of the State Party concerned.[29]

After each visit, the Committee shall draw up a report on the facts found during the visit and it shall transmit to the State Party concerned its report containing any recommendations.[30] The Committee may consult with the State Party with a view to suggest improvements in the protection of persons deprived of their liberty.[31] The information gathered by the Committee in relation to a visit, its report and its consultations with the Party concerned shall be confidential.[32] However, the Committee shall annually submit a general report to the Committee of Ministers on its activities which shall be transmitted to the Consultative Assembly and to any non-Member State of the Council of Europe which is a party to the Convention and make a public statement, if necessary, on the report.[33] Thus, the committee has the authority to visit a Member State where it deems that a person's liberty has been violated. When such intention is expressed by the committee it becomes obligation on the State Party to provide facilities and access to visit such places. Although the Committee has no judicial authority, yet it can report to the Committee of Ministers regarding its visit to a country.

11.1.3 Charter of Fundamental Rights of the European Union, 2000

The structure and composition of the European Union is different from that of Council of Europe and all the members of the Council of Europe is not members of the European Union. However, there is a close relationship between Council of Europe and European Union. The Parliament Assembly of Council of Europe adjoins the European Parliament of European Union at Strasbourg in France. The European Court of Human Rights situated at Strasbourg in France is part of the Council of Europe structure. A similar European Union Court is located in Luxemburg for the matters connected only with European Union. The former court abides to the European Convention on Human Rights adopted by the Council of Europe, while the later abides to the Charter of the Fundamental Rights of the European Union. The purpose for the creation of the separate Charter for European Union is evident from the preamble of the Charter of the Fundamental Rights which provides "the peoples of Europe, in creating an ever closer union among them, are resolved to share a peaceful future based on common values" and to strengthen the protection of fundamental rights in the light of changes in society, social progress and scientific and technological developments.[34] Charter of the Fundamental Rights consists of 54 articles in 7 chapters. First chapter deals with human dignity and it guarantees right to life,[35] prohibits torture and other cruel or inhuman treatment.[36] Chapter 2 deals with freedoms and it guarantees, *inter alia*, right to liberty and security of a person.[37] However, it does not provide for the procedural guarantee in the event of arrest or detention of a person as is provided in other conventions. It also lacks provisions for the enforceability and monitoring mechanisms. Since it is a document created by the European Union, as and when there is a violation of rights guaranteed by the Charter, they can approach the court in Luxemburg created under the treaty of the European Union. However, it confirms the authority of other European Treaties and Conventions including European Convention on Human Rights. The preamble of the Charter provides:

> "This Charter reaffirms, with due regard for the powers and tasks of the Community and the Union and the principle of subsidiarity, the rights as they result, in particular, from the constitutional traditions and international obligations common to the Member States, the Treaty on European Union, the Community Treaties, the European Convention for the Protection of Human Rights and Fundamental Freedoms, the Social Charters adopted by the Community and by the Council of Europe and the case-law of the Court of Justice of the European Communities and of the European Court of Human Rights"

In fact, there is no restriction for an aggrieved party to approach the European Court of Human Rights from the Council of Europe or from the European Union as is evident from the preamble. However, only an aggrieved person from the European Union can approach the European Union Court in Luxemburg. It appears that the Charter is a corollary to the other

271

international and regional instruments for the effective protection of the human rights within the European Union community.

11.2 THE INTER-AMERICAN REGIONAL SYSTEM

The Inter-American regional system operates among the member countries of American continent. It also stands for the protection and promotion of human rights. The system works based on: a) American Declaration of the Rights and Duties of Man 1948; b) American Convention on Human Rights 1969; c) Inter-American Convention to Prevent and Punish Torture 1985; and d) Inter-American Convention on the Forced Disappearance of Person 1994. The Organization of American States can be considered as the beginning for the establishment of the Inter-American regional system in relation to the protection and promotion of human rights.[38] The Organization of American States constituted the Inter-American Commission on Human rights in 1959. The Commission was behind making the Inter-American Convention on Human rights, 1969 and the Convention came into force in 1978.[39] There are 35 Organization of American Member States, 25 having ratified the convention and 20 having recognized the jurisdiction of the Court established under the convention.[40]

11.2.1 American Convention on Human Rights, 1969

Though American Declaration of the Rights and Duties of Man, 1948 pre-dates the Universal Declaration of Human Rights and European Convention on Human Rights, it did not in itself establish the American regional settings in relation to human rights protection nor did it provide a mechanism for supervision and enforcement. This led to the adoption of American Convention on Human rights in 1969. It was only after the adoption of the American Convention

272

on Human rights in 1969 there were better mechanisms for supervision and enforcement for the protection of human rights.

The American Convention on Human Rights is the treaty based on the Declaration of the Rights and Duties of Man 1948, sometimes referred to as the Pact of San Jose, Costa Rica. The American convention contains specific rights to life,[41] liberty,[42] human treatment[43] and judicial protection by laws.[44] Article 33 provides for the establishment of Inter-American Commission on Human Rights and the Inter-American Court of Human Rights. The Commission shall consist of as many members as the member countries of the Organization of American States.[45] The Commission has power to make recommendations to the Governments of the Member States for the adoption of progressive measures in favor of human rights within the framework of their domestic law and constitutional provisions as well as appropriate measures to further the observance of those rights; to request the Governments of the Member States to supply it with information on the measures adopted by them in matters of human rights; to take action on petitions and other communications pursuant to its authority under the provisions of Articles 44 through 51 of the Convention; and to submit an annual report to the General Assembly of the Organization of American States.[46] Article 44 makes it clear that any person or group of persons, or any non-governmental entity legally recognized in one or more Member States of the Organization, may lodge petitions with the Commission containing complaints of violation of the rights covered under the Convention. Thus, a single individual can file a complaint against the State which has violated or not taken any appropriate action against the violation of human rights.

Article 52 provides for the constitution of a 7 Judge Inter-American Court of Human Rights. The Commission shall appear in all cases before the Court.[47] It is provided under Article 61 that only the States Parties and the Commission shall have the right to submit a case to the Court. Thus, an individual or groups cannot have direct access with the court. It is only through the commission that their cases are filed before the court. If the Court finds that there has been violation of a right or freedom protected by this Convention, the Court shall have authority to rule that the injured party be ensured the enjoyment of his right or freedom that was violated and if appropriate, it shall order that fair compensation be paid to the injured party.[48] Sub-article 2 of Article 63 further provides that in cases of extreme gravity and urgency, and when necessary to avoid irreparable damage to persons, the Court shall adopt such provisional measures as it deems pertinent in matters it has under consideration. Thus, the Court has ample discretionary powers to decide the issues that may arise in connection with human rights violations under the Convention. Unlike European Convention on Human Rights where individual person can approach the European Court of Human Rights directly, the individuals do not have direct access to the court though they have access to Human Rights Commission which represent in the Court.

11.2.2 *Inter-American Convention on the Forced Disappearance of Persons*

The Inter-American Convention on the Forced Disappearance of Persons, 1994 was made due to the forced disappearances and abuse of human rights that were widespread in Latin and South America for much of the twentieth century. The police and other law enforcement officials within many National States played a vital role in the forced disappearance cases. The preamble of the Convention states that Organization of American States' Members were disturbed by the persistence of the forced disappearance of persons, which affronted the conscience of the

274

hemisphere; and concerned at violations of numerous non-derogable and essential human rights in the American and UN Declarations, and in the American Convention on Human Right. Article I of the Convention provides that the Member State Parties undertake not to practice or tolerate forced disappearances. Article II defines forced disappearance as:

> ...the act of depriving a person or persons of his or their freedom, in whatever way, perpetrated by agents of the state or by persons or groups of persons acting with the authorization, support, or acquiescence of the state, followed by an absence of information or a refusal to acknowledge that deprivation of freedom or to give information on the whereabouts of that person, thereby impeding his or her recourse to the applicable legal remedies and procedural guarantees

Thus, forced disappearance includes four essential elements;

- a) depriving persons of their freedom in whatever way;
- b) perpetration by or with the support of the State;
- c) absence of information and refusal to acknowledge occurrences;
- d) impedance or negation of legal and procedural remedies

The Convention makes it clear that forced disappearance could not be treated as political offences[49] and criminal prosecutions would not be subject to statutes of limitation,[50] i.e. they could be prosecuted at any time in the future, with no defense of 'superior orders'. Convention is categorical in stating that war, threats of political instability, or other public emergencies, would not justify the crime of disappearance of persons,[51] and detainees should be held in an officially recognized place of detention.[52] Convention casts a duty on the States Parties to establish and maintain official up-to-date registries of the detainees and to make them available to relatives, judges, attorneys, any other person having a legitimate interest, and other authorities.[53] Complaint regarding the alleged forced disappearance shall be made to the Inter-American Commission on Human Rights.

Article XIV provides that when the Inter-American Commission on Human Rights receives a petition or communication regarding an alleged forced disappearance, its Executive Secretariat shall urgently and confidentially address the respective government, and shall request that government to provide as soon as possible information as to the whereabouts of the allegedly disappeared person. Many cases of forced disappearances occur due to political rivalry and it occurs with the aid of police or other law enforcement machineries and hence, State Government may need to suppress such issues. The Inter- American regional settings provides fairly good procedure in the event of forced disappearances to bring the matter before the Inter-American Commission on Human rights.

11.3 AFRICAN REGIONAL SYSTEM

The regional African human rights system is based on the African Charter on Human and Peoples' Rights, shortly known as the "African Charter" or "Banjul Charter", which entered into force on October 21, 1986 upon ratification by a simple majority of Member States of the Organization of African Unity.[54]The Organization of African Unity was the regional body of the African States until 2002.[55] In 2002, the Organization of African Unity was disbanded and new African Union was launched in Durban, South Africa, to replace the Organization of African Unity. The new African Union is structured broadly modelling the European Union[56] and it, *inter alia*, provides the objective as to promote and protect human rights and human dignity among the African Countries effectively.

11.3.1.   African Charter on Human and Peoples' Rights

The African Charter on Human and Peoples' Rights 1981 contains three parts. The first part of the Charter deals with rights and duties, second part deals with measures of safeguard and the third part with general provisions. Preamble of the Charter states that it has been created in pursuance of Charter of the Organization of African Unity, which stipulates that "freedom, equality, justice and dignity are essential objectives for the achievement of the legitimate aspirations of the African people and for the establishment of bodies to promote and protect human and peoples' rights." The preamble has reference to Universal Declaration of Human Rights and UN Charter. Article 4 of the African Charter states that human beings are inviolable. It guarantees right to life and prohibit arbitrary deprivation of it. Article 5 provides for the respect of the inherent dignity of human beings and prohibits all forms of torture, cruel, inhuman or degrading punishment and treatment. Article 6 provides the right to liberty and the security of person and it further guarantees that no one may be deprived of his freedom except for reasons and conditions previously laid down by law. In particular, it provides no person may be arbitrarily arrested, detained or tortured. Article 7 guarantees a right to an appeal to competent national organs against acts of violation of fundamental rights, the right to defense and to be defended by counsel of one's choice. These are the important safeguards that the Charter provides from arbitrary arrest, illegal detention, torture, *etc*. These safeguards are similar with the Universal Declaration of Human Rights, International Covenant on Civil and Political Rights and European Convention on Human Rights. However, what matters is how the system works and how effectively the rights are enforced. In order to assess the effectiveness, it would be better to see the mechanisms that are provided by the Charter and the Protocols.

11.3.1.1. Enforceable mechanism

The African Charter provides for the constitution of African Commission on Human and Peoples' Rights for the promotion and protection of human rights in Africa.[57] In 1998, the Protocol to the African Charter for the establishment of an African Court of Human and Peoples'

Rights was adopted by the Organization of African Unity. However, the African Court of Human and Peoples' Rights came into being only in January, 2004 with the ratification by fifteen Member States.[58] On July 1, 2008, at the African Union Summit of Heads of State and Government in Sharm El Sheikh, Egypt, the African Court of Human and Peoples' Rights was merged with the African Court of Justice.[59] The court is now known as the African Court of Justice and Human Rights.[60] However, the African Court of Justice Human Rights is not functional yet.[61] So the only enforceable mechanism available is through African Commission on Human and Peoples' Rights

i. African Commission on Human and Peoples' Rights

The African Charter provides for the constitution of eleven members Human Rights Commission.[62] The main function of the Commission is to ensure protection of human and peoples' rights within the region.[63] There are two mechanisms provided under the charter for the enforceability of the rights, *namely,* (i) Inter-State communications, and (ii) Communication from other sources.

(a) Inter- State Communications

If a State Party has good reasons to believe that another State Party to the Charter has violated the provisions of the Charter, it may intimate by written communication to that State Party regarding the violation. Within three months of the receipt of the communication, the State to which the communication is addressed shall give a written explanation or statement elucidating the matter to the complained State Party.[64] If the issue is not settled within three months through bilateral negotiations or by any other peaceful procedure, either State shall have the right to submit the matter to the Commission.[65] Article 50 provides that the Commission deals with a matter only when all the domestic remedies have been exhausted, unless it is obvious to the Commission that the procedure of achieving these remedies would be unduly prolonged. The Commission may require the States concerned to provide it with all relevant information. The concerned State may represent before the Commission and submit written or oral representation.[66] The Commission will try to reach an amicable solution based on the respect of human and peoples' rights. Thereafter, the Commission shall prepare, within a reasonable period of time, a report stating the facts and its findings. The report shall be sent to the States concerned and communicated to the Assembly of Heads of State and Government.[67] While transmitting its report, the Commission may make such recommendations as it deems necessary to the Assembly of Heads of State and Government.[68] It is submitted that the authority available to the Commission is only amicable settlement. If there is no possibility of amicable settlement, the Commission has no power to enforce its decision. To this extent, it is a weak enforceable mechanism.

(b) Communication from other sources

The Charter does not specifically provide that individual can make complaints to the Commission. However, the Charter provides that before each session of the Commission, its Secretary "shall make a list of the communications other than those from the States Parties ... and transmit them to the Members of the Commission, who shall indicate which communication should be considered by the Commission".[69] Further, the Charter provides for fulfilling certain criteria before submitting communications such as (i) the communication must indicate the author (ii) it must be submitted only after all domestic remedies have been exhausted "unless it is obvious that this procedure is unduly prolonged"; (iii) it must be submitted "within a reasonable period from the time local remedies are exhausted", *etc.* These criteria points towards making

279

individual communications to the Commission. Here again, the authority available to the Commission is only to resort to amicable settlement. Thus, the Commission is very weak in enforcing its decisions.

Thus, there exists a super-national mechanism for the protection of human rights for African countries. The model adopted by the African system is more or less similar to that of European system, but functionally is far away from the European system. European arrangement is much more advanced from the enforceability point of view of human rights; whereas the African system is not even up to the level. It is submitted that the African human rights protection mechanism requires much work and task to make the enforceability of human and peoples' rights more effective.

11.4 THE MINSK CONVENTION

The Commonwealth of Independent States Convention on Human Rights 1995, shortly MINSK convention, is an association of those former Soviet Union States which cannot become members of the Council of Europe as they are outside the European territory. Since these States cannot become part of European Convention of Human Rights, they rightly decided to have a separate convention for the protection of human rights within their region and hence, formed the MINSK Convention. The MINSK Convention was opened for signature on 26th May 1995 at MINSK in Russia.[70] The Convention guarantees right to life,[71] liberty and security of person,[72] and prohibits torture and cruel, inhuman or degrading treatment[73]. It provides that anyone who is arrested shall be informed, at the time of his arrest, in a language which he understands, of the reasons for his arrest.[74] Everyone who is deprived of his liberty by arrest or detention, in accordance with national legislation, shall be entitled to have the lawfulness of his arrest or

280

detention examined by a court.[75] It also provides that any person who is deprived of his liberty shall be entitled to humane treatment and to respect for his dignity as a human being.[76] Persons who have been subjected to unlawful arrest or detention shall be entitled to compensation in accordance with national legislation for the damage caused.[77]

Article 6 provides procedural guarantee in the event of deprivation of liberty of any person that are enshrined by the convention. The Article 6 states:

1. Everyone shall have the right to liberty and security of person. No one shall be deprived of his liberty save in the following cases and in accordance with a procedure established by national legislation:
    (a) the lawful detention of a person after conviction by a competent court;
    (b) the lawful arrest or detention of a person;
    (c) the lawful detention of a minor for the purpose of referring his case for investigation, sentencing or trial.

2. Everyone who is arrested shall be informed, at the time of his arrest, in a language which he understands, of the reasons for his arrest.

3. Everyone who is deprived of his liberty by arrest or detention, in accordance with national legislation, shall be entitled to have the lawfulness of his arrest or detention examined by a court.

4. Everyone who is deprived of his liberty shall be entitled to humane treatment and to respect for his dignity as a human being.

Persons who have been subjected to unlawful arrest or detention shall be entitled, in accordance with national legislation, to compensation for the damage caused.

In fact, the Convention is very elaborate in providing protection from arbitrary arrest, illegal detention, torture and other inhuman treatment, *etc.* It also elaborates the procedure while making arrest or detention of a person. Thus, the Convention takes care of unlawful arrest, illegal detention, torture, *etc.*, and provides for measure for compensation in case of damage caused due such unlawful arrest or detention.

The control mechanism comprises the Human Rights Commission of the Commonwealth of Independent States, which monitors practices of the States by issuing recommendations.[78]With a view to effectively monitoring the fulfillment of the human rights obligations entered into by Member States a "regulations on the Human Rights Commission of Commonwealth of Independent States" was adopted on 24th September 1993 in consonance with Article 34 of the Commonwealth of Independent States Convention. Article 10 of the Regulation provides that the decisions of the Commission shall take the form of understanding, conclusions and recommendations. The Commission shall submit annual activity report to the council of Heads of State of the Commonwealth of Independent States.[79] However, the operational aspect of Commission is at minimal level as the regional setting is not a full-fledged one.

11.5 ARAB REGIONAL SYSTEM

The Arab regional system works for the protection of human rights in Muslim countries in the Middle Eastern region. The protection system is mainly based on the Arab Charter on Human Rights, 2004. However, before the Charter of 2004, there were attempts to have a protection system in the region. The first document in this regard is the Cairo Declaration on Human Rights, 1990.

11.5.1 The Cairo Declaration on Human Rights

The Cairo Declaration on Human Rights, 1990 is considered to be the Arab world's pioneer in respect of human rights protection documents. It was adopted after the conference held in Cairo in 1990. The declaration contains the preamble and 25 articles, and issued to serve as general guidance for Member States of League of Arab States[80]in the field of human rights. It is expressed in Islamic religious terms, referring to the human family descended from Adam, subordinate to Allah, with life being a God-given gift and it is thus guaranteed.[81] Article 20 declares that it is not permitted without legitimate reason to arrest an individual, or restrict his freedom, to exile or to punish him. It further prohibits from physical or psychological torture or to any form of maltreatment, cruelty or indignity. All rights and freedoms stipulated in the Declaration are subject to the *Shari'ah*, the only source of reference for explanation or clarification of any of its articles.[82] It is submitted that by a simple gaze at the provisions of the declaration it can be seen that at one place the declaration provides that physical or psychological torture or any form of maltreatment, cruelty or indignity is prohibited. At another place it provides that the declaration shall be subject to *Shari'ah* which provides for amputation in case of theft, a kind of cruel and inhuman punishment. Due to these inconsistencies, this declaration has attracted much criticism due to the superfluous dominance of Islamic religious tenets in limiting the enjoyment of human rights.

11.5.2.   *Arab Charter on Human Rights, 2004*

Considering the widespread criticisms on the Cairo Declaration, League of Arab States considered the matter and decided to adopt a separate document for the effective protection of human rights within the region. As a result an Arab Charter on Human Rights was adopted by the Arab League in 1994.[83] It was also widely criticized by many human rights organisations both within the region and beyond as failing to meet international human rights standards.[84] This has resulted into the adoption of a new version of Arab Charter on Human Rights at the Arab summit in Tunis in 2004.[85] The 2004 Charter in its preamble refers the Arab world as the birthplace of civilization and cradle of religions, and rejects racism and Zionism. It acknowledges the eternal principles of brotherhood established by the *Shari'ah*[86] and other divinely revealed religions. The preamble further expresses belief in the rule of law and reaffirms the principals of the UN charter with the international Bill of Human Rights, together with the Cairo Declaration on Human Rights in Islam, 1990. The 2004 Arab Charter on Human Rights is a binding treaty since it has entered into force in March 15, 2008 due to the ratification of it by 7 Arab States.[87]

Article 5 of the Charter guarantees the right to Life. Article 8 prohibits torture or cruel, inhuman or degrading treatment or punishment. Article 14 guarantees right to liberty and security of person and prohibit any person to be arrested, searched or detained without a legal warrant. It states:

1. Every individual has the right to liberty and security of person and no one shall be arrested, searched or detained without a legal warrant.
2. No one shall be deprived of his liberty except on such grounds and in accordance with such procedures as are established by law.
3. Anyone who is arrested shall be informed at the time of arrest, in a language which he understands, of the reasons for his arrest, and shall be promptly informed of any charges against him. Anyone who is arrested has a right to contact his relatives.
4. Anyone who has been deprived of his liberty by arrest or detention is entitled to be subjected to a medical examination, and shall be informed of such right.
5. Anyone arrested or detained on a criminal charge shall be brought promptly before a Judge or other officer authorized by law to exercise judicial power, and shall be entitled to trial within a reasonable time, or to release. The release may be subject to guarantees to appear for trial. It shall not be a general rule that persons awaiting trial shall be held in custody.
6. Anyone who is deprived of his liberty by arrest or detention shall be entitled to proceedings before a court, in order that a court may decide without delay on the lawfulness of his arrest or detention, and order his release if the arrest or the detention is not lawful.
7. Anyone who is the victim of unlawful arrest or detention shall be entitled to compensation.

Thus, the Arab Charter provides safeguards and procedural guarantees in the event of deprivation of liberty such as the right to information about the grounds of arrest, right to know the charges, right to be medically examined and right to be produced before the ordinary court. It also guarantees a right to claim compensation, if anyone is aggrieved by unlawful arrest or detention. The Charter provides for the constitution of an Arab Committee on Human Rights for the effective protection of human rights. Unfortunately, it has not been constituted so far.

It is submitted that the Charter 2004, like Cairo Declaration, also suffers from superfluous religious tenets into the enjoyment of human rights. The Arab human rights documents appears to be more of cultural than of universal due to the religious subjugation of human rights. However, it provides for the protection of persons from arbitrary arrest, illegal detention, torture, *etc.* But the main criticism connected with the Charter is that it does not provide any effective mechanism for the enforcement of rights guaranteed in the Charter.[88] No serious measure has been taken to constitute Arab Committee on Human Rights for the effective protection of rights under the Charter.

11.5.3   *ASIA*

Probably Asia is the only continent which does not have regional human rights documents like that of European, Inter- American or African systems. It is submitted that Asia does not have a unified document, may be because of the reason that it is too large and culturally diverse to allow similar or equivalent document. However, in January 2001, the Association of Asian Parliaments for Peace is scheduled to hold a conference in the Cambodian capital, Phnom Penh, to adopt a proposed Asian Human Rights Charter.[89] Three efforts have been made to formulate a human rights document for the region. Asian Human Rights Commission, a Hong Kong-based Non- Governmental Organization, drafted the first one; Forum Asia, the Bangkok-based Non- Governmental Organization, attempted the second for the Association of South East Asian Nations region. The Association of Asian Parliaments for Peace has made a draft Charter but it attracted much criticism as that itself has clothed with the authority to monitor and enforceability.[90] It is not an easy task to formulate a unified regional Charter for Asia due to the vast diversities that exist in the continent and in many countries. However, it is submitted that the

285

argument of cultural, religious, ideological or linguistic diversities cannot be a sound ground for not having a human rights institution for the protection of human rights.

11.6 CONCLUSION

In concluding, it is submitted that there exist different regional systems for the protection of human rights, some of which are effective while some are not. Among the regional systems, European system can be considered as very successful one. It is successful due to the fact that it provides efficient mechanism for the redressal of the grievances and violations through a full-fledged super-national Court system. What is more significant is that individuals whose rights have been violated and is not satisfied by the remedy provided by the national tribunal can directly approach European Court of Human Rights. The decision of the court is binding on all Member States. The successfulness of the system supplements to the fact that it provides an effective monitoring mechanism by the Committee of Ministers of the Council of Europe to see that the decision of the Court has been implemented by the Member State. Although the Europe has divergent ideologies and legal systems, yet the Court functions productively. The European Union system and the Charter of Fundamental Rights can be seen as a positive measure for providing further protection and effective remedy within European Union and Community.

The Inter-American regional system is more complex than the European regional system. The Inter-American system is based on the Declaration and the Convention. In this system, the Commission hears cases, makes visits and prepares country reports on the human rights position of Member States. Human rights violations in Europe tend to be individual rather than collective whereas in the American continent there have been repeated and large scale gross violations and hence, the inter-American system focuses collective violations too. Under European system, even an individual can directly approach the European Court of Human Rights to redress his grievance against the State action. However, this is not available in the Inter-American system. There is no enforcement procedure in the American system and decisions are not necessarily accepted as legally bindings, whereas in Europe the Committee of Ministers of Council of Europe guarantees that the decision of the European Court of Human Rights is implemented effectively. This shows that the European system is more acceptable in terms of effectiveness and enforceability.

The African system, though not fully functional, has been trying to follow the footsteps of the Council of Europe system. In the African regional system the only enforceable mechanism available is through African Commission on Human and Peoples' Rights. However, due to diverse political situations that exist among the Member Nations within the Union makes it more complex for the monitoring and remedial mechanisms in this system. Further, the Member Nations are not as transparent and responsible as the Member Nations of Council of Europe. This adversely influences people not to bring cases of violation before the Commission. Even when case is brought and decision is rendered, there is no efficient mechanism for monitoring that the decision is properly implemented or complied with by the Member Nations.

Though the MINSK Convention has been adopted and entered into force for the protection and promotion of human rights particularly for the former Soviet Union Nations which are not part of Council of Europe, it is not fully operational in the first place. Secondly, there is no effective Court mechanism to enforce it. The only mechanism provided is for the establishment of Human Rights Commission. It is submitted that there are possibilities for effectively working of the system in future since there is no other effective system available for them in the region to remedy the human rights violations.

The Arab Charter elaborately provides provisions for the protection of human rights, dignity and freedoms. However, the major problem with it is that it provides human rights and freedoms within the four walls of Islam and *Shari'ah*. It is because of this reason there is wide criticism about the human rights protection under Arab Charter. Though the Arab Charter is not functional, at least it is in existence, while the Asian Charter is not even in existence even after repeated attempts. Thus, scenario of regional countries systems is diverse in its scope, application and level of effectiveness and enforceability in the protection of human rights.

Endnotes

[1] In 1949, the Treaty of London established the Council of Europe based on principles of pluralist democracy, human rights, and the rule of law.

[2] Halstead, Peter, *The Comprehensive Guide to All Facts of Human Rights*, Hodder Arnold, UK, p. 21,(2010).

[3] However, it did not contain some provision that were provided under International Covenant on Civil and Political Rights in relation to right to self-determination or minority group rights.

[4] Art. 2.

[5] Art. 5.

[6] *Ibid.*

[7] Art. 3.

[8] Art. 15.

[9] The original structure of mechanism for handling cases provided for a two-tier system of rights protection, which included the European Commission of Human Rights which was constituted in 1954 and the European Court of Human Rights which was constituted in 1959. The dichotomy between the two institutions initially worked well since the Court dealt with a relatively small caseload. However, the caseload facing the court grew from 16 cases between 1960 and 1975 to 119 cases in 1997 alone (*See* Steven Greer, *European Convention on Human Rights: Achievements, problems and prospects*, Cambridge University Press, (2006), pp. 17-18). On 1 November 1998, Protocol 11 of the European Convention on Human Rights came into force, eliminating the Commission of Human Rights and restructuring a new European Court of Human Rights and replacing the former system. Although the European Commission on Human Rights became obsolete, it held an important role in assisting the

European Court of Human Rights from 1954 to 1998. Their role was to consider if a petition was admissible to the Court. If so, the Commission would examine the petition to determine the facts of the case and look for parties that could help settle the case in a friendly manner. If a friendly settlement could not take place, the Commission would issue a report on the established facts with an opinion on whether or not a violation had occurred to the Court. Thus the Commission acted independently and at the same time supported the Court before it has been abolished. After 1998, there exists only the European Court of Human Rights in settling the disputes that arise from within member States.

[10]The European Court of Human Rights stands as a Super national Court among the Member Countries of the Council of Europe, some of which follow adversarial system such as England, Ireland and Scotland while some others follow inquisitorial system such as German, France, Italy, Belgium, Italy and so on. The European Court of Human Rights was not very active until 1980s due to the fact that the court existed in between the two known block of countries with ideologies of communism and capitalism and two known procedural systems *viz.*, adversarial and inquisitorial. After the disintegration of Soviet Russia many eastern and central European Countries joined (Hungary joined Council of Europe in 1990, Poland in 1991, Bulgaria in 1992; and Estonia, Lithuania, Slovenia, the Czech Republic, Slovakia, and Romania all joined in 1993. Latvia, Albania, Moldova, Ukraine, and the Former Yugoslav Republic of Macedonia became members in 1995, while Russia and Croatia joined the following year. The newest members of the Council of Europe are Georgia (1999), Armenia and Azerbaijan (2001), Bosnia and Herzegovina (2002), and Serbia and Montenegro (2003) the Council of Europe. The number of cases of human rights violations that were brought before the Court increased suddenly. During and after 90s the European Court of Human Rights became active and gave authoritative judgments that have far reaching effects in the protection and promotion of Human rights.

[11]European Convention on Human Rights, Art. 26.

[12]The Court normally sits as a Chamber of nine judges, including one from the country in question, but in rare instances can seat a Grand Chamber consisting of 21 judges.

[13] Expanded from seven originally by Protocol 11.

[14] Expanded from seventeen originally by Protocol 11.

[15]Article 28 of the European Convention on Human Rights.

[16]European Convention on Human Rights, Art. 50.

[17] The Committee of Ministers is the main decision-making body of the COE. It is composed of the Foreign Affairs Ministers of all member States.

[18] See *Supra n.*16.

[19] *Ibid*

[20]The European Convention for the Prevention of Torture was adopted in 1987 and came into force in 1989; hereinafter referred as "European Convention against Torture".

[21] See Art. 1, ECPT.

[22] See Art. 18, ECPT.

[23] See Art. 4, ECPT.

[24] *Supra n.*15.

[25] *See* Art. 4, ECPT.

[26] *See* Art. 8 (1), ECPT.

[27] *See* Art. 8 (2), ECPT.

[28] *See* Art. 8 (3) &(4), ECPT.

[29] *See* Art. 8 (5), ECPT.

[30] *See* Art. 10, ECPT.

[31] *Ibid.*

[32] *See* Art. 11, ECPT.

[33] *See* Art. 12, ECPT.

[34] *See* Charter of Fundamental Rights of the European Union, 2000.

[35] *See* Art. 2.

[36] *See* Art. 4.

[37] *See* Art. 6.

[38] The Organization of American States originated in the International Union of American Republics in 1890, but was established in its modern form at the 1948 Bogota conference. The 1948 charter entered into force in 1951, and was subsequently amended by the protocols of Buenos Aries 1967, Cartagena de India 1985, Washington 1992, and Managua 1993 (*See* Charter of the Organization of American States). It has a number of objectives, including; strengthening peace and security on the continent; promoting democracy; providing for common action against aggression; and seeking solution to political, juridical and economic problems (*See* Preamble of the Charter of the Organization of American States). It operates through general assembly annual meetings, consultation between foreign ministers,and has a General secretariat and permanent council[38] located in Washington DC.

[39] *Supra n.* 2.

[40] Lúcio Martins Rodrigues, *Sixty years after the Universal Declaration: navigating the contradictions*, International Journal on Human Rights,Cidade University, Brazil, p. 7, (2008).

[41] *See* Art. 4.

[42] *See* Art. 7.

[43] *See* Art. 5.

[44] *See* Art. 25.

[45] *See* Art. 35.

[46] *See* Art. 41.

[47] *See* Art. 57.

[48] *See* Art. 63(1).

[49] *See* Art. V.

[50] *See* Art. VII.

[51] *See* Art. X.

[52] *See* Art. XI.

[53] *See* Art. XI.

[54] The African Charter was adopted in 1981 by the 18th Assembly of Heads of State and Government of the OAU, the official body of African states. It is also known as the Banjul Charter because a final draft of it was produced in Banjul, the capital of the Gambia

[55] By the Charter of the Organization of African Unity since its adoption in 1963

[56] Sicurelli, Daniella. *"The European Union as a Model for the African Union - Effectiveness and Limits of European Norm Promotion"*, Paper presented at the annual meeting of the International Studies Association's 50th Annual Convention *"Exploring the Past, Anticipating the Future"*, New York, (Feb 15-18, 2000), p.5

[57] African Charter on Human and Peoples' Rights, Art. 30.

[58] *Id.*, Art.31

[59] African Court of Justice is the Court for African Union for all matters; *See* Gina Bekker, *Recent Developments in the African Human Rights System 2008-2009*, Human Rights Law Review, 9 (4), (2009), pp. 674.

[60] By the time the Constitutive Act of the African Union was adopted in 2000, the African Court on Human and Peoples' Rights was already legally established through the Protocol to the African Charter on Human and People's Rights which was adopted in 1998. The Constitutive Act created the Court of Justice of the African Union as one of the African Union organs. In July 2006, the African Union Assembly decided that the Court of Justice of the African Union and the African Court on Human and Peoples' Rights should be merged to form the African Court of Justice and Human Rights. By then, the Protocol of the African Charter on Human and People's Rights had entered into force in January 2004 and judges of the Court had been elected by the Assembly in January 2006. The Human Rights Court became operational on the understanding that, once the Protocol on the Statute of the African Charter on Human and People's Rights enters into force, the merged Court will commence full operations. However, the current situation in African regional settings is that although the African Court on Human and Peoples' Rights is established, it is not operational; *See* Gina Bekker, *Recent Developments in the African Human Rights System 2008-2009*, Human Rights Law Review, 9 (4), (2009), pp. 674.

[61] George MukundiWachira ,*African Court on Human and Peoples' Rights: Ten years on and still no justice (2008)*, p.2.

[62] Art. 31.

[63] Art. 45.

[64] Art. 47.

[65] Art. 48.

[66] Art. 51.

[67] Art. 52.

[68] Art. 53.

[69] Art. 55(1).

[70] *See* Commonwealth of Independent States Convention on Human Rights and Fundamental Freedoms; originally signed by Armenia, Belarus, Georgia, Kyrgyzstan, Moldova, Russia and Tajikistan and subsequently ratified by the Russian Federation, Tajikistan and Belarus.

[71] Article 2 of Commonwealth of Independent States Convention on Human Rights and Fundamental Freedoms

[72] Art. 4.

[73] Art. 5.

[74] Art. 5(2).

[75] Art. 5(3).

[76] Art. 5(4).

[77] Art. 5.

[78] Art. 34.

[79] Art. 11, regulations on the Human Rights Commission of commonwealth of Independent States

[80] The *Arab League* was founded on 22 March 1945 by a group of Arab *countries*, namely Egypt, Lebanon, Iraq, Saudi Arabia, Syria, and Yemen. The Arab League currently has 22 members. The main goal of the league is to attain closer the relations among member States and co-ordinate collaboration between them, to safeguard their independence and sovereignty, and to consider in a general way the affairs and interests of the Arab countries.

[81] *See* Art. 2, Cairo Declaration of the Human Rights.

[82] *See* Art. 24, Cairo Declaration of the Human Rights.

[83] M. Rishmawi, ***The Revised Arab Charter on Human Rights: A Step Forward?***,Human Rights Law Review, Vol.(5) (2005), 368.

[84]*Ibid.*

[85]MervatRishmawi, *The Arab Charter on Human Rights and the League of Arab States: An Update,* Human Rights Law Review, Oxford University Press (2010), p.170.

[86] Islamic Personal Law.

[87] The States that ratified the Charter are Algeria, Bahrain, United Arab Emirates, Jordan, Libya, Palestine, and Syria. The Yemen and Qatar ratified recently this Arab Charter. *See* Mohammed Amin Al-Midani,*The Enforcement Mechanisms of the Arab Charter on Human Rights and the Need for an Arab Court of Human Right,* Regional Human Rights Mechanisms, The European Convention and the Arab Charter, International Conference, Bologna (Italy), P.3, December 2-3, 2008.

[88] *Ibid, See Supra n.*82.

[89] Human Rights Features, *The Proposed Asian Human Rights Charter: No Rights at the End of This Tunnel,* 11 November 2000, *available at:*<http://www.hrdc.net/sahrdc/hrfeatures/HRF27.htm> (Visited on March 11, 2011)

[90] *Ibid.*

292

Chapter 12

UNITED NATION'S GUIDELINES ON THE EXERCISE OF POLICE POWERS

The police and law enforcement machinery is the most important weapon in the hands of the State administration to enforce law and order whenever necessary in the day-to-day affairs within a State domain. The constructive mission of the police in the society strengthens the rule of law within the territory. However, the unfettered powers that are entrusted with the police may be abused by the police to the prejudice of the individuals and the community. Any police activity or operation that achieves results through unlawful or inhumane action is a complete negation of the purposes and principles of policing.[1] Since there used to be large number of violations of human rights by police globally, specifically in developing countries, UN and other International Agencies have been attempting to provide a minimum level of standard of human rights protection that has to be guaranteed by police within any Nation. The objective is that the minimum standard must be kept by all police men under any circumstances. The most important areas where there require the police to be entrusted with wide powers are interrogation, arrest without warrant and pre-trial detention. Taking into consideration of such circumstances and situations that is prevalent in different parts of the world the UN has come up with a number of declarations, conventions, covenants, code of conducts, basic principles for providing guidelines to control the exercise of police powers during the course of investigation, interrogation, arrest and pre-trial detention.

12.1. Investigation

During investigation police officials may suspect one or more persons who may have roles in the crime. In order to guide and control police and other law enforcement officials in the exercise of their powers the UN has adopted the Code of Conduct for Law Enforcement Officers in 1979. The resolution in which the Code of Conduct was adopted recognizes the importance and relationship of functions of law enforcement officials and the manner of exercising such functions by them with its direct impact on the quality of life for individuals, as well as for society as a whole.[2] While the General Assembly stressed the important task that the law enforcement officials were performing, it also pointed out the potential abuse of power in the discharge of their duties.[3] Article 2 specifies that law enforcement officials in the performance of their duty shall respect and protect human dignity and maintain and uphold the human rights of all persons.

The connotation of these provisions has broad spectrum for the fair criminal investigation process. Generally, as part of investigation the police require to make searches in order to discover materials that are subject of crime and to seize those materials. The searches, especially of persons, and their homes and other properties including vehicles and interceptions of correspondence, telephone messages or other communications must be strictly legal and necessary for the legitimate law enforcement purpose.[4] The protection of privacy is reinforced by Article 4 of the UN Code of Conduct which provides that matters which are of confidential nature shall be kept confidential by the law enforcement officials. Thus, the police officers are not supposed to conduct searches or seizure arbitrarily. They shall also not disclose the confidential information about a person's private affairs or matters that are injurious to his reputation or honour unless it is so essential for the crime investigation.

12.2. Interrogation

Interrogation by police is one of the areas where there exist continuing controversies of arbitrariness or abuse of powers. In many developing countries, police employs gruesome methods in order to extract facts and information about the crimes without taking into consideration the human dignity and human rights of accused, witnesses or detainees. The Declaration on the Protection of All Persons from Enforced Disappearance[5] provides that no pressure, physical or mental, shall be exerted on suspects, witnesses, or victims in attempting to obtain information.[6] It further provides that the duration of the process of any interrogation, the intervals between the interrogations, the identity of the officials who conducted the interrogations, other persons present, *etc.*, shall be recorded in the prescribed form[7] and a detained person or his counsel shall have access to such information.[8] It is prohibited to take undue advantage of the situation of a detained or imprisoned person for the purpose of compelling him to confess, to incriminate himself otherwise or to testify against any other person.[9] No detained person while being interrogated shall be subject to violence, threats or methods of interrogation which impair his capacity of decision or his judgment.[10] Thus, there are clear stipulations and guidelines that may be followed by the Police during investigation and interrogation under the UN scheme.

12.3. Arrest

Arrest is that quarter which is controversial in the pre-trial stage procedure in almost every country as the arresting process inevitably affects the deprivation of liberty of a person. In developing countries, most frequently, police abuses such powers of arrest thereby violating the human rights of people, and in many countries, police arrests innocent people at the instance of State machineries. It is due to these reasons that the UN has set guidelines, basic principles, standard rules and code of conducts that must be kept by the police in the event of arrest.

The UN adopted the "Body of Principles for the Protection of All Persons under Any Form of Detention or Imprisonment1988"[11] for providing effective safeguards for all persons under arrest or detention and to be treated in a humane manner with respect for the inherent dignity of the human person.[12] It provides that the authorities which arrest a person or investigate the case is required to exercise only those powers that are granted to them under the law and the exercise of these powers shall be subject to recourse to a judicial authority.[13] "The Principles on the Effective Prevention and Investigation of Extra-legal, Arbitrary and Summary Executions" also provides for ensuring strict control over police officials making arrest and detention. The principle reads:

> In order to prevent extra-legal, arbitrary and summary executions, Governments shall ensure strict control, including a clear chain of command over all officials responsible for apprehension, arrest, detention, custody and imprisonment, as well as those officials authorized by law to use force and firearms.[14]

The arrested person shall be informed of the reasons for his arrest at the time of arrest and shall be promptly informed of any charges levelled against him.[15] It casts a duty to duly record: (a) the reasons for the arrest; (b) the time of the arrest, the taking of the arrested person to a place of custody and his first appearance before a judicial or other authority; (c) the identity of the arresting official/s concerned; and (d) a precise information concerning the place of custody.[16] Such records shall be communicated to the detained person, or his counsel, if any, in the form prescribed by law.[17] It is also the duty of the arresting official to provide with the information on and an explanation of his rights and how he can avail himself of such rights at the time of his arrest.[18] Promptly after the arrest, the arrested person shall be entitled to notify or to require the competent authority to notify members of his family or other appropriate persons of his choice of his arrest and of the place where he is kept in custody.[19] Where an arrested person does not adequately understand the language used by the authorities responsible for his arrest, the communication and information shall be provided in a language understandable by the arrested or detained person.[20] He shall be entitled to communicate with and consult his legal counsel[21] and shall be provided adequate time and facilities for consultation with his legal counsel.[22] The rights contained herein are similar with Constitutional and legal safeguards provided under the Constitution of India, the Indian Criminal legal Framework and the principles laid down by the Hon'ble Supreme Court of India in *D.K. Basu*'s case. It is interesting to note that even 10 years before the Supreme Court has given the guidelines, the UN has laid down these fair procedures of arrest.

12.3.1.   *Use of Force*

The police officials may encounter situations whereby the use of force becomes inevitable and, hence, they are entrusted with such powers to use force. However, the power at some police hands may be abused. The UN Code of Conduct for Law Enforcement Officials, 1979 in Article 3 regulates and controls the use of force. It sets out that the use of force is not to be considered as a general rule rather it implies only an exception. It should be used only when strictly necessary and to the extent required for the performance of their duty.[23] It implies that police officials may be authorized to use force as is reasonably necessary under the circumstances for the prevention of crime or in effecting or assisting the lawful arrest of offenders or suspected offenders.[24] The UN Code of Conduct for Law Enforcement Officials envisions that the National law, in many countries, ordinarily restricts the use of force by the law enforcement officials in accordance with the principle of proportionality and it is to be understood that such national principles of proportionality are to be respected in the interpretation of this provision.[25]

12.3.2.   Use of Firearms

Use of force sometimes requires use of firearms and the UNCode of Conduct for Law Enforcement Officials warns that the use of firearms should be considered only as an extreme measure.[26] Every effort should be made to exclude the use of firearms. The general principle should be not to use fire arms as far as possible. If circumstances are such that suspected offender offers armed resistance or otherwise jeopardizes the lives of others and less extreme measures are not sufficient to restrain or apprehend the suspected offender[27] use of fire arms becomes inevitable and can be used only to the extent of minimum level needed. In every instance in which a firearm is discharged, a report should be made promptly to the competent authorities.[28] Thus, UN Code of Conduct for Law Enforcement Officials provides effective regulation and control in the use of fire arms by making the use only in exceptional circumstances inevitably warranted by the situation. When such fire arms are used, obligation is cast on the officials using the fire arms to report the matter promptly to higher and competent authorities.

In addition to the UN Code of Conduct for Law Enforcement Officials, there is another UN Basic Principles which specifically deal with the use of force and firearms by the law enforcement officials in any National State. The Basic Principles on the Use of Force and Firearms by Law Enforcement Officials, 1990[29] provides that the law enforcement officials in carrying out their duty should apply non-violent means as far as possible before resorting to the use of force and firearms.[30]Principle 5 stipulates the circumstances to use the fire arms wherein it is unavoidable. It provides:

> Whenever the lawful use of force and firearms is unavoidable, law enforcement officials shall:
>
> (a) Exercise restraint in such use and act in proportion to the seriousness of the offence and the legitimate objective to be achieved;
>
> (b) Minimize damage and injury, and respect and preserve human life;
>
> (c) Ensure that assistance and medical aid are rendered to any injured or affected persons at the earliest possible moment;
>
> (d) Ensure that relatives or close friends of the injured or affected person are notified at the earliest possible moment.

Where injury or death is caused due to the use of force and firearms, the official should report the incident promptly to their superiors.[31] The UN Principles on Use of Force & Firearms casts a duty on the Government to ensure that arbitrary or abusive use of force and firearms by law enforcement officials is punished as a criminal offence under their National law.[32] It specifies the exceptional circumstances where the law enforcement officials may use firearms such as to arrest a person presenting a danger and resisting their authority, or to prevent his escape, and only when less extreme means are insufficient to achieve these objectives.[33]

The police may also use fire arms in self-defence or defence of others against the imminent threat of death or serious injury or to prevent the perpetration of a particularly serious crime involving grave threat to life, where there are no other alternatives available to prevent the criminal.[34] The UN Principles on Use of Force and Firearms also provides the procedure to be followed in the event of use firearms such as (a) the police officials must identify themselves as such; (b) they must give a clear warning of their intent to use firearms if the criminals do not surrender; and (c) sufficient time shall be given for the warning to be observed. However, these principles are not needed to be observed when the circumstances are such that it would unduly place the police officials at risk or would create a risk of death or serious harm to other persons, or would be clearly inappropriate or pointless in the circumstances of the incident.[35] Principle 11 provides certain guidelines whenever the rules and regulations are made by National States on the use of firearms. It states:

> Rules and regulations on the use of firearms by law enforcement officials should include guidelines that:
>
> (a) Specify the circumstances under which law enforcement officials are authorized to carry firearms and prescribe the types of firearms and ammunition permitted;
>
> (b) Ensure that firearms are used only in appropriate circumstances and in a manner likely to decrease the risk of unnecessary harm;
>
> (c) Prohibit the use of those firearms and ammunition that cause unwarranted injury or present an unwarranted risk;
>
> (d) Regulate the control, storage and issuing of firearms, including procedures for ensuring that law enforcement officials are accountable for the firearms and ammunition issued to them;
>
> (e) Provide for warnings to be given, if appropriate, when firearms are to be discharged;
>
> (f) Provide for a system of reporting whenever law enforcement officials use firearms in the performance of their duty.

Thus, the UN recognizes significance of the role of police in any society, on the one hand, but on the other hand it provides guidelines to take serious considerations and stringent control over the possible illegal arrests, unlawful use of force and firearms. The UN intends only that the minimum level of human rights and human dignity must be kept by all police in all countries.

12.1.4 Detention/Custody

Detention/Custody of a person is inevitable in many cases for different reasons such as prevention of further crime, to produce before the judicial authority, to collect evidences, *etc.* What the UN envisages in such unavoidable circumstances is to keep the dignity of human beings and non-interference with the recognized fundamental human rights of detainees by the police and other law enforcement officials. The Body of Principles for the Protection of All Persons under Any Form of Detention or Imprisonment, 1988 provides that all persons under any form of detention shall be treated in a humane manner and with respect for the inherent dignity of the human person.[36]Principle 2 of the UN Principles of Detention or Imprisonment provides that the detention shall only be carried out strictly in accordance with the provisions of the law and by competent officials or persons authorized for that purpose.[37] Any form of detention and all measures affecting the human rights of person under any form of detention shall be ordered by, or be subject to the effective control of a judicial authority.[38] The authority which keeps a person under detention is required to exercise only the powers granted to them under the law and the exercise of these powers shall be subject to recourse to a judicial authority.[39] Any detained person should be provided with information on and an explanation of his rights and how he can avail himself of such rights.[40] No person shall be kept in detention without affording an opportunity of being heard by judicial or other authority.[41]

Interviews and communications between a detained person and his legal counsel may be within sight, but not within the hearing of police official.[42] It is prohibited to take undue advantage of the situation of a detained person for compelling him to confess or to incriminate himself otherwise or to testify against any other person.[43] Detainees shall be kept in humane facilities, designed to preserve health, and shall be provided with adequate food, water, shelter, clothing, medical services, exercise and items of personal hygiene.[44] Principle 24 affords for proper medical examination to be offered to a detained person as promptly as possible after his admission to the place of detention, and thereafter whenever necessary, that too free of charge.

The UN Principles on the Use of Force & Firearmsprovides that the Law enforcement officials are not permitted to use firearms against persons in custody or detention except in self-defence or in the defence of others against the immediate threat of death or serious injury, or when strictly necessary to prevent the escape of a person in custody or detention presenting the danger referred to in principle 9. [45] Principle 34 of the UN Principles of Detention or Imprisonment provides that whenever the death or disappearance of a detained or imprisoned person occurs during his detention or imprisonment, an inquiry into the cause of death or disappearance shall be held by a judicial or other authority. This may be initiated either on its own motion or at the instance of a member of the family of such a person or any person who has knowledge of the case.[46] It stretches to the extent of circumstances which warrants that such an inquiry shall be held on the same procedural basis whenever the death or disappearance occurs shortly after the termination of the detention.[47] Principle 34 provides that the findings of such inquiry or a report should be made available upon request, unless doing so would jeopardize an ongoing criminal investigation.Principle 35 of the UN Principles of Detention or Imprisonment further provides that any damage incurred because of acts or omissions by a public official contrary to the rights contained in these principles shall be compensated according to the applicable rules on liability provided by domestic law. Thus, illegal detentions are controlled by making payment of compensation to the victim of illegal detention.

Thus, considering the helplessness of the persons under detention by the organized and mighty police in any country, the UN has made efforts to make guidelines, principles and rules that may be taken into consideration by the National States for controlling the police keeping a person under detention. The significance lies in the fact that a duty is cast on the detaining official to provide facilities for the detained person to consult with his legal counsel, and communicate with his family or friend.

12.1.5.   *Torture*

In many countries, police employ torture or cruel and inhuman treatment against persons under arrest and custody. Many developed countries have absolutely prohibited torture by law. Article 5 of the UN Code of Conduct for Law Enforcement Officials prohibits any kind of torture not only of inflicting but instigating and tolerating it also.[48] It bars invoking superior orders or exceptional circumstances as a justification for torture or such other acts. Commentary to the Article 5 states that the prohibition is derived from the UN Declaration Against Torture. The UN Torture Convention[49] casts an obligation on the State Parties to take effective measures to prevent torture,[50] to criminalize all acts of torture,[51] and to investigate thoroughly the complaint or suspicious circumstances of torture.[52] The UN Torture Declaration and the UN Torture Convention later resulted into the adoption of the UN Principles of Detention or Imprisonment which also prohibits any person under detention to be subjected to torture or to cruel, inhuman or degrading treatment or punishment.[53] Thus, the UN totally bans any form of torture or employing any cruel or inhuman methods by police. Significant fact that must be noted here is that no justification whatever might be cannot be raised by police for employing torture or other cruel or inhuman methods against persons.[54] This has been expressly provided in both the UN Code of Conduct and the UN Principles of Detention or Imprisonment.

303

12.1.6.   *Non-Custodial Measures*

The United Nations Standard Minimum Rules for Non-custodial Measures 1990, shortly

known as "The Tokyo Rules",[55] is adopted, *inter alia*, to promote the use of non-custodial

measures and to provide minimum safeguards for such persons. The Tokyo Rules provides that

the Member States should develop non-custodial measures within their legal systems to provide

other options for detentions, thus reducing the use of detention.[56] It also provides that when

implementing the Rules, Member States should ensure a proper balance between the rights of

individual offenders, the rights of victims, and the concern of society for public safety and crime

prevention.[57] The selection of a non-custodial measure should be based on an assessment of

established criteria after due consideration of the nature and gravity of the offence, the

personality and background of the offender, the purposes of sentencing and the rights of

victims.[58] Decisions on the imposition of non-custodial measures should also be subject to

review by a judicial or other competent independent authority, upon application by the

offender.[59] The offender should be entitled to make a request or complaint to a judicial or other

competent independent authority on matters affecting his individual rights in the implementation

of non-custodial measures.[60] The dignity of the offender subject to non-custodial measures

should also be protected at all times.

12.1.6.1.   Pretrial Disposing of Offenders

Pre-trial disposing of the offenders is one of the effective non-custodial measures. Rule 5

of the Tokyo Rules provides regarding the pre-trial dispositions of offenders. It provides, *inter*

alia, that where appropriate and compatible with the legal system the police should be empowered to discharge the offender if they consider that it is not necessary to proceed with the case.[61] For the purpose of deciding upon the appropriateness of discharge the Standard Minimum Rules requires the Member States to develop a set of established criteria within each legal system.[62] Rule 6 provides that the pre trial detention shall be used as a last resort with due regard to investigation of the alleged offence and for the protection of society and the victim.[63] Rule 6 provides:

> 1). Pre-trial detention shall be used as a means of last resort in criminal proceedings, with due regard for the investigation of the alleged offence and for the protection of society and the victim.
>
> 2). Alternatives to pre-trial detention shall be employed at as early a stage as possible. Pre-trial detention shall last no longer than necessary to achieve the objectives stated under rule 5.1 and shall be administered humanely and with respect for the inherent dignity of human beings.
>
> 3).The offender shall have the right to appeal to a judicial or other competent independent authority in cases where pre-trial detention is employed.

Thus, if alternatives to detention are possible that method should be resorted to first rather than arrest and detention. The person under custody shall have the right to judicial recourse about the justifiability of pre-trial detention.

12.1.7.   *Women and Special Procedures*

Women as vulnerable category in any society require special attention, status and protection. Realizing the situation, the UN has made various principles, declarations and conventions which deal with women such as Declaration on Elimination of All forms of Discrimination Against Women, Convention on Elimination of All forms of Discrimination Against Women, *etc.*, as guidelines to be adopted by any National States. These instruments, *inter alia*, provides guidelines for the police in dealing with women. Arrested or detained women should not be discriminated, and should be protected from all forms of violence or exploitation.[64] Women detainees must be supervised and searched by female officers and staff only.[65] Women should be detained separately from male detainees.[66] Pregnant women and nursing mothers should be provided with special facilities in detention.[67] Thus, it is submitted that the international instruments set for women primarily focuses the non-discrimination of women by police officials; secondly, special status of women must be kept by all police at all times; and thirdly, as vulnerable members of the society special protection and support shall be provided to them always.

12.1.8. *Juvenile Offenders and Special Procedures*

Juvenile offenders require special kind of treatment and procedure due to their vulnerable character, lower mental strength and easily susceptible nature to undesirable situations. The 1959 UN Declaration on the Rights of the Child declares that "humankind owes the child the best it has to give"[68] and sets out ten principles which provided a framework for children's rights. The Convention on the Rights of the Child 1989, defines a child as a person who has not attained the age of 18 years.[69] Article 3 of the Convention on the Rights of the Child provides that in all actions concerning children, "the best interests of the child" shall be the primary consideration. Article 37 casts obligation on the State Parties to ensure on juvenile offenders that torture is not employed nor arbitrarily or unlawfully deprived of his liberty.[70]Every child deprived of liberty should be treated with humanity and respect for the inherent dignity of the human person, and in a manner which takes into account the needs of persons of his or her age.It should be noted that all the procedural safeguards that are available to adults shall equally be applicable in the case of juvenile persons such as presumption of innocence,[71] right to be informed promptly about the charge with which is indicted,[72] right to have the matter determined without delay by a competent judicial authority,[73] *etc.* The Convention on the Rights of the Child is enforceable and works only as a guideline within the Member Nations. The UN Rules for the Protection of Juveniles Deprived of Their Liberty[74] provides that it is only when there is absolute necessity that child's liberty is deprived of and put in institution.

The United Nations Standard Minimum Rules for the Administration of Juvenile Justice1985,[75] popularly known as "The Beijing Rules" elaborately deals with minimum requirement that has to be complied with under all circumstances in the event of dealing with juvenile offenders. It defines 'juvenile offender' as a child or young person who is alleged to have committed or who has been found to have committed an offence.[76]

In the case of arrest or apprehension of a juvenile, the parents or guardian shall be immediately notified of such apprehension, and, where such immediate notification is not possible, the parents or guardian shall be notified within the shortest possible time thereafter.[77] A judge or other competent official should consider the issue of release without delay.[78] The police, dealing with juvenile cases should be empowered to dispose of such cases, at their discretion, without recourse to formal hearings. In order to best fulfill their functions, police officers who frequently or exclusively deal with juveniles or who are primarily engaged in the prevention of juvenile crime should be specially instructed and trained.[79] The UN Guidelines for the Prevention of Juvenile Delinquency, 1990[80] shortly known as "the Riyadh Guidelines", also stresses the aspect of providing training for the law enforcement officials dealing with juvenile delinquents. It provides that the Law enforcement and other relevant personnel, of both sexes, should be trained to be familiar with and use programmes and referral possibilities for the diversion of young persons from the justice system.[81]

If a detained or imprisoned person is a juvenile or is incapable of understanding his entitlement, the competent authority should, on its own initiative, undertake the notification referred to in this principle. Juveniles under pre-trial detention shall be entitled to all rights and guarantees of the UN Standard Minimum Rules for Prisoners adopted by the United Nations.[82] Thus, The UN provides a number of guidelines in the case of protection of juveniles from arrest, detention and interrogation.

12.1.9.   *Victims of Crime and Abuse of Power*

The protection of victims of crime due to abuse of power had been a critical area for the UN and on 29th November, 1985 the UN has adopted the Declaration of Basic Principles of Justice for Victims of Crime and Abuse of Power.[83] The Declaration defines 'victims' of abuse of power as persons who, individually or collectively, have suffered harm, including physical or mental injury, emotional suffering, economic loss or substantial impairment of their fundamental rights, through acts or omissions that do not yet constitute violations of national criminal laws but of internationally recognized norms relating to human rights.[84] Principle 19 persuades the States to incorporate into the national legal systems norms forbidding abuse of power and prescribing remedies to victims of such abuses. In particular, the remedies should include restitution and/or compensation, and necessary material, medical, psychological and social assistance and support.[85] It further provides that States should periodically review existing legislation and practices to ensure their responsiveness to changing circumstances, should enact and enforce, if necessary, legislation proscribing acts that constitute serious abuses of political or economic power, as well as promoting policies and mechanisms for the prevention of such acts, and should develop and make readily available appropriate rights and remedies for victims of such acts.[86] It provides that victims and witnesses are to be treated with compassion and

308

consideration.[87] No person shall be compelled to confess or to testify against themselves.[88] Investigatory activities shall be conducted only lawfully and with due cause.[89] Commentary (b) to Article 6 of the UN Code of Conduct for Law Enforcement Officers also provides that the law enforcement officials shall also secure medical attention for victims of violations of law or of accidents occurring in the course of violations of law. Thus, the UN makes guideline, stipulations and remedies that are essential for the victims of crime and abuse of power.

12.1.10.   Complaints, Reporting and Reviewing Procedures

The police enjoy immense powers in any State jurisdiction and they tend to abuse those powers. The mechanism for complaint, reporting or review procedure is predominantly warranted in the cases of police actions against people. The system can work well only when there is effective complaint procedure or efficient reporting and reviewing course of action on the police actions. The UN Principles of Detention or Imprisonment provides that in order to supervise the strict observance of relevant laws and regulations, places of detention shall be visited regularly by qualified and experienced persons appointed by, and responsible to, a competent authority distinct from the authority directly in charge of the administration of the place of detention.[90] A detained person shall have the right to communicate freely and in full confidentiality with the persons who visit the places of detention subject to reasonable conditions to ensure security and good order in such places.[91]

Principle 32 of the UN Body of Principles for the Protection of Persons provides that a detained person or his counsel should be entitled to take proceedings at any time according to domestic law before a judicial authority to challenge the lawfulness of his detention. The proceedings shall be simple and expeditious and at no cost for detained persons having inadequate means.[92] The detaining authority shall produce without unreasonable delay the detained person before the reviewing authority.[93] Principle 33 provides that a detained person or his counsel shall have the right to make a request or complaint regarding his treatment, in particular, in case of torture or other cruel, inhuman or degrading treatment, to the authorities responsible for the administration of the place of detention and to higher authorities and, when necessary, to appropriate authorities vested with reviewing or remedial powers. The article further provides in cases where neither the detained person nor his counsel has opportunity to exercise his rights, a member of the family of the detained person or any other person who has knowledge of the case may exercise such rights.[94] Confidentiality of the request or complaint shall be maintained if so requested by the complainant.[95] Every request or complaint shall be promptly dealt with and replied to without undue delay. If the request or complaint is rejected or in case of inordinate delay the complainant shall be entitled to bring it before a judicial or other authority.[96] Principle 33 (4) further guarantees that neither the detained person nor any person on his behalf complaining shall suffer prejudice for making a request or complain.

12.1.10.1. Review and Reporting in the Use of Firearms

The UN Principles on Force & Firearms also provides provisions for effective reporting and review procedures. It provides that the Governments and law enforcement agencies shall establish effective reporting and review procedures for all incidents where injury or death is caused by the use of force and firearms.[97] It further provides that rules and regulations for the use of fire arms made by officials should contain a guideline for a system of reporting to superior officials. [98] For incidents reported pursuant to these principles, Governments and law enforcement agencies shall ensure that an effective review process is available and that independent administrative or prosecutorial authorities are in a position to exercise jurisdiction in appropriate circumstances.[99] In cases of death and serious injury or other grave consequences, a detailed report shall be sent promptly to the competent authorities responsible for administrative review and judicial control.[100] Persons affected by the use of force and firearms or their legal representatives shall have access to an independent process, including a judicial process.[101] In the event of the death of such persons, their dependants can invoke this provision accordingly.[102] Governments and law enforcement agencies shall ensure that superior officers are held responsible if they know, or should have known, that law enforcement officials under their command are resorting, or have resorted, to the unlawful use of force and firearms, and they did not take all measures in their power to prevent, suppress or report such use.[103]

Article 25 provides a guarantee to the official who, in compliance with the UN Code of Conduct and the provisions of the UN Principles on Force & Firearms, refuse to carry out an order to use force and firearms, or who report such use by other officials and casts a duty on Governments and law enforcement agencies to ensure that no criminal or disciplinary sanction is imposed on such law enforcement officials. It further makes clear that defense of obedience to superior orders should not be a defense if law enforcement officials knew that an order to use force and firearms resulting in the death or serious injury of a person was manifestly unlawful and had a reasonable opportunity to refuse to follow it. In any case, responsibility also rests on the superiors who gave the unlawful orders.[104] Thus, the UN Principles on Force & Firearms provides an effective review and reporting mechanism in the use of fire arms by law enforcement officials. It also provides that these basic principles should be adopted by Government of States to ensure that use of force and firearms are regulated properly within their jurisdiction.

311

12.1.10.2. Acts Contrary to UN Principles of Detention

The UN Principles of Detention or Imprisonment provides three important measures in the event of occurrence of any act contrary to these principles. (i) It provides that States should prohibit by law any act contrary to the rights and duties contained in these principles, make any such act subject to appropriate sanctions and conduct impartial investigations upon complaints; (ii) Officials who have reason to believe that a violation of this Body of Principles has occurred or is about to occur shall report the matter to their superior authorities and, where necessary, to other appropriate authorities or organs vested with reviewing or remedial powers; (iii) Any other person who has ground to believe that a violation of this Body of Principles has occurred or is about to occur shall have the right to report the matter to the superiors of the officials involved as well as to other appropriate authorities or organs vested with reviewing or remedial powers.[105]

12.1.10.3.   Acts Contrary to UN Code of Conduct for Law Enforcement Officials

The UN Code of Conduct also provides that Law enforcement officials who have reason to believe that a violation of the provisions of the UN Code of Conduct has occurred or is about to occur shall report the matter to their superior authorities and, where necessary, to other appropriate authorities or organs vested with reviewing or remedial power.[106] Law enforcement officials shall report violations within the chain of command and take other lawful action outside the chain of command only when no other remedies are available or effective.[107] It also guarantees that the law enforcement officials shall not suffer administrative or other penalties because they have reported that a violation of the Code has occurred or is about to occur.[108]

reviewing or remedial power" refers to any authority or organ existing under national law, whether internal to the law enforcement agency or independent thereof, with statutory, customary or other power to review grievances and complaints arising out of violations within the purview of this Code. In some countries, the mass media may be regarded as performing complaint review functions similar to those described in commentary (c).[109] Law enforcement officials may be justified if, as a last resort, bring violations to the attention of public opinion through the mass media.[110] It is to be noted that the UN, considering the role of mass media, gives standing for the reporting of police violation by them. Thus, the UN has provided reporting by the police officers about violation of human rights committed by other police officers. But if his reporting is not fruitful he may be justified in bringing the matter to the notice of the media.

12.2.   Conclusion

As James Madison said in Federalist Papers "If men were angels, no government would be necessary. If angels were to govern men, neither external nor internal controls on government would be necessary."[111] But we are not angels. This may be absolutely true with the police. The UN, therefore, puts the efforts to provide guidelines to keep minimum standards to the law enforcement officials in dealing with investigation, interrogation, arrest and detention of people. The Standard Minimum Rules for Non-custodial Measures sets out a number of rules that the National State may make use of in order to avoid the pre-trial detention. It provides that the pre-trial detention may be used as a last resort. The UN Code of Conduct for Law Enforcement Officers sets out a number of conduct rules that the National States must adopt into their legal system. It also prohibits any kind of torture by law enforcement agencies not only of inflicting but instigating and tolerating it also. The UN Principles of Detention or Imprisonment further provides a number of principles that National State may make rules in the cases of detention and imprisonment. It provides that if any damage incurred because of acts or omissions by a public official contrary to the rights contained in these principles must be compensated according to the applicable rules on liability provided by domestic law.

The Basic Principles on the Use of Force and Firearms by Law Enforcement Officials sets out guidelines for the use of firearms against persons. However, police officials are not permitted to use fire arms against a person in custody or detention except in self-defense or in the defense of others against the immediate threat of death or serious injury. The Declaration on the Protection of All Persons from Enforced Disappearance provides that National States must ensure that no pressure, physical or mental, is exerted on suspects, witnesses, or victims in attempting to obtain information. It further provides that the duration of interrogation, the intervals between the interrogations, the identity of the officials who conducted the interrogations, other persons present, *etc.*, should be recorded in the prescribed form. The United Nations Standard Minimum Rules for the Administration of Juvenile Justice, 1985 directs a number of safeguards and special treatments to be taken by the National States in the cases of arrest and detention of juveniles. Similarly, UN Standard Minimum Rules for Prisoners provides a number of safeguards for women in custody also.Thus, the UN has made elaborate guidelines in order to control the exercise of police powers and avoid abuse of such powers within any National State.However, the point is not that there are the UN Body of Principle or the UN Standard Minimum Rules or Code of Conduct, but the point is to what extent the National States are incorporating into their legal systems and how effectively they are implemented. This determines the success of these of rules and principles.

Endnotes

[1] *Ihsan and M. BedriEryilmaz, Police Professional Ethics (2002), p.4; See also* RalphCrawshaw, *Human Rights and Policing,* The Journal of Turkish Weekly (2005).

[2] United Nations Criminal Justice Information Network, *Use and Application of the Code of Conduct for Law Enforcement Officials, Including the Basic Principles on the Use of Force and Firearms,* Crime Prevention and Criminal Justice Division, United Nations Office at Vienna(1999), p.6.

[3] *Ibid.*

[4] High Commissioner for Human Rights, *Human Rights and Law Enforcement:Manual on Human Rights Training for the Police,* Professional Training Series No.5 (1995), P.62 .

[5] Hereinafter "the UN Declaration on the Enforced Disappearance".

[6] Declaration on the Enforced Disappearance, Art. 13 (3);*See* for similar protection principle 15of thePrinciples on the Effective Prevention and Investigation of Extralegal, Arbitrary and Summary Executions [hereinafter "the UN Principles on Summary Executions"]; Art. 2 of the UN Code of Conduct on the basic duties of law enforcement officials with regard to all persons (including victims, witnesses and suspects) whether conducting investigations or otherwise; Art. 13 of the Convention against Torture and Other Cruel, Inhuman or Degrading Treatment or Punishment [hereinafter "the UN Torture Convention"] includes a special provision that in cases of allegation of torture witnesses be protected against ill-treatment or intimidation. For more specific information regarding the rights of victims to appropriate treatment and sensitivity, *see* Principles 4, 5 and 6(d) of the Declaration of Basic Principles of Justice for Victims of Crime and Abuse of Power [hereinafter "the UN Declaration for Victims"]; on the rights of suspects and other detained persons during investigation and interrogation, *see* Principles 1, 17, 18, 21, 23 and 36 of the Principles of Detention or Imprisonment. *See cited* United Nations High Commissioner or Human Rights, *International Human Rights Standard for Law Enforcement: A pocket Book on the Human Rights for the police*(1997), p.18.

[7] Body of Principles for the Protection of All Persons under Any Form of Detention or Imprisonment, Principle 23(1); hereinafter referred also as "the UN Principles of Detention or Imprisonment".

[8] *Id.,* Principle 23(2).

[9] *Id.,* Principle 21 (1).

[10] *Id.,* Principle 21 (2).

[11] The United Nations General Assembly in its 76th plenary meeting adopted by Resolution No: A/RES/43/173 on 9 December 1988.

[12] The UN Principles of Detention or Imprisonment, Principle 1.

[13] *Id.,* Principle 9.

[14] The Principles on the Effective Prevention and Investigation of Extra-legal, Arbitrary and Summary Executions 1989, Principle 2.

[15] The UN Principles of Detention or Imprisonment, Principle 10.

[16] *Id.*, Principle 12 (1).

[17] *Id.*, Principle 12 (2).

[18] *Id.*, Principle 13.

[19] *Id.*, Principle 16.

[20] *Id.*, Principle 14.

[21] *Id.*, Principle 18 (1).

[22] *Id.*, Principle 18 (2); however Principle 18 (3)provides that the right of such persons to be visited by and to consult and communicate, without delay or censorship and in full confidentiality, with his legal counsel may not be suspended or restricted except in exceptional circumstances to be specified by law when it is considered indispensable by a judicial or other authority in order to maintain security and good order.

[23] The UN Code of Conduct, Art. 3.

[24] The UN Code of Conduct for Law Enforcement Officials, commentary (a), Art. 3.

[25] *Id.*,commentary (b), Art. 3.

[26] *Id.*,commentary (c), Art. 3.

[27] *Ibid.*

[28] *Ibid.*

[29] Hereinafter called as "the UN Principles on Force & Firearms" was adopted by the Eighth United Nations Congress on the Prevention of Crime and the Treatment of Offenders, in Havana in September 1990 and accepted by the General Assembly in its resolution 45/166 of 18 December 1990, were formulated in order to provide effective regulation on the use of force and firearms by law enforcement officials.[29]

[30] The UN Principles on Force & Firearms,Principle 4.

[31] *Id.*,Principle 6.

[32] *Id.*,Principle 7.

[33] *Id.*, Principle 9.

[34] *Ibid.*

[35] *Id.*, Principle 10.

[36] The UN Principles of Detention or Imprisonment, Principle 1.

[37] *Id.*, Principle 2.

[38] *Id.*, Principle 4.

[39] *Id.*, Principle 9 .

[40]*Id.,* Principle 13.

[41]*Id.,* Principle 11.

[42]*Id.,* Principle 18 (4).

[43]*Id.,* Principle 21 (1).

[44]International Covenant On Civil and Political Rights, Art. 10(1); The UN Principles of Detention or Imprisonment, Principles 1, 22, 24, 25, and 26; Standard Minimum Rule for the Treatment of Prisoners, Rules 9-14, 15-16, 17-19, 20, 21, 22-26, 66, 82-83, 86-88, and 91; Article 6 of the UN Code of Conduct casts a duty on the Law enforcement officials to ensure the full protection of the health of persons in their custody and, in particular, to take immediate action to secure medical attention[44] whenever required. Commentary (b) to the article provides that law enforcement officials must take into account the judgment of medical personnel when they recommend providing the person in custody with appropriate treatment.

[45]The UN Principles on the use of Force & Firearms, Principle 16; Principle 17 states that Principle 15 and 16 are without prejudice to the rights, duties and responsibilities of prison officials, as set out in the UN SMR for Prisoners, particularly rules 33, 34 and 54.

[46]*Id.,* Principle 34.

[47]*Ibid.*

[48]The Art.5 of the UN Code of Conduct for Law Enforcement Officials provides "No law enforcement official may inflict, instigate or tolerate any act of torture or other cruel, inhuman or degrading treatment or punishment, nor may any law enforcement official invoke superior orders or exceptional circumstances such as a state of war or a threat of war, a threat to national security, internal political instability or any other public emergency as a justification of torture or other cruel, inhuman or degrading treatment or punishment".

[49] *The UN Convention against Torture*

[50]The UN Torture Declaration, Art.4 ;the UN Torture Convention, Art. 2.

[51]*Id.,* Art. 7; the UN Torture Convention, Art. 4.

[52]*Id.,* Art. 9; the UN Torture Convention, Art. 13.

[53]The Principle 6 appendix provides that the term "cruel, inhuman or degrading treatment or punishment "should be interpreted so as to extend the widest possible protection against abuses, whether physical or mental, including the holding of a detained or imprisoned person in conditions which deprive him, temporarily or permanently, of the use of any of his natural senses, such as sight or hearing or of his awareness of place and the passing of time.

[54]The UN Principles of Detention or Imprisonment, Principle 6.

[55]The United Nations Standard Minimum Rules for Non-custodial Measures [hereinafter "the Tokyo Rules"], G.A. Res. 45/110 of 14 December 1990.

[56]The Tokyo Rules, Rule 1.5.

[57]*Id.,* Rule 1.4.

[58]*Id.,* Rule 3.2.

[59]*Id.,* Rule 3.5.

[60]*Id.,* Rule 3.6.

[61]*Id.,* Rule 5.1.

[62]*Ibid.*

[63]*Id.,* Rule 6.1.

[64]Universal Declaration of Human Rights (UDHR), Art. 2; International Covenant on Civil and Political Rights (International Covenant on Civil and Political Rights), articles 2 and 3; Code of Conduct, articles 1 and 2; Convention for Elimination of all forms of Discrimination Against Women (CEDAW), Art.15; Declaration on Discrimination against Women, articles 1 and 6; Principles on Detention or Imprisonment, Principle 5.

[65]The UN Standard Minimum Rules for Prisoners, Rule 53.

[66]*Ibid.*

[67]*Id.,* Rule 23.

[68]The UN Declaration on the Rights of Child, Preamble, paragraph 5.

[69]Convention on the Rights of Child, Art.1.

[70]Art.37 of the Convention on the Rights of the Child provides "The States Parties shall ensure that (a) No child shall be subjected to torture or other cruel, inhuman or degrading treatment or punishment. Neither capital punishment nor life imprisonment without possibility of release shall be imposed for offences committed by persons below eighteen years of age;(b) No child shall be deprived of his or her liberty unlawfully or arbitrarily. The arrest, detention or imprisonment of a child shall be in conformity with the law and shall be used only as a measure of last resort and for the shortest appropriate period of time;(c) Every child deprived of liberty shall be treated with humanity and respect for the inherent dignity of the human person, and in a manner which takes into account the needs of persons of his or her age. In particular, every child deprived of liberty shall be separated from adults unless it is considered in the child's best interest not to do so and shall have the right to maintain contact with his or her family through correspondence and visits, save in exceptional circumstances;(d) Every child deprived of his or her liberty shall have the right to prompt access to legal and other appropriate assistance, as well as the right to challenge the legality of the deprivation of his or her liberty before a court or other competent, independent and impartial authority, and to a prompt decision on any such action.

[71]Convention on the Rights of Child, Art.40 2(b) (i).

[72]*Id.,* Art.40 2(b) (ii).

[73]*Id.,* Art. 40 2(b) (iii).

[74]Adopted by the General Assembly resolution 45/113 of 14 December 1990

[75]Adopted by General Assembly by Resolution 40/33 of 29 November 1985;Adopted by General Assembly by Resolution 40/33 of 29 November 1985; The Beijing Rules are deliberately formulated so

as to be applicable within different legal systems and, at the same time, to set some minimum standards for the handling of juvenile offenders under any definition of a juvenile and under any system of dealing with juvenile offenders.

[76]However, Beijing Rules does not specifically say who is a child. Different legal systems follow different age limit to determine the criminal responsibility and hence, the Beijing Rules leaves it to the national legal system to determine the same:; the age limit of 12 years for Canada, Greece, Netherlands; 13 years—France, Israel, New Zealand (except for murder/ manslaughter where the age limit of 10 applies); 14 years—Austria, Germany, Italy and many Eastern European countries; 15 years—Denmark, Finland, Iceland, Norway, Sweden; 16 years—Japan, Portugal, Spain; 18 years—Belgium, Luxembourg and 7 years- India, Myanmar, Pakistan, Nigeria, South Africa;

[77]The Beijing Rules, Rule 10.1.

[78]*Id.*,Rule 10.2.

[79]Commentary Rule 12 draws attention to the need for specialized training for all law enforcement officials who are involved in the administration of juvenile justice. As police are the first point of contact with the juvenile justice system, it is most important that they act in an informed and appropriate manner. While the relationship between urbanization and crime is clearly complex, an increase in juvenile crime has been associated with the growth of large cities, particularly with rapid and unplanned growth. Specialized police units would therefore be indispensable, not only in the interest of implementing specific principles contained in the present instrument (such as rule 1.6) but more generally for improving the prevention and control of juvenile crime and the handling of juvenile offenders.

[80]Adopted and proclaimed by General Assembly resolution 45/112 of 14 December 1990.

[81]The United Nations Guidelines for the Prevention of Juvenile Delinquency (The Riyadh Guidelines), Guideline 58.

[82]The UN Standard Minimum Rules for Prisoners, Rule 13.3.

[83]Hereinafter "the UN Declaration for Victims of Crime".

[84]The UN Victims Declaration, Principle 18.

[85]*Id.*, Principle 19.

[86]*Id.*, Principle 21.

[87]*Id.*, Principle 4.

[88]Universal Declaration of Human Rights, Art.11(1); International Covenant on Civil and Political Rights, Art.14(3)(g); The UN Principles of Detention or Imprisonment, Principle 21(1).

[89]Code of Conduct, Art.4; The UN Principles of Detention or Imprisonment, principles 21, 23, 36; UN Principles on Summary Executions, principles 9, 10 and 11.

[90]The UN Principles of Detention or Imprisonment, Principle 29 (1).

[91]*Id.*, Principle 29 (2).

[92]*Id.*, Principle 32 (2).

[93]*Ibid.*

[94]*Id.*, Principle 33 (2).

[95]*Id.*, Principle 33 (3).

[96]*Id.*, Principle 33 (4).

[97]The UN Principles on Force & Firearms, Principle 6.

[98]*Id.*, Principle 11(f).

[99]*Id.*, Principle 22.

[100]*Ibid.*

[101]*Id.*, Principle 23.

[102]*Ibid.*

[103]*Id.*, Principle 24.

[104]*Id.*, Principle 26.

[105]The UN Principles of Detention or Imprisonment, Principle 7.

[106]The UN Code of Conduct, Art. 8.

[107]*Id.*, Commentary (b) to Art. 8.

[108]*Ibid.*

[109]*Id.*, commentary (d) to Art. 8.

[110]*Ibid.*

[111]James Madison, *The Structure of the Government Must Furnish the Proper Checks and Balances between the Different Departments*, The Federalist papers No. 51, Independent Journal, (1978).

Chapter 13

CONCLUSION

The concept of human rights is as old as the coming into existence of human beings on earth. These rights are inherent in every person by virtue of his birth. However, these rights were referred to as natural rights until recently. In the eighteenth and nineteenth centuries in Europe several philosophers such as Thomas Paine, John Stuart Mill and Henry David Thoreau proposed the concept of "natural rights", the rights belonging to a person by nature by virtue of being born as human being. The concept of human rights emerged as a solemn premise after the Second World War due to the barbarous atrocities and massacre committed by Nazi Germany prior to and during the War. Although the expression "human rights" came into general use after the Second World War, yet Henry David Thoreau is considered to first use the expression "human rights" in the previous century. The concept of human rights can be traced from Western Philosophy to Stoic natural law doctrines. The ideas that originated with Zeno of *Citium* and the Stoics teachings that there were pervasive laws of nature and hence, the Man's conduct should be measured in accordance with those laws have roots in the development of the concept of human rights.

The real concept of protection of human rights started emerging from England with the signing of the *Magna Carta* in 1215. The *Magna Carta* provided that the King would follow the legal procedure before His official's arrest, detain or punish a person. The procedural safeguard provided in the *Magna Carta* was further broadened in the Petition of Rights, 1628 which provided protection against arbitrary arrest and detention by affirming that no person may be

321

imprisoned without showing a cause for the arrest and detention. The Virginia Declaration of Rights 1776, though not provided provisions against arbitrary arrest and detention, but asserted that all people have certain inherent rights such as right to life and liberty which they enjoy as human beings and such rights cannot be "compacted, deprived or divested from their posterity". The American Declaration of Independence, 1776 elaborated the rights guaranteed by the Virginia Declaration of Rights and it declared that (i) man possess certain inalienable rights of life, liberty and pursuit of human happiness, and (ii) the purpose of the government is to secure those inalienable rights. Following the American Declaration of Independence, the French Declaration also provides that men are born free, equal with the rights to liberty, property and security; but the French declaration specifically granted freedom from unlawful arrest or imprisonment. Overwhelmed by the genocide and atrocious acts committed by the Nazi Germany during the Second World War when the United Nations' Charter was drafted, it incorporated the spirit of these declarations in its preamble to uphold and protect human rights, human dignity and worth of the human personality.

Torture, unlawful arrest, illegal detention, false implication, *etc.*, are the chief areas of human rights violations committed by the police. Among these, torture is the most aggravated form of violation of human rights committed by the police. It varies from simple beating to causing death in custody. Police in India are generally blamed of employing the methods of torture for different reasons. They employ "third degree methods" to collect evidences from the accused. But the evidence collected by torturing human beings is not justifiable from the human rights point of view, and often violates norms of human rights protection. Some police officers are rough and rude by nature and finds pleasure in torturing his fellow beings who are caught in their net. Pre-set offensive attitudinal behavioural pattern developed through training or years of

322

experience by the police also results into the violations. Some Police officials have the false notion that they can keep their dignity and obtain respect from people only when they horrifythe people by showing rude behavior or undignified attitudes towards accused or witnesses or even to general public. Corruption, political nexus or personal bias in particular cases under investigation may also cause violations of human rights by the police. They also employ torture on individuals who stand against the police officer's abuse of power. The extreme form of torture in custody is causing death of a person by the police. Asian Centre for Human Rights in its report "Torture in India 2009" states that from April 2001 to March 2009 *i.e.*, during the past 8 years, an estimated 1,184 persons were killed in police custody in India. Most of the victims were killed as a result of torture within the first 48 hours of being taken into custody. This depicts the picture of violation of human rights by the police taking place in the country.

At international level, there were many attempts to protect the human rights. The major documents that deal with protection of persons from the violation of human rights by the police are the Universal Declaration of Human Rights, the International Covenant on Civil and Political Rights and Convention Against Torture. These documents provide protection from torture, arbitrary arrest, illegal detention, illegal search and seizure, *etc*. However, the Universal Declaration of Human Rights does not provide any mechanism to enforce the violations of the human rights. The Covenant on Civil and Political Rights and the Convention Against Torture contains provision for the enforcement of human rights. The mechanisms provided under these documents are 'State Reporting', 'Inter-State Communications' and 'Individual Complaint' mechanisms. In fact, State Reporting and Inter-State communications cannot be considered as an effective enforcement mechanism as these mechanisms provide only the mode of decision making by conciliations and negotiations. They are more of a compromise than a mechanism of

323

enforcement. Individual communication mechanism again is very weak, since the decision making Committees can only give an opinion, on the basis of its findings, to the State and the aggrieved individual. If the State is not complying with the opinion expressed, the Committees have no authority to compel the State to act in accordance with the opinion. India follows dualist system for the implementation of International treaties, declarations, conventions, *etc.*, into its *corpus juris* and hence, Act of Parliament is essential to incorporate it. However, the Supreme Court of India held that the International treaties, declarations and conventions can be applied by the courts in India, even in the absence of an Act of Parliament, if the provisions of such instruments are not inconsistent with Municipal law of India. Thus, even in the absence of Act of Parliament, such convents and declarations are enforceable in India if there is no inconsistency with the Constitution and the law of India.

The Constitution of India provides protection from the violation of human rights by the police. Clause (3) of Article 20 which provides prohibition against self- incrimination, Article 21 which guarantees right to life and personal liberty, and Article 22 which provides safeguards against arbitrary arrest and detention are the significant constitutional provisions in this regard. The right to remain silent is not expressly provided under the Indian Constitution. The Supreme Court held that the right to remain silent is implied under Article 20 (3).The dynamic interpretation that has been given to Article 21 in *Maneka Gandhi*'s case has widened the horizons of human rights jurisprudence in India and the Supreme Court held that Article 21 takes within it sweep right to live with human dignity, right against inhuman treatment, right against torture, right to compensation in case of death in police custody right against hand cuffing, *etc.*Article 22 provides safeguards against arbitrary arrest and detention. Article 22 (1) and (2) provides that the arrested person has a right to know the grounds of arrest, to consult and to be defended by a lawyer, to be produced before a Magistrate within twenty-four hours.In *Joginder Kumar's* case and *D.K. Basu's* case the Supreme Court has laid down detailed procedures to be complied with in making the arrest such as to inform about the arrest to a friend, relative or other person who is known to him, where he is being detained, *etc*. Further, it has been made obligation to the arresting officer to inform the arrested person about this right. In the event of preventive detention Article 22 (4) provides that no preventive law shall authorize a person to be detained for more than three months, and in exceptional situations the period of detention can be extended for more than three months after obtaining an opinion from the advisory body constituted for this purpose. The Article 22(5) of the Constitution provides two categories of protection in the event of preventive detention, *namely*, (i) the grounds on which the detention order is passed must be communicated to the detenue as soon as possible; and (ii) earliest opportunity of making representation against the detention order shall be provided.

There are many statutes in India which provide protection from torture, arbitrary arrest, unlawful detention, interrogation, false implication and vexatious searches and seizures by the police. The Code of Criminal Procedure provides provisions that are to be followed in making arrest, detention, search and seizure. The new Amendment to the Code of Criminal Procedure in 2008 and 2010 made significant changes in the arrest and detention matters such as police to compulsorily record the reasons both for making as well as for not making an arrest in respect of offences carrying punishment up to 7 years, first the officer issue a 'notice of appearance' before making arrest in these cases, prepare a memorandum of arrest which shall be attested by at least one witness and counter signed by the person arrested, *etc.*The Indian Penal Code does not provide an exclusive definition of "torture" nor does it prescribe punishment as such for torture committed by the police officers. The Indian Penal Code provides very few specific provisions such as Sections 330 and 331 which provide punishment for causing hurt or grievous hurt to extort confession or to compel restoration of property respectively and Section 376 (2) (a) which provides punishment for committing rape in police custody. Since the police commit torture and other atrocities in the custody where there are no witnesses other than police personnel, the general provisions of the Indian Penal Code have proved to be inadequate in order to bring the erring police officers to justice. The Indian Evidence Act bans the admissibility of confessions made to police or confession made to any person while in the custody of police altogether.

The Indian Police Act which was enacted in 1861 during the period of British rule to coerce and suppress people who stood against the rule is still followed in India. Many Commissions and Committees such as Dharma Veera Commission (National Police Commission), Reibero Commission, Soli Sorbjee committee, *etc.*, recommended to the reform of law relating to the police. However, the recommendation of these commissions and Committees were not implemented by the Government of India. Hence, the Supreme Court in *Prakash Singh's* case gave directions with specific guidelines to the Government to reform police Acts both at the Centre and the States. Consequent to the directives of the Supreme Court, the Kerala Government has passed new Kerala Police Act in 2011 totally replacing by the Kerala Police Act, 1960. The New Act contains provisions for taking care of human rights and human dignity of individuals. The Act provides for the establishment of a Police Establishment Board for posting, promotion and transfer of employment of police, State Security Commission for effectively improving the police department, Police Complaint Authorities at State and the District level to redress the grievances against police actions. National Human Rights Commission in India and State Human Rights Commissions in many States including Kerala have established in accordance with the provisions of Protection Human Rights Act, 1993. These institutions work as recommendatory body for the greater protection and promotion of human rights. The National Human Rights Commission has dealt with many death and torture cases in police custody which would not have come to lime light but for the involvement of the Commission. There are no procedural hurdles of formal court procedure and lawyerings in the case of these institutions to redress a grievance against the police. The major problem that these institutions suffer is that they cannot execute their decisions.

The Empirical study reveals that the extent of violation of human rights by the police in Kerala is very high. The study reveals that in around 80 percent arrests made by the police are unlawful. The major areas where the police do not follow the procedural requirement not informing the grounds of arrest, not issuing the notice of appearance before making an arrest, not informing the relatives or friends about the arrest and not asking whether the arrest be informed to any friends or relatives. Handcuffing is prohibited by the New Amendment to Code of Criminal Procedure and also the Supreme Court unless there is an exceptional circumstance of suspecting that the arrestee may escape. However, study reveals that police continue to hand cuff persons (11.03 percent of the arrestees) unnecessarily. Illegal detention by the police is also very common in Kerala. The study reveals that more than 60 percent cases the arrested persons were not produced before the Magistrate within 24 hours. What is more astonishing is that in 97.06 percent cases, the police did not inform the arrestees about their right to consult a lawyer. In majority cases, the police did not inform the venue of detention (78.67 percent) to the relatives or friends.

Torture has been prohibited by the Supreme Court. However, the study reveals that 17.24 percent tortures are still employed for extracting information, 8.81 percent are employed due to the political influence of the opposite party, 8.09 percent by reason of the bribes paid by the

327

opposite party, 5.88 percent for admitting guilt and 5.51 percent as retaliation for standing against abuse of power by the police. Torture also affects health and earning capacity. Among the victims of torture, 43.12 percent victims had bad impact on health, out of which for 12.83 percent victims, the torture affected negatively on the earning capacity. However, the majority police officers favour torture. 68.18 percent responded that torture is necessary to elicit facts from hardened and habitual offenders. Majority police officers are of the opinion that the custody time of 24 hours for producing the accused before the Magistrate is too short. Within this time it is difficult to investigate the crime, collect evidences from different places, interrogate different witnesses, make recovery of the weapons used to commit crime, prepare statements and records, *etc*. Hence, they consider torture as a short cut. Further, 48.13 percent of the police officers affirmed that torture is necessary where a person commits a cruel and heinous crime. They believe that even if the court punishes, criminals do not suffer any kind of pain that they have inflicted on the victim of crime, and the pain is really inflicted only by torture. However, the top level police officials do not support this view. Majority of them opined that police have no authority to torture any person. They suggest that the police should act in accordance with law, not by emotions.

Majority of the victims and human rights activists expressed their dissatisfaction with the Kerala State Human Rights Commission. More than 80 percent of the victims and activists expressed their dissatisfaction on the remedy given by the Commission and enforceability of the decisions of the Commission. 87.87 percent victims and 90.81 percent activists responded that the Commission is an ineffective body and should be dismissed. However, the Members of the Kerala State Human Rights Commission opined that they provide remedy in appropriate cases within the legal frame work. Nonetheless, they admit that since it is a recommendatory body, it cannot execute its decisions, it can only recommend to the Government, and hence, implementation of the decision of the Commission may not be effective.

Thus, in summary, the study reveals that there takes place violations of human rights by the police in Kerala State in different ways such as unlawful arrest, illegal detention, torture, false implication, failure in taking action on complaints, *etc*. The extent of violation is very high in unlawful arrest and illegal detention. The police recurrently employ third degree methods, even though torture is prohibited. These violations take place irrespective of Constitutional guarantees, criminal procedural requirements, and the direction of Supreme Court in different cases. Hence, it is submitted that the major problem lies not with the laws but with the implementation of laws.

The comparative analysis on the protection of human rights in different regional systems of the world such as Europe, inter-American, African, *etc*., reveals that these systems guarantee the protection from torture, arbitrary arrest, illegal detention, *etc*. However, the enforceability mechanism in some regional systems is very effective while in some it is not. Among the regional systems, European system is very successful one due to the efficient mechanism for the redressal of the individual grievances of violations through a full-fledged super-national European Court of Human Rights system. Under the European system, even an individual can directly approach the European Court of Human Rights to redress his grievance against the State action. However, this is not available in the Inter-American system. There is no enforcement procedure in the American system and the decisions are not necessarily accepted as legally bindings in this system. In the African regional system the only enforceable mechanism available is through African Commission on Human and Peoples' Rights. However, due to diverse political situations that exist among the Member Nations within the Union makes it more complex for the monitoring and remedial mechanisms in this system. Though the Minsk convention or the Commonwealth of Independent States Convention on Human Rights 1995 provides elaborate safeguards against violations of human rights by the police, the system is not fully operational in the first place. Secondly, there is no effective Court mechanism to enforce it. The only mechanism provided is for the establishment of Human Rights Commission. Though the Arab Charter is not operational, at least, it is in existence, while the Asian Charter is not even in existence even after repeated attempts. Thus, the scenario of regional systems for the protection of human rights is diverse in its scope, application, level of effectiveness and enforceability in the protection of human rights.

The UN has made Code of Conduct for Law Enforcement Officers, the Basic Principles on the Use of Force and Firearms by Law Enforcement Officials, Body of Principles for the Protection of All Persons under Any Form of Detention or Imprisonment, The Standard Minimum Rules for Non-custodial Measures, *etc,* which work as guidelines for National States for making laws in their respective Nations. The Standard Minimum Rules for Non-custodial Measures sets out a number of rules that the National State may make use of in order to avoid the pre-trial detention. It provides that the pre-trial detention shall be used as a last resort. The UN Code of Conduct for Law Enforcement Officers sets out a number of conduct rules that the National States must adopt into their States. It also prohibits any kind of torture by law enforcement agencies not only of inflicting but instigating and tolerating it also. The UN Principles of Detention or Imprisonment further provides a number of principles that National State may make rules in the cases of detention and imprisonment. It provides that if any damage incurred because of acts or omissions by a public official contrary to the rights contained in these principles must be compensated according to the applicable rules on liability provided by domestic law. The Basic Principles on the Use of Force and Firearms by Law Enforcement Officials sets out guidelines for the use of firearms against persons. However, they are not permitted to use firearms against a person in custody or detention except in self-defense or in the defense of others against the immediate threat of death or serious injury. The Declaration on the Protection of All Persons from Enforced Disappearance provides that National States must ensure that no pressure, physical or mental, is exerted on suspects, witnesses, or victims in attempting to obtain information. It further provides that the duration of the process of any interrogation of a detained person and of the intervals between the interrogations as well as the identity of the officials who conducted the interrogations and other persons present shall be recorded in the prescribed form. The United Nations Standard Minimum Rules for the Administration of Juvenile Justice, 1985 directs a number of safeguards and special treatments to be taken by the National States in the cases of arrest and detention of juveniles. Similarly, UN Standard Minimum Rules for Prisoners provides a number of safeguards for women in custody. Thus, the UN has made elaborate guidelines in order to control exercise of police powers and avoid abuse of such powers within any National State.

Suggestions and Recommendations

In the interest of effective protection of human rights from being violated by police, the researcher makes the following suggestions and recommendations:

1. 'Torture' in police custody should be defined in the Indian Penal Code and severe punishment ought to be prescribed for it. Currently, torture by police as such is not made an offence though general provisions such as hurt, grievous hurt, assault, *etc.*, form the torture.

331

2. The 'burden of proving' custodial torture should be shifted to the police officer who is accused in a crime of torture in custody. There is always lack of independent witnesses in custodial torture. Even if someone is present, the police by coercion or otherwise influence such witnesses to favour their side and hence, the victims of torture are always in a disadvantageous position to prove their side. Consequently, the accused police officer escapes from justice.

3. The Indian Penal Code should be amended to incorporate to punish a police officer who refuses or fails to record, without reasonable cause, a First Information Report or who do not conduct investigation properly in a case. The Law Commission's 84th Report recommended that any police officer who refused or without reasonable cause failed to record a First Information Report be subject to imprisonment for a term of one year or fine or both.

4. Currently, Sections 197 and 132 of the Code Criminal Procedure require the prior sanction of the government before prosecuting public servants for any offence alleged to have been done in discharge of their official duty. The immunity given as per these provisions to the police officers as public servant should be withdrawn in the cases of violation of human rights committed by the police. The National Police Commission's 8th Report also recommended for the withdrawal of the immunity given to police officers under Sections 197 and 132 of the Code Criminal Procedure.

5. Kerala Police Act should be amended to constitute a separate independent body not composed of any police officers to inquire into the corruption charges levelled against any police officer. Currently, corruption charges against police are enquired into by Vigilance wing of the police department where the police officers from other wings

are transferred and placed. This reduces the efficient investigation of corruption charges levelled against police officers.

6. State Security Commission as provided under Section 24 of the KeralaPolice Act should be constituted immediately with functional independence.

7. Currently, the Kerala Police Act empowers theGovernment to interfere with fully or partially for rejecting or modifying any recommendations made by the State Security Commission. Such interferences of the Government reduce the independence of the Commission. Hence, Section 24 (5) of the Kerala Police Act should be amended in order to make the State Security Commission independent from political interference.

8. Indian Penal Code should be amended to provide severe punishments for perjury for witnesses turning hostile during trial in the cases where the police officer is the accused. The Law should also provide procedure for Magistrate/ Judges to order separate investigations into the suspicious circumstances such as influence, coercion, promise, *etc.*, which led to the turning hostile.

9. Delay in the disposal of cases also affords greater opportunity for the accused to win over the witnesses by threats or inducements. So the law with special procedure should be made to provide time bound investigation and trial in all cases human rights violation by the police.

10. National Human Rights Commission and State Human Rights Commissions should be given tribunal like power to implement its findings and decisions particularly in the matters of violations of human rights by the police. Currently, the National Human Rights Commission and State Human Rights Commissions operate only as recommendatory bodies.

11. Protection of Human Rights Act should be amended to provide clear demarcations of jurisdictions of the National Human Rights Commission and the State Human Rights Commissions to inquire into cases.

12. The National Human Rights Commission should be given appellate power from the cases arising from the State Human Rights Commissions. Currently, the National Human Rights Commission does not have appellate power.

13. A sitting Judge of the High Court should always be made as chairperson of the Kerala State Human Rights Commission in order to improve the efficiency of the Commission.

14. Domestic enquiries related with human rights violations by the police should be made more transparent and be completed within three months from the date of occurrence, and the result of the enquiry should be made known to public through the media. Currently, the domestic enquiry conducted by a superior police officer on a complaint against his subordinates impedes the propriety due to the departmental brethren solidarity among officers.

15. The Kerala Police Departmental Enquiries (Punishment and Appeal) Rules, 1958 should be amended to incorporate a presumption of complicity in all cases where the superior officer, even after the incident came to his knowledge, does not institute disciplinary action against a subordinate police officer who has committed violation of human rights.

16. The Prevention of Terrorism Act should be amended to create a separate and independent body consisting of Judges of High Court/ District Court to monitor each

and every case where the police make arrest and detention of persons invoking such laws.

17. Currently, it is the discretion of the Government to give sanction if the victim of police excesses requests that he may engage a lawyer of his choice at his own expense. The Government has authority even to refuse to give permission for it. Rules should be amended to make it mandatory for the Government to give sanction if such a request is made by a victim.

18. A separate Act should be made consolidating the protection of human rights from being violated by the Police officials. The Act should define 'torture' and other offences in the custody and outside custody, prescribe special and speedy procedures for redressal, shift burden of proof from victims to the accused officials, specify the authorities competent to investigate and decide, provide severe punishments for the violations, *etc.*

19. India should initiate that South Asian Association for Regional Cooperation (SAARC) countries should have a regional system for the protection of human rights within the region like that of European Union or Inter-American or African system which provide protection through a supra- national body .

20. India should make law in tune with the "UN Declaration of Victims of Crime and Abuse of Power" to prevent abuse of power by the police. Such law should also prescribe remedies such as restitution and/or compensation, and necessary material, medical, psychological and social assistance and support to the victims of such abuses.

21. India should make law in tune with the "UN Body of Principles for the Protection of All Persons under Any Form of Detention or Imprisonment" laying down clear procedure for recording the process of any interrogation of a detained person, the duration of interrogation, the intervals between the interrogations, the identity of the officials who conducted the interrogations and other persons present at the interrogation.

22. In tune with the "UN Convention Against Torture" and the "UN Code of Conduct for Law Enforcement Officers", India should make laws for punishing police officers who inflicts torture. The Law should also punish instigators of torture. It should also punish those who did not reasonably take any steps to prevent the torture that took place in their presence.

23. The Government and the Police Department should make appropriate steps to implement the laws and Supreme Court guidelines on arrest, detention, search and seizure effectively. The Government and the Police Department should, for achieving this purpose, create an efficient monitoring mechanism within the Department at State and District level.

24. Victims of violations of human rights by police shall be given free legal services at the expenses of the State to engage a lawyer of his own choice in all cases of human rights violation by the police.

25. A team of expert psychologists should periodically give training to police officers so that the traditional colonial attitudinal behaviour towards common man can be transformed.

26. Periodic in-service training, seminar, workshop, *etc.*, on human rights should be imparted to all police officers. This will sensitize and inculcate respect for human rights in them and also improve police-public relations.

27. The capacity building of the investigating officers should be improved though proper training including the strengthening of the crime-investigation curriculum at police academies, training low-ranking officers to assist in crime investigations, and providing basic forensic equipment to every police officer. Torturing accused person in order to elicit facts in a crime is a cruel and barbarous practice and should not be used as a short cut method in crime investigation. If crime investigators are intelligent and efficient, the valuable information can be gathered through proper and scientific investigations without violating the human rights and human dignity of persons.

CPSIA information can be obtained
at www.ICGtesting.com
Printed in the USA
LVHW051655240523
747950LV00019B/54